SEQUENCE DANCING

THE LATE MICHAEL GWYNNE

SEQUENCE DANCING

By

MICHAEL GWYNNE

Championship Adjudicator Modern, Latin and Sequence Dancing
Examiner and Fellow, International Dance Teachers Association
(Modern, Latin and Sequence Dancing)
Life Member, Imperial Society of Teachers of Dancing
(Modern, Latin and Sequence Dancing)

FOREWORD BY

LEONARD MORGAN

Chairman, The Official Board of Ballroom Dancing

A & C BLACK · LONDON

Second edition 1985
A & C Black (Publishers) Ltd
35 Bedford Row, London WC1R 4JH

© 1985, 1963, 1965, 1971 Michael Gwynne

This title originally published 1971
Pitman Publishing Ltd

(Much of the material in this book has been taken from the same author's
Old Time and Sequence Dancing, first published in 1950 by Sir Isaac
Pitman and Sons Ltd, several times reprinted but long out of print.)

British Library Cataloguing in Publication Data

Gwynne, Michael
  Sequence dancing.—2nd ed.
  1. Ballroom dancing
  I. Title
  793.3′3 GV1753

  ISBN 0-7136-2750-6

ISBN 0-7136-2750-6

Printed in Great Britain at the
University Press, Cambridge

CONTENTS

vi

FOREWORD
to the Second Edition

IT would seem incongruous in these days of loud beat music, flashing lights, Punk Rock and Break dancing to publish this revised edition of Michael Gwynne's *Sequence Dancing*; a style of dancing based on tuneful music, graceful movement and, may I add, good manners.

In the years leading to the Second World War social dancing was an amalgam of genuine Old Time dances (the Lancers was still being danced) and a new style referred to as Modern dancing. The Foxtrot and Tango were captivating the public and Latin dances could not be ignored. Following the war there was an extraordinary resurgence of interest in Old Time and Sequence dancing due in no small measure to the famous B.B.C. programme 'Those were the Days'. Booms can be self-destructive and the proliferation of new Sequence dances brought confusion and some frustration to the dancing thousands. The Official Board of Ballroom Dancing, the national authority for ballroom dancing in Great Britain, appointed a Sequence Advisory committee upon which all recognised Dance Teachers' Associations were represented. The committee standardised dances and technique and brought about comprehension and development.

Today, Old Time and Sequence dancing is as popular as ever with numerous schools of dancing and clubs catering for the requirements of all grades – from the casual social dancer who wants to dance (and possibly sing) his way through happy evenings with friends, to the keen dancer who finds enjoyment and achievement in entering for amateur medal tests and to the dedicated competition dancer who thrills us all with the grace and beauty of his movement.

The love of Sequence dancing is not confined to Great Britain. British teachers frequently visit the Continent; for a long time Australia has enjoyed our dances and there is considerable interest in the U.S.A. and other countries. Dancing can be the key to a new life of fun and friendship and it is becoming more widely known that it is the nicest possible way to keep fit.

Michael Gwynne, a highly qualified and most respected teacher of dancing, was a life-long observer of the dance scene. He contributed to its progress and this book is evidence of his knowledge as a technician and his unique ability to use the written word to describe movement. This new edition of his book will be of value to all Sequence dancers. It describes forty-eight dances, including all the recognised adult and junior Old Time championship dances and a variety of other popular dances, many of which are included in the Medal Tests syllabuses of Dance Teachers' Associations.

Sadly, Michael Gwynne is no longer with us. He passed away after completing his work on this book. It is a good book from a good man.

LEONARD MORGAN

Chairman, The Official Board of Ballroom Dancing.
President, The International Council of Ballroom Dancing.
Vice-President, The International Dance Teachers Association.

PREFACE

In the preface to my *Old Time and Sequence Dancing*, first published in 1950, I said "It is my endeavour in this present volume to describe many of the Sequence Dances which are popular today." Twenty years later this is still my endeavour. During the last two decades dancing has not remained static and many of the new dances, particularly the type of dance known as Modern Sequence, are achieving great popularity with the public. In 1965 a Slow Modern Waltz Sequence— the Magenta Waltz—was voted the most popular of all modern sequences by the readers of *Dance News*.

An up-to-date textbook must therefore reflect these changes, and the most useful of these new dances are included in this book, which also includes much material from my *Old Time and Sequence Dancing*, which is now out of print.

Any reader who learns the dances described in the following pages will experience no difficulty in learning any new dances that may subsequently become popular, since all the movements that are danced in the original Old Time or in the Modern Sequence style are adequately described. The foot charts and other illustrations were specially designed to supplement the descriptive matter and will enable the reader to learn the dances easily and accurately.

Michael Gwynne

INTRODUCTORY SECTION

Why is dancing so fascinating?

This is a question I am frequently asked, and one which I frequently ask myself. That it is a fascinating art is beyond all question of doubt, but, as to why, everybody seems to have a different answer. Movement to rhythm and melody, the pattern of the movement and the feet, the co-ordination of the senses—all combine in some intangible manner to make a dance.

Almost everybody has some sense of rhythm. This means that almost everybody can dance, provided, of course, an attempt to do so is made. Some people learn very rapidly, others slowly. The slow ones, incidentally, usually become the best dancers. Everybody who can dance enjoys it, and goes on enjoying it.

The difference between the good dancer and the competition dancer is not generally understood. Unless you have the build of a Greek god or goddess it is wise to leave competitions alone. The essential difference lies in the incontrovertible fact that competitions are judged entirely on the appearance of a couple, and you can without any question of doubt be a better dancer than you appear to be. The greatest value to be derived from competitions is in the creation of an ideal to be aimed at. In the same way as the tailor's dummy sets off the desirable merits of a suit or costume, so does the competition dancer set the standard of appearance. Good dancing goes on for all time.

Teachers of dancing have two main teaching methods; they can "build" from the shoulders downwards or "build" from the feet upwards. Either method may give satisfactory results.

The expert teacher adopts a combination of both methods according to the characteristic physical make-up of the pupil. To correct the placing of a step will invariably move the body to the proper position, whilst correct travel or movement of the body will achieve the correct foot position.

The position of the body should be upright, with the shoulders back and the head erect, not inclined forward. The muscles throughout the body should be flexible and not rigid. Avoid stiffness and cultivate free and easy movement.

Foot Positions. There are five essential foot positions. In three of these the feet are together. In two the feet are apart, or open.

The Closed Positions

First Position.   Heels placed together—toes turned outward.

Third   „   Heel of foot placed against instep of the other foot.

Fifth   „   Heel of foot placed against toe of the other foot.

The Open Positions

Second   „   Either foot placed to the side.

Fourth   „   Either foot placed straight forward or straight back.

In all the positions the feet are placed at an angle of 90 degrees to each other.

Reference to the foot charts will amplify these notes.

Try to master the 3rd and 5th positions. These present the greatest amount of difficulty, and occur most frequently when dancing. The other positions

FIFTH REAR POSITION

may be acquired more easily as the various dances are learnt.

A 6th position may be mentioned. This is the parallel position and it occurs in almost all dances, although it has, in practice, more particular application to the Tangos. The position is a natural one, with the feet either apart or together with the inside edges of the feet in line or parallel to each other. The toes are *not* turned outward.

In the construction of sequence dances certain body positions and short phrases of one or two bars' duration frequently recur. It will facilitate the learning of the dances if some information on those that are the most used is, as it were, isolated and learnt separately.

Pas Glissé. This is a movement of two steps. Step one foot to the side and then close the other foot to the 3rd position front, without transferring the weight of the body to the closing foot. The closing foot will then move to another position, either a point position or as a definite step into another movement.

Footwork: to side on inside edge of ball of foot, lower to inside edge of foot and then take the weight to the whole foot. The closing is made with slight pressure on the ball of foot; do not lower the heel.

Pas Glissade. This is the Pas Glissé but with transference of weight to the closing foot, thus leaving the rear foot free to move into the next movement.

Footwork: close with pressure on ball of foot, then lower to the whole of foot. As the heel of the closing foot is lowered, the heel of the rear foot is slightly raised from the floor.

This will give a softer action to the movement.

In both the Pas Glissé and the Pas Glissade the body is inclined slightly over the closing foot.

The Balancé. A movement of two steps. Step forward, then close other foot to 3rd or 5th position rear, without transferring the weight of the body to the closing foot.

Footwork: pressure on the heel when moving forward, transferring the weight to the whole foot, with the body upright. As the close is made, brace the muscles at the waist and rise to the ball of the

FIFTH POINT

forward foot. Lower the heel of the forward foot as the rear foot moves backward into the next movement.

The balancé is also danced with the first step moving backward. Rise to the ball of rear foot as front foot closes to 3rd or 5th front position. Lightly

6

lower heel of rear foot as front foot moves forward into the next movement.

The closing is made in both instances with slight pressure on the ball of foot.

Another type of balancé is occasionally used. Step backward, then close the other foot to a 5th position rear, i.e. move the toe of the forward foot to the heel of the supporting leg, and after holding the foot in position for the rhythm period continue by stepping the closing foot backward.

The Point Position. This is a foot movement—the toe is moved into position without transference of weight. The toe is turned outward with slight pressure on the outside edge of the foot in the open positions.

The 5th point position is taken with only the tip of the toe on the floor, the turning out action being felt more strongly with the knee than with the foot. The 5th point position is illustrated opposite.

The Chassé. Literally this means a chasing step, and in practice the movement occurs in many forms. There are, however, two very common chassés.

Step forward, close the other foot to a 3rd position rear and transfer the weight, then step the forward foot again forward.

A parallel chassé consists of a step to the side, forward or diagonally forward, closing the other foot to a parallel position with transference of weight, then moving the first foot again in a side or forward direction.

Promenade Position. This term is used to indicate that the man's right hip and lady's left hip are touching, the opposite sides of the bodies being opened out so that the bodies form a "V" shape. In some dances the "V" is opened out to a wider position between the bodies without hip contact.

The hold is always a waltz or tango hold when a promenade position is used.

When dancing in promenade position the man will move to his left, the lady to her right.

Counter or Contra Promenade Position. The inversion or opposite of promenade position. Man's left hip and lady's right hip are in contact, the opposite sides of the bodies being opened out so that the bodies form a "V" shape.

The waltz or tango hold is retained although the man's right arm may be moved slightly to allow more freedom of movement.

When dancing in contra promenade position the man will move to his right, the lady to her left.

Fallaway Position. A promenade position but both partners moving backward.

Brush. Refers to the track of the foot when moving from a position where the feet are apart, to another position where the feet finish apart. The moving foot closes or almost closes to the standing foot.

Check. A step in which the body travel is arrested, then moving to the opposite direction.

Rhythm. Few people find difficulty in hearing the pulse or accented beats in music.

When you listen to dance music try to hear the bass instruments, particularly the double bass, bass drum and the pianist's left hand. Note also that certain beats are more strongly accented than others.

The Waltz has three beats to a bar of music, the first being the most strongly accented—ONE, two, three, 3/4 is the time signature of the music.

Common time, 4/4, has four beats to the bar—ONE, two, three, four. The third beat is invariably stressed a little more than the second and fourth. Each beat is called a quick, four quicks to a bar. Two of these quicks used together for only one step is called a slow. The dancer can dance 2 slows, 1 slow and 2 quicks, or 4 quicks to a bar of common time. 2/4 time is used for Tangos. The dancer, instead of counting one and two and, may count one, two, three, four, as this is easier. In Lancers and Quadrilles the steps are normal marching steps, 2 steps to a bar.

Tempo. Indicates the number of bars of music played in a minute—the speed of the music.

The Waltz. Most of the Round Dances include a few bars of waltzing, and in many this is danced to common time, the feet moving to a rhythm of 1 and 2—1 and 2.

The Steps of the Natural Turn.

Beat 1. Glide L.F. across L.O.D., turning to R.
Beat 2. Bring toe of R.F. to heel of L.F., still turning.
Beat 3. Pivot round to R., changing feet to opposite position. Finish with weight on L.F.
Beat 1. Glide R.F. to 4th pos.
Beat 2. Turning to R., L.F. to side.
Beat 3. Still turning, draw R.F. up to L.F.

Lady dances the second group of steps while man is dancing the first group, and vice versa.

9

The Steps of the Reverse Turn.

Beat 1. L.F. to *4th pos*.
Beat 2. Turning to L., R.F. to side.
Beat 3. Still turning, draw L.F. up to R.F.
Beat 1. Glide R.F. across L.O.D., turning to L.
Beat 2. Bring toe of L.F. to heel of R.F., still turning.
Beat 3. Pivot round to L., changing feet from that position to opposite position. Finish with weight on R.F.

Lady dances the second group of steps while man is dancing the first group, and vice versa.

Each complete turn has six steps.

The Pas de Valse.

An important group of three steps.

Step forward—step forward—close opposite foot to a rear position.

Step back—step back—close opposite foot to a front position.

It is used as a link between waltz turns, and occurs in many dances in which the movement is danced solo. When danced solo it is a much more travelled movement than when waltzing.

Bow and Curtsy. This is customary during the introductory music, usually of four bars.

The man bows normally by stepping with L.F. to the side (or *rear position*). Close R.F. to L.F. *3rd pos. front*, L. arm lowered to L. side of the body, R. arm drawn across the body, the hand towards L. hip. Recover normal position by stepping forward R.F. towards partner and closing L.F. to R.F. *3rd pos.* (*front* or *rear*). In Tangos and Saunters many men prefer to close the feet to a *parallel position* instead of the *3rd position*.

The Curtsy is dealt with in detail on page 14.

Abbreviations used in the Descriptions.

R.	Right.	Q.	Quick.
L.	Left.	Diag.	Diagonal(ly).
L.F.	Left Foot.	b.o.f.	Ball of foot.
R.F.	Right Foot.	w.f.	Whole foot.
L.O.D.	Line of Dance.	W.W.	Without weight
Pos.	Position.	C.B.M.P.	Contra body movement position.
S.	Slow.		

ALIGNMENT

THIS term has three distinct meanings in dancing, and it is most important that they are completely understood.

(1) The relationship of the feet to the body.

(2) The relationship of the body to the ballroom.

(3) The pattern of a series of steps, or a movement in relation to the ballroom.

The first is covered in the foot positions already given, and although there are intermediate positions these are clearly explained in the descriptions.

The second refers to the part of the ballroom you are facing. If you stand and face the outside wall squarely the term used is "facing wall," and if you stand facing squarely to the centre you are "facing centre," which, of course, is the same position as "backing wall."

To understand the "diagonals," stand square to the wall, with the feet together and toes turned outwards at an angle of 90 degrees. This is the first position of the feet, a right angle. Note that the left foot is pointing diagonally to wall down L.O.D., and the right foot is pointing diagonally to wall against L.O.D. Transfer the weight of the body to the left foot, and then move the right foot to the left foot with the feet parallel. The body will now face diagonally to wall down L.O.D.

A movement can be taken in a diagonal direction, but often the body does not face the diagonal direction of the movement. This applies particularly to movements in the promenade position.

A study of the two pages of foot prints which follow will amplify the above.

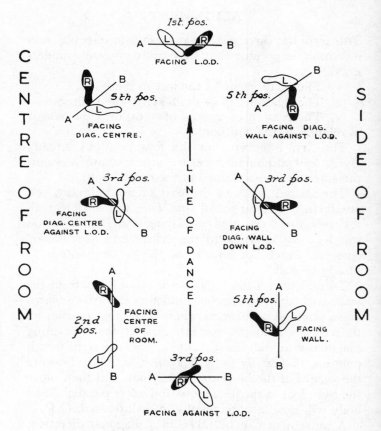

CENTRE OF ROOM

SIDE OF ROOM

1st. pos.

A L R B

FACING L.O.D.

5th pos.

R
B
A
L

FACING
DIAG. CENTRE.

5th pos.

L
B
A
R

FACING DIAG.
WALL AGAINST L.O.D.

3rd pos.

A R
L
B

FACING
DIAG. CENTRE
AGAINST L.O.D.

3rd pos.

A
L R
B

FACING
DIAG. WALL
DOWN L.O.D.

LINE OF DANCE

2nd pos.

A
R
L
B

FACING
CENTRE
OF
ROOM.

5th pos.

A
R L
B

FACING
WALL.

3rd pos.

A R L B

FACING AGAINST L.O.D.

POSITION OF THE BODY IN RELATION TO THE FEET
Line *A–B* represents the shoulder line.

12

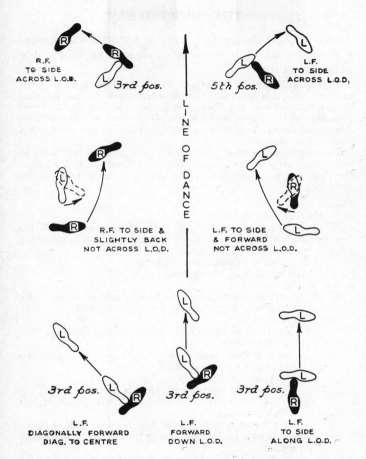

POSITION OF A STEP IN RELATION TO THE ROOM AND LINE OF DANCE

THE CURTSIES

THESE should be danced with grace and expression. Footwork and body movement should be in rhythm with the dance.

The hands play an important part. Hold the gown lightly between the fingers, with the knuckles and fingers pointing downwards towards the floor, not raised from the wrist. Head poise should be upward looking at your partner, not at the floor. Additional notes are added in several of the dances of which a curtsy forms a part.

Footwork consists of 2, 3, or 4 steps according to the dance in which the curtsy occurs. In practice it can begin on either foot— the descriptions which follow are given as beginning on the right foot.

Count

4   R.F. to side *2nd pos.*

L.F. back with a rondé action to *4th pos. rear.* The L. toe on the floor, knee turned outward without transferring weight to the foot. Relax—plié R. knee.

L.F. forward straightening R. knee.

R.F. close to L.F. *1st or 3rd pos.*

3   R.F. to side *2nd pos.*

L.F. back with a rondé action to *4th pos. rear.* Relax—plié on R. knee. Straighten R. knee and leg and

Close L.F. to R.F.

Turn can be made to R. as the close is danced.

3   R.F. to side *2nd pos.*

L.F. back with a rondé action to *4th pos. rear.* Take the weight back to the L.F. and

Close R.F. to L.F.

Turn can be made as the close is taken.

2   This is sometimes called a "Bob" or "Charity" Curtsy—it is a half curtsy.

Step forward or to side with either foot. Move opposite foot to a *4th pos. rear* flexing the leg that is in front of the body.

A rondé action can be used as the leg moves to the *4th pos. rear*—it will not be so emphasized as in the other forms of curtsy.

Straighten the flexed knee and move the rear foot into the next movement or figure.

THE WALTZ

UNDOUBTEDLY the Old Time or Rotary Waltz is the most vital single element in Old Time Dancing. It is the basis of the round dances in which waltz steps occur and is in itself a complete dance with a character and atmosphere of its own.

The foot positions are derived from ballet dancing but modified to fit the ballroom dances of to-day, the continuous turning of the body throughout each part of the turn, the foot placings, and the correct use of the knees, have combined to make a dance of immense fascination and charm.

Time 3/4. Three beats in a bar.

Tempo. Music should be played at 42 bars per minute.

Hold.—Man's R. hand under partner's L. shoulder blade, fingers together towards centre of lady's back.

Man's L. hand at shoulder height, palm of hand inward and upward.

Lady's L. hand rests on partner's arm towards the shoulder, the fingers grouped together. Lady's R. hand rests in man's L. hand.

A light hip contact should be maintained between the partners when dancing and although the lady is very slightly towards her partner's R. side she should avoid the common tendency to move to her L. Try to keep as square to partner as possible.

Parts of a Turn	The Rotary Turn The Progressive Turn	A complete turn
Linking Movement	The Pas de Valse or forward waltz	Is danced when changing from a turn to the opposite turn.

The beginner is urged to make sure that he has memorized the five elementary foot positions. Both lady and man should each learn the three groups of steps, practising them individually until they can be danced easily; this time is not ill-spent as in many of our old-time dances solo waltzing occurs.

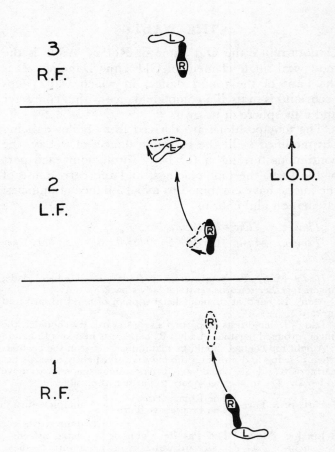

3
R.F.

2
L.F.

L.O.D.

1
R.F.

WALTZ. PROGRESSIVE NATURAL TURN

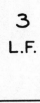

3
L.F.

2
R.F.

L.O.D.

1
L.F.

WALTZ. ROTARY NATURAL TURN

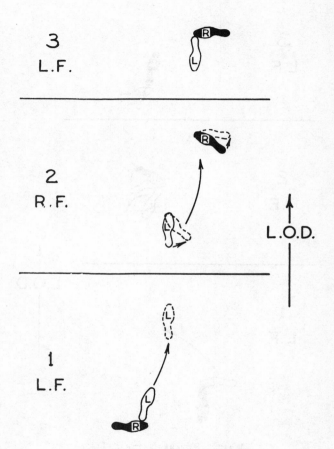

3
L.F.

2
R.F.

L.O.D.

1
L.F.

WALTZ. PROGRESSIVE REVERSE TURN

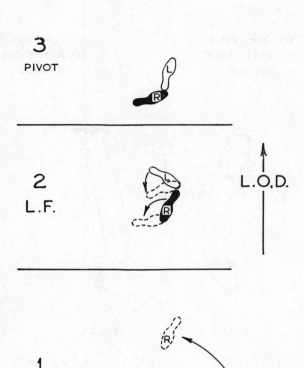

3
PIVOT

2
L.F.

L.O.D.

1
R.F.

WALTZ. ROTARY REVERSE TURN

19

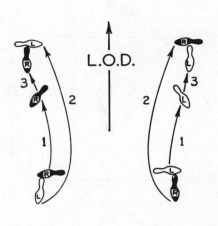

FOLLOW WITH
ROTARY TURN
NATURAL.

FOLLOW WITH
ROTARY TURN
REVERSE.

L.O.D.

START.

START.

R.F. L.F. R.F.
AFTER
PROGRESSIVE REVERSE TURN.

L.F. R.F. L.F.
AFTER
PROGRESSIVE NATURAL TURN.

WALTZ. PAS DE VALSE (LADY)

20

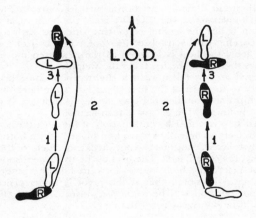

FOLLOW WITH
PROGRESSIVE TURN
NATURAL.

FOLLOW WITH
PROGRESSIVE TURN
REVERSE.

L.O.D.

START.

L.F. R.F. L.F.
AFTER
ROTARY REVERSE TURN.

START.

R.F. L.F. R.F.
AFTER
ROTARY NATURAL TURN.

WALTZ. PAS DE VALSE (MAN)

THE WALTZ (*contd.*)

The aspirant for competition and medal test honours should carefully study the following technical points; the novice can gain more proficiency when he or she has begun to combine the turns and to get the feel of the dance.

The Rotary Part of the Turn

This is the most difficult part of the turn to control. The first step always moves across the L.O.D.; since the body turns as the step is taken it has the feeling of moving sideways with a slight outwards curving to the track of the foot. The ball of the foot skims the floor, the heel is lowered as the next step moves, the knee relaxes slightly as the leg takes the weight.

The second step is taken with a slightly bent knee bringing the toe only to the heel of the first step. Keep the knee out and bring the hip and shoulder back as the leg is moving, begin to straighten the knee as the weight is transferred.

The third step is rather a continuation of the turn through the soles of both feet (technically known as a pivot). With both knees very slightly relaxed, continue the outwards movement of the knee until the pivot is completed. The heel of the third step is lowered to the floor before the body moves forward into the progressive turn. It should be noted that if the pivot is underturned the resulting foot position will be a 3*rd pos.*, instead of the 5*th pos.*, which should be danced when waltzing.

The Progressive Part of the Turn

The first step is not a long step and is taken rather across the body and underneath the partner.

The second step is somewhat lateral in movement, it is the most travelled step of the turns.

The third step is a closed step (5*th pos.*).

THE WALTZ (*contd.*)

Amalgamation of the Turns when Dancing

This presents little difficulty if the man remembers that his forward Pas de Valse follows the Rotary part of a turn. The Pas de Valse when waltzing is used as a preparatory movement in which the rotary action of the body turn is checked, thus smoothing the entry into the "opposing" turn.

The man controls the pattern of the dance. As a further guide to the interpretation of the Waltz his steps are given with the *approximate* body positions on each step.

Commence facing L.O.D.

Count	**Pas de Valse on L.F.**
1	L.F.
2	R.F. (toe pointing down L.O.D.) face diag. centre down L.O.D.
3	Close L.F. to R.F., *3rd pos. rear*, face diag. centre down L.O.D.

Natural (Right) Progressive Turn

1	R.F. Face diag. to centre down L.O.D. finish facing slightly diag. to wall down L.O.D.
2	L.F. Diag. to wall down L.O.D. body turning to face towards wall.
3	R.F. Wall—finish Facing diag. wall against L.O.D.

Natural (Right) Rotary Turn

1	L.F. Face diag. wall against L.O.D. finish facing slightly diag. to centre against L.O.D.
2	R.F. Diag. to centre against L.O.D. body turning to face towards centre.
3	L.F. Centre—finish Facing diag. to centre down L.O.D.

Repeat the last six steps until you wish to change, then—

Count	**Pas de Valse on R.F.**
1	R.F. Face diag. centre down L.O.D., finish almost facing down L.O.D.
2	L.F. (toe pointing down L.O.D.) face diag. wall down L.O.D.
3	Close R.F. to L.F. *3rd rear*, face diag. wall down L.O.D.

23

Count	**Reverse (Left) Progressive Turn**
1	L.F. Face diag. wall down L.O.D., finish facing slightly diag. to centre down L.O.D.
2	R.F. Diag. to centre down L.O.D. body turning to face towards centre.
3	L.F. Centre—finish Facing diag. to centre against L.O.D.
1	R.F. Face diag. to centre against L.O.D., finish facing slightly diag. to wall against L.O.D.
2	L.F. Diag. to wall against L.O.D. body turning to face towards wall.
3	R.F. Wall—finish facing diag. to wall down L.O.D.

Repeat the last six steps until you wish to change then commence again with the pas de valse on L.F.

Lady dances progressive turn when man is dancing rotary turn.

Lady dances rotary turn when man is dancing progressive turn.

Lady dances backward pas de valse (as man moves forward) closing on third step to a *3rd pos. front*.

Important Note

When the music is played at a fast tempo a slight loss of alignment occurs, the curving of the Pas de Valse is not so emphasized, the muscles of the upper part of the body tend to anticipate the opposite turn earlier.

Dance round the corners of the ballroom with Natural (Right) Turns very slightly underturning them, if three or four complete turns are used it will be found easier to maintain the *5th positions* which are the characteristic essential to footwork in this dance.

The man also dances a Pas de Valse moving backward down L.O.D. This must be danced as well as the Forward Pas de Valse in Championship Competitions.

Essentials of Footwork

Progressive Part of Turn.
1. Heel—ball of foot.
2. Ball of foot.
3. Ball of foot—whole foot.

Rotary Part of Turn
1. Ball of foot—whole foot (ball again on 3).
2. Toe—ball of foot.
3. Ball of foot—whole foot.

There is foot and body rise on the 2nd beat of the bar. This occurs when dancing the Rotary Turn immediately after the toe of the 2nd step is in position. Rise is felt slightly earlier on the Progressive Turn.

WALTZ HOLD (HOLD No. 1)

THE ROTARY CHASSÉ (TWO STEP)

An important movement danced to 2/4 and 4/4 time, which forms part of many tangos and foxtrots, and can be danced as an alternative to waltzing in the Maxina and similar dances. It is usually danced as a form of Natural (Right) Turn.

Count		**Man**	
		Commence facing square to wall.	
1	Q	L.F. to side across L.O.D., turning to R.	(b.o.f.)
2	Q	Close R.F. to L.F. *parallel pos.*	(b.o.f.)
		Lower R. heel and step.	
3	S	L.F. back down L.O.D. turning to R.	(b.o.f. lower to w.f.)
4	Q	R.F. to side, toe pointing diag. to centre down L.O.D.	(b.o.f.)
5	Q	Close L.F. to R.F. *parallel pos.*	(b.o.f.)
6	S	R.F. forward down L.O.D.	(heel)
		Most dancers use a slight foot swivel on the ball of L.F. as the R.F. moves forward.	

		Lady	
4	Q	R.F. to side.	(b.o.f.)
5	Q	Close L.F. to R.F. *parallel pos.*	(b.o.f.)
6	S	R.F. forward down L.O.D.	(heel)
1	Q	L.F. to side across L.O.D.	(b.o.f.)
2	Q	Close R.F. to L.F. *parallel pos.*	(b.o.f.)
		Lower R. heel and step.	
3	S	L.F. back down L.O.D.	(b.o.f. lower to w.f.)

When dancing a series of rotary chassés the body will be facing to centre on the 4th step, the R.F. will move into position with the toe almost pointing down L.O.D.; the body completes the turn as the following close is made. A slight loss of alignment will occur on the 3rd step (L.F. back) when dancing at fast speed—the foot will tend to move leftwards. Avoid this when dancing the Royal Empress Tango and the slower dances.

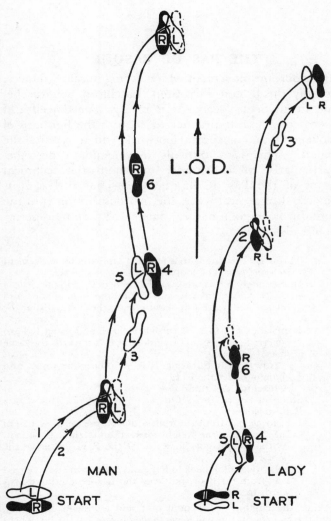

L.O.D.

MAN

START

LADY

START

Rotary Chassé to Right

27

THE PAS DE BASQUE

An important movement which occurs in many dances, notably the Boston Two Step, Latchford Schottische, and in all Scots Reels. It is rarely danced well and needs considerable practice to acquire the lightness of movement and accurate footwork which typifies the expert. This is a difficult movement to describe, particularly to a beginner to whom the technical terms of the Pas de Basque mean but little. It is described in several ways, the first description is in the actual wording of a natural dancer, a teaching description is also given.

Count

1   Throw L.F. to side with a forward semicircular movement to a *2nd pos.* The foot leaves the floor slightly.

and   Immediately release the weight from R.F. bringing it to a *5th pos. front*, take weight on to the ball of foot and release L.F. raising it slightly from the floor, still in the *5th pos.*

2   Replace weight to L.F., raising R. knee and bring R.F. to *5th aerial pos.*, toe pointing downwards towards the same place.

       Now repeat throwing R.F. to other side to R. and changing over the feet.

       A teaching description—

       Stand in *1st pos.*, Toes Out.

1   R.F. to side *2nd pos.*

2   L.F. to *5th pos.* front (in front of R.F.), use only the ball of L.F. and take the weight forward on to the ball of foot. As the weight goes forward let the R.F. *just* leave the floor.

3   Let the weight fall back to R.F. and at the same time release L.F. from the floor, but keep the L. toe pointing downwards to the floor.

Alter the rhythm to a count of 1 and 2 instead of 1, 2, 3, hold the 2nd count, this will leave the leg in front of the body bent

and the toe pointing downwards an inch or so from the floor, and the other foot flat.

Keep the knees turned outwards resisting any tendency to turn the body, the body does not turn in dancing normal ballroom movements.

The action on the first step is as follows: the track of the foot moves through an arc, curve the foot slightly forwards as it goes to the side; it is important that it goes to the side, and not to the side and slightly back, or to the side and slightly forward. Throw the leg into the 2*nd pos.* with a loose knee action, allowing the other foot to leave the floor. At the end of the first step the ball of foot takes the weight in the 2*nd pos.*, the other foot is slightly in the air over the 5*th pos. front.*

The second step: take the weight on to the toe in the 5*th pos.*, the weight is momentarily on the toes of both feet, rear foot leaves the floor slightly.

Take the weight on to the rear foot, immediately releasing the forward foot from the floor, bend the knee limply with the toe pointing downward only an inch or so from the floor, and prepare the balance of the body to move towards the side and in the opposite direction to the first step, initiating the repeat on the opposite feet.

Technical Descriptions

Jeté with demi-rondé to 2*nd pos.*
Assemblé to 5*th front* ball of foot.
Slight plié and coupé in place.
Finish 5*th en l'air.*

Half circle away L.F.
Bring other foot in front heels raised.
Pressure on ball of front foot, hop on rear foot with a springing movement, cut front foot from the floor, and at the same time raise front knee with the toe pointing downwards.
A pas de basque consists of a Jeté—Assemblé—Coupé.

Veleta. Commencing Position (Hold No. 2)

VELETA

ARTHUR MORRIS, B.A.T.D. TIME 3/4—TEMPO 42
Music published by Francis Day & Hunter, Ltd.

A ROUND dance in waltz time of immense charm and character; practise this dance both for its movement and technical value.

It is described in four sections, each of 4 bars, a 16 bar sequence.

Commencing position—Man facing diag. to wall down L.O.D. Lady facing diag. to centre down L.O.D. Feet placed *3rd pos. front*, man L.F. in front of R.F. the L.F. pointing down L.O.D., lady R.F. in front of L.F. the R.F. pointing down L.O.D., bodies about 2 feet apart.

Man's L. hand placed on L. hip, fingers closed together and forward, the thumb behind the hip.

Lady with her R. hand holds her gown away from the body to the side.

Man holds partner's L. hand in his R. hand, palm of R. hand being uppermost, the fingers of lady's L. hand resting downwards on man's R. hand. The joined hands are raised to a level slightly above the man's shoulder, arms are curved, elbows pointing downwards and slightly outwards (backwards).

Section One
Pas de Valse—Inwards Waltz Turn—Pas Glissade— Pas Glissé

Count	Man	Bar
1	L.F. forward down L.O.D. turn to L. to face down L.O.D. (heel).	
2	R.F. forward, toe pointing down L.O.D. face diag. to centre (b.o.f.).	
	Both of these steps are taken with a strong forward swing of the body the R. hip and shoulder leading, the raised arms are carried forward until they are in front of the body, the man should resist any attempt to force the hands forward, the hands move forward as a result of the shoulder swing.	
3	Close L.F. to R.F. *3rd pos. rear* (b.o.f. lower to whole foot before next step moves).	1

31

Count	**Man**	Bars
1	R.F. forward down L.O.D. turn R. to face L.O.D. toe pointing down L.O.D. (heel).	
2	L.F. forward down L.O.D. toe pointing diag. to wall (b.o.f.). Continuing to turn to R. on ball of L.F.	
3	Close R.F. to L.F. *3rd pos. front*, toe of L.F. will finish pointing to wall, R.F. pointing against L.O.D. (b.o.f. lower heel before next step moves). Finish facing diag. to wall against L.O.D. The body turn will bring the arms back and past the shoulders through the original position, then release the hold taking partner's R. hand in L. hand raising the joined hands just above shoulder level, place R. hand on R. hip.	2
1	L.F. to side along L.O.D. (b.o.f. then w.f.).	
2, 3	Close R.F. to L.F. *3rd pos. front* incline body slightly over the foot (b.o.f. lower to w.f. before next step moves).	3
1	L.F. to side along L.O.D. (b.o.f. then w.f.).	
2, 3	Close R.F. to L.F. *3rd pos. front* incline body slightly over the foot (b.o.f. do not lower to w.f. pas glissé).	4

Lady

1	R.F. forward down L.O.D. turn to R. to face down L.O.D. (heel).	
2	L.F. forward, toe pointing down L.O.D. face diag. to wall (b.o.f.).	
3	Close R.F. to L.F. *3rd pos. rear* (b.o.f. lower to whole foot before next step moves).	1
1	L.F. forward down L.O.D. turn L. to face L.O.D. toe pointing down L.O.D. (heel).	
2	R.F. forward down L.O.D. toe pointing diag. to centre (b.o.f.). Continuing to turn to L. on ball of R.F.	
3	Close L.F. to R.F. *3rd pos. front* toe of R.F. will finish pointing to centre, L.F. pointing against L.O.D., finish facing diag. to centre against L.O.D. Gown in L. hand (b.o.f. lower heel before next step moves).	2
1	R.F. to side along L.O.D. (b.o.f. then w.f.).	
2, 3	Close L.F. to R.F. *3rd pos. front* incline body slightly over the foot (b.o.f. lower to w.f. before next step moves).	3
1	R.F. to side along L.O.D. (b.o.f. then w.f.).	
2, 3	Close L.F. to R.F. *3rd pos. front* incline body slightly over the foot (b.o.f. do not lower to w.f. pas glissé).	4

32

VELETA. END OF SECOND BAR

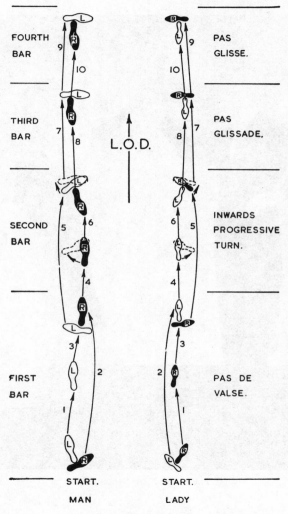

FOURTH BAR

PAS GLISSE.

THIRD BAR

PAS GLISSADE.

L.O.D.

SECOND BAR

INWARDS PROGRESSIVE TURN.

FIRST BAR

PAS DE VALSE.

START.
MAN

START.
LADY

VELETA. BARS 1 TO 4

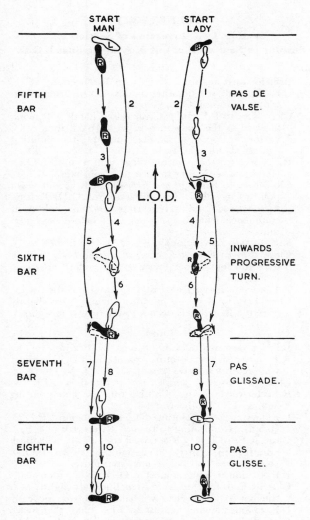

FIFTH
BAR

PAS DE
VALSE.

L.O.D.

SIXTH
BAR

INWARDS
PROGRESSIVE
TURN.

SEVENTH
BAR

PAS
GLISSADE.

EIGHTH
BAR

PAS
GLISSE.

VELETA. BARS 5 TO 8

Section Two (Inversion of Section 1)
Similar to first section but moving against L.O.D.

Count	Man	Bars

Count	**Man**	Bars
1	R.F. forward against L.O.D. turn R. (heel).	
2	L.F. forward, toe pointing against L.O.D. face diag. centre against L.O.D. (b.o.f.).	
3	Close R.F. to L.F. *3rd pos. rear* raised hands will swing forward as the body turn is made (b.o.f. then w.f.).	5
1	L.F. forward against L.O.D. turn L., toe pointing against L.O.D. (heel).	
2	R.F. forward, toe pointing diag. wall against L.O.D. (b.o.f.). Continuing to turn to L. on ball of R.F.	
3	Close L.F. to R.F. *3rd pos. front* toe of R.F. will finish pointing to wall, L.F. pointing down L.O.D. Release hold between 2nd and 3rd steps, and take hold as at commencement (b.o.f. lower heel before next step moves).	6
1	R.F. to side moving against L.O.D. (b.o.f. then w.f.).	
2, 3	Close L.F. to R.F. *3rd pos. front* incline body slightly over the foot (b.o.f. lower to w.f. before next step moves).	7
1	R.F. to side moving against L.O.D. (b.o.f. then w.f.).	
2, 3	Close L.F. to R.F. *3rd pos. front* incline body slightly over the foot (b.o.f. do not lower to w.f. pas glissé).	8

Lady

Count		Bars
1	L.F. forward against L.O.D. turn L. (heel).	
2	R.F. forward, toe pointing against L.O.D. face diag. wall against L.O.D. (b.o.f.).	
3	Close L.F. to R.F. *3rd pos. rear* (b.o.f. then w.f.).	5
1	R.F. forward against L.O.D. turn R. toe pointing against L.O.D. (heel).	
2	L.F. forward, toe pointing diag. centre against L.O.D (b.o.f.). Continuing to turn to R. on ball of L.F.	
3	Close R.F. to L.F. *3rd pos. front* toe of L.F. will finish pointing to centre, R.F. pointing down L.O.D. (b.o.f. lower heel before next step moves).	6
1	L.F. to side moving against L.O.D. (b.o.f. then w.f.).	
2, 3	Close R.F. to L.F. *3rd pos. front* incline body slightly over the foot (b.o.f. lower to w.f. before next step moves).	7
1	L.F. to side moving against L.O.D. (b.o.f. then w.f.).	
2, 3	Close R.F. to L.F. *3rd pos. front* incline body slightly over the foot (b.o.f. do not lower to w.f. pas glissé).	8

VELETA (*cont.*)

Section Three

Natural Waltz Turn opening out to an open contra promenade position, and two Pas Glissades

Count	Man		Bars
	Take partner with normal waltz hold.		
1, 2, 3	Dance rotary part of turn	L.F. R.F. L.F.	9
1, 2, 3	Dance progressive part of turn, closing 5*th pos. front* release R. hand from partner's waist at end of the 3rd step, and place it on R. hip.		10
1	L.F. to side along L.O.D. toe pointing to wall, R. toe pointing against L.O.D. (b.o.f. lower to w.f. before next step moves).		
2, 3	Close R.F. to L.F. 3*rd pos. front* incline body slightly over the foot (b.o.f. lower to w.f. before next step moves).		11
1	L.F. to side along L.O.D. (b.o.f. lower to w.f. before next step moves).		
2, 3	Close R.F. to L.F. 3*rd pos. front* incline body slightly over the foot (b.o.f. lower to w.f. pas glissade).		12

Lady

Count	Lady		Bars
1, 2, 3	Dance progressive part of turn	R.F. L.F. R.F.	9
1, 2, 3	Dance rotary part of turn, L.F. R.F. L.F., pivoting to 5*th pos.* Finish with R.F. pointing down L.O.D., L.F. pointing to centre. Dance the last step by rather forcing the R. knee outwards to attain the 5*th pos.*, the body will very slightly underturn in anticipation of the leftwards turn of the body used on the first step of the following pas glissade. Partner will release his R. hand on third step.		10
1	R.F. to side along L.O.D. toe pointing to centre (b.o.f. lower to w.f. before next step moves).		
2, 3	Close L.F. to R.F. 3*rd pos. front* incline body slightly over the foot (b.o.f. lower to w.f. before next step moves).		11
1	R.F. to side along L.O.D. (b.o.f. lower to w.f. before next step moves).		
2, 3	Close L.F. to R.F. 3*rd pos. front* incline body slightly over the foot (b.o.f. lower to w.f. pas glissade). Note lady takes gown in L. hand when in contra promenade.		12

37

Section Four
Four bars natural waltz turn, finishing in commencing position

Count	**Man**		Bars
	Take partner with normal waltz hold.		
1, 2, 3	Dance rotary part of R. turn	L.F. R.F. L.F.	13
1, 2, 3	Dance progressive part of R. turn	R.F. L.F. R.F.	14
1, 2, 3	Dance rotary part of R. turn	L.F. R.F. L.F.	15
1	R.F. forward, slightly diag. to centre, toe pointing down L.O.D. (heel).		
2	L.F. forward down L.O.D. a short step, body facing diag. to wall down L.O.D. (b.o.f.).		
3	Close R.F. to L.F. 3rd *pos. rear* (b.o.f. then w.f.).		16

The last three steps are a shortened pas de valse, take care in the placing of the 2nd step L.F. forward, the foot should be placed in LINE with the lady's R.F. On second step release the hold, and take commencing position on 3rd step.

Lady

Swivelling to R. on inside edge of ball of L.F. as the upright position is recovered step forward diag. to centre.

1, 2, 3	Dance progressive part of R. turn	R.F. L.F. R.F.	13
1, 2, 3	Dance rotary part of R. turn	L.F. R.F. L.F.	14
1, 2, 3	Dance progressive part of R. turn	R.F. L.F. R.F.	15
1, 2, 3	Dance rotary part of R. turn	L.F. R.F. L.F.	16

Pivot on last bar to 3rd *pos.* front. Finish body facing diag. to centre down L.O.D. Man will release hold during this turn preparing to repeat the sequence.

Notes. Man and Lady. Brace the muscles at the waist as the body swings forward, between the 2nd and 3rd steps of the pas de valse and inwards waltz movements.

Lady. The hand holding the gown during the glissades and glissés 3/4, 7/8, 11/12 bars, bring the hand down on the 1st beat of the bar, raise on 2nd and 3rd beats. As the hand is raised move it away from the body outwards and upwards, the hand is curved downwards, the elbow slightly bent, the upwards and downwards movement emanating from the shoulder.

LATCHFORD SCHOTTISCHE

MADAME M. OLDBURY, B.A.T.D. TIME 4/4—TEMPO 24

Music published by Francis Day & Hunter, Ltd.

DESCRIBED in three sections each of 4 bars—12 bar sequence. Commencing position is similar to the Veleta (Hold No. 2).

Section One

Count	Man	Bars
1	L.F. forward down L.O.D. toe pointing down L.O.D. (b.o.f. then w.f.).	
2	Close R.F. to L.F. *3rd pos. rear* (b.o.f. then w.f.).	
3	L.F. forward (b.o.f. then w.f.).	
4	*Point* R.F. forward *4th pos.* (toe). Turn head to R. and look towards partner on 3rd and 4th steps. Slight R. shoulder lead.	1
1	R.F. back against L.O.D. *4th pos. rear* toe pointing to wall, head facing L.O.D., slight shoulder turn to R. (inwards).	
2	Close L.F. to R.F. *3rd pos. front* (b.o.f. then w.f.).	
3	R.F. back against L.O.D. *4th pos. rear* toe pointing diag. to wall down L.O.D.	
4	Close L.F. to R.F. *3rd pos. front* toe pointing slightly diag. to centre down L.O.D. (b.o.f. do not lower heel).	2
1, 2	Pas de basque on L.F. (slight turn to L. to face down L.O.D.) Turn head to R. and look towards partner.	
3, 4	Pas de basque on R.F. Slight turn to R. to face diag. wall down L.O.D. (Pas de basque, see Boston Two Step.)	3
1, 2	Reverse progressive waltz turn (outwards)	L.F. R.F. L.F.
3, 4	Reverse rotary waltz turn	R.F. L.F. R.F. 4

Release R. hand at end of progressive turn but do not lower, retain in position in the air taking partner's hand again towards completion of the rotary turn.

Man and lady turn heads inwards on 1st pas de basque, on 2nd, lady turns head outwards, man down L.O.D.

LATCHFORD SCHOTTISCHE (contd.)
Section One

Count	Lady	Bars
1	R.F. forward down L.O.D. toe pointing down L.O.D. (b.o.f. then w.f.).	
2	Close L.F. to R.F. *3rd pos. rear* (b.o.f. then w.f.).	
3	R.F. forward (b.o.f. then w.f.).	
4	*Point* L.F. forward *4th pos.* (toe). Turn head to L. and look towards partner on 3rd and 4th steps. Slight L. shoulder lead.	1
1	L.F. back against L.O.D. *4th pos. rear* toe pointing to centre down L.O.D., head facing L.O.D., slight shoulder turn to L. (inwards).	
2	Close R.F. to L.F. *3rd pos. front* (b.o.f. then w.f.).	
3	L.F. back against L.O.D. *4th pos. rear* toe pointing diag. to centre down L.O.D.	
4	Close R.F. to L.F. *3rd pos. front* toe pointing slightly diag. to wall down L.O.D. (b.o.f. do not lower heel).	2
1, 2	Pas de basque on R.F. (slight turn to R. to face down L.O.D.), turn head to L. and look towards partner.	
3, 4	Pas de basque on L.F. to face L.O.D. (slight turn to L. to face diag. centre down L.O.D.), turn head to R. looking outwards.	3
1, 2	Natural progressive waltz turn (outwards). R.F. L.F. R.F.	
3, 4	Natural rotary waltz turn L.F. R.F. L.F.	4

Man will release lady's L. hand during the outwards waltzing, retain in position in the air so that man can take the hand again towards end of turn.

Section Two

Count   **Man and Lady**   Bars

Repeat first, second, and fourth bars (the pas de basque is not repeated).

Man and lady should slightly underturn the rotary waltz turn but finish in a 5*th pos.* facing towards each other. (Man facing wall, lady facing centre.)

The Bow and Curtsy

Man

1   L.F. to side along L.O.D. 2*nd pos.* (b.o.f. then w.f.).

2   Close R.F. to L.F. 3*rd pos. front* (b.o.f.). Bow to partner with R. arm across body. L. arm lightly swinging on L. side of body.

3   R.F. forward towards partner *inter.* 4*th pos.* (heel) preparing the arms to assume a waltz hold.

4   Close L.F. to R.F. 3*rd pos. rear* (b.o.f.) do not transfer   8
weight. Assume normal waltz hold.

Lady

1   R.F. to side along L.O.D. 2*nd pos.* plié (b.o.f. then w.f.).

2   L.F. back a short 4*th pos. rear* slight rondé (toe).

3   L.F. forward towards partner (heel).

4   Close R.F. to L.F. 3*rd pos. front* (b.o.f.) do not transfer   8
weight.

As the curtsy is made on second step, look at partner.

Section Three

Man and Lady

Bars

Dance four bars of waltz (natural turns) opening out to commencing position on last bar in similar manner to the Veleta.   9–12

BOSTON TWO STEP

TOM WALTON

TIME 6/8—TEMPO 48—16 BAR SEQUENCE

Music published by Francis Day & Hunter, Ltd.

COMMENCING position similar to the Veleta partners facing diagonally inwards. Headlines down L.O.D.

Count	**Man**	Bars
1, 2	Pas de basque outwards, L.F., R.F., L.F., body turn to L. to face down L.O.D. (⅛ turn).	1
3, 4	Pas de basque inwards, R.F., L.F., R.F., body turn to R. to face diag. wall down L.O.D. (⅛ turn).	2
1, 2, 3	March forward along L.O.D. (heel). L.F., R.F., L.F. (toes pointing down L.O.D.).	3–4
4	Turn to face diag. wall against L.O.D. (⅜ turn R.) on ball of L.F. The R.F. will move very slightly towards L.F. *inter*. 4th *pos*. Do not lower R. heel. Release hold and take partner's R. hand in L. hand.	
1, 2	Pas de basque outwards, R.F., L.F., R.F., body turn to R. to face against L.O.D. (⅛ turn).	5
3, 4	Pas de basque inwards, L.F., R.F., L.F., body turn to L. to face diag. wall against L.O.D. (⅛ turn).	6
1, 2, 3	Moving against L.O.D. march forward (heel). R.F., L.F., R.F. Turn a quarter turn to L. to face partner and wall on ball of R.F.	7–8
4	Close L.F. to R.F. *parallel pos*. without weight. Assume double hold.	
1, 2	Pas de basque to L., L.F., R.F., L.F., facing partner.	9
3, 4	Pas de basque to R., R.F., L.F., R.F., facing partner.	10
1	L.F. to side along L.O.D. toe pointing to wall.	
2	Close R.F. to L.F. *parallel pos*. (w.f.).	11
3	L.F. to side along L.O.D. toe pointing to wall.	
4	Close R.F. to L.F. *parallel pos*. (w.f.).	12
	Assume waltz hold. Dance four bars natural waltz, similar to last four bars of Veleta.	13–16

The head. Turn head to R. and look at partner on 1st bar. Look down L.O.D. 2nd bar.

Turn head to L. and look at partner on 5th bar, look forward on 6th bar.

BOSTON TWO STEP (*contd.*)

Count	Lady	Bars
1, 2	Pas de basque outwards, R.F., L.F., R.F., body turn to R. to face down L.O.D. ($\frac{1}{8}$ turn).	1
	Pas de basque inwards, L.F., R.F., L.F., body turn to L. to face diag. centre down L.O.D. ($\frac{1}{8}$ turn).	
1, 2, 3	March forward along L.O.D. (heel).	2
	R.F., L.F., R.F. (toes pointing down L.O.D.). Turn to face diag. centre against L.O.D. ($\frac{3}{8}$ turn L.) on ball of R.F. The L.F. will move very slightly towards R.F. *inter 4th pos.* Do not lower L. heel. Partner will change the hold.	3–4
1, 2	Pas de basque outwards, L.F., R.F., L.F., body turn to L. to face against L.O.D. ($\frac{1}{8}$ turn).	5
3, 4	Pas de basque inwards, R.F., L.F., R.F., body turn to R. to face diag. centre against L.O.D. ($\frac{1}{8}$ turn).	
1, 2, 3	Moving against L.O.D. march forward (heel).	6
	L.F., R.F., L.F. Turn a quarter turn to R. to face partner and centre on ball of L.F.	
4	Close R.F. to L.F. *parallel pos.* Partner will take double hold.	7–8
1, 2	Pas de basque to R., R.F., L.F., R.F., facing partner.	9
3, 4	Pas de basque to L., L.F., R.F., L.F., facing partner.	10
1	R.F. to side along L.O.D. toe pointing to centre.	
2	Close L.F. to R.F. *parallel pos.* (w.f.).	11
3	R.F. to side along L.O.D. toe pointing to centre.	
4	Close L.F. to R.F. *parallel pos.* (w.f.).	12
	Partner will assume normal waltz hold and dance four bars natural waltz turns. Open out on last bar to commencing position in similar manner to the Veleta.	13–16

The head. Turn head to L. and look at partner on 1st bar, turn to R. outwards on 2nd bar.

Turn head to R. on 5th bar and look at partner, turn to L. outwards on 6th bar.

TANGO HOLD (HOLD No. 4)

44

LOLA TANGO

ARTHUR WANTLING, E.S.T.D. TIME 2/4—TEMPO 30/32
Music published by Francis Day & Hunter, Ltd.

A CHAMPIONSHIP dance that is now well established, it is deservedly popular with all grades of dancers. 16 bars described in four sections of 4 bars. Almost all the forward steps are heel led, the exceptions are noted. The hold is the same as that of the Royal Empress Tango.

Section One

The Walks

Count	Man	Bars
SSS	Forward L.F., R.F., L.F. down L.O.D.	
Q	R.F. forward.	
Q	Close L.F. to R.F. *parallel pos.* (w.f.).	1–2
SSS	Forward R.F., L.F., R.F. down L.O.D.	
Q	L.F. forward.	
Q	Close R.F. to L.F. *parallel pos.* (w.f.).	3–4

Turn the body very slightly to L. to face between centre diag. and L.O.D. and by pressure on L. side of partner's body, turn lady into *promenade pos.* The forward steps are taken with a heel lead immediately lowering to the flat of the foot, the closes are made without a definite heel lead, step them into position rather sharply on the flat of the foot, giving the effect of a slight pause before the next step is taken.

Lady

Count	Lady	Bars
SSS	Back R.F., L.F., R.F.	
Q	L.F. back.	
Q	Close R.F. to L.F. *parallel pos.* (w.f.).	1–2
SSS	Back L.F., R.F., L.F.	
Q	R.F. back.	
	Swivelling slightly to R. on inside edge of R.F.,	
Q	Close L.F. to R.F. (w.f.) *parallel pos.*	3–4

45

LOLA TANGO (*contd.*)

The lady should finish facing diag. to centre against L.O.D.
The backward steps need care; the toe will meet the floor first,
then lower to the whole foot as the weight is carried over the
supporting leg. Close rather sharply avoiding too much use of the
toe.

Section Two

The Promenade

Count	Man	Bars
	Promenade moving on a line diag. to centre.	
S	L.F. to side in *promenade pos.* (heel).	
S	Cross R.F. over L.F. (heel).	5
Q	L.F. to side in *promenade pos.* (heel).	
Q	Cross R.F. over L.F. (heel).	
Q	L.F. to side in *promenade pos.* (heel), swivel slightly to R. on flat of L.F. after the weight has been transferred.	
Q	Close R.F. to L.F. *parallel pos.* inside edge of whole foot without transferring weight. Finish in *contra promenade pos.* facing towards wall, relax the R. knee slightly, loosen the hold of the R. arm, and bring L. hand in and over the L. shoulder, elbows curved rather acutely. L. hip will be in contact with partner's R. hip.	6
	Promenade (invert) moving on a line diag. to wall against L.O.D. retracing the line of the previous promenade.	
S	R.F. to side in *contra promenade pos.* (heel).	
S	Cross L.F. over R.F. (heel).	
Q	R.F. to side in *contra promenade pos.* (heel).	
Q	Cross L.F. over R.F. (heel).	
Q	R.F. to side in *contra promenade pos.* (heel), Swivelling very slightly to L. on flat of R.F.	
Q	Close L.F. to R.F. *parallel pos.* inside edge of whole foot without transferring weight. Turn partner square, finish facing diag. to wall down L.O.D.	8

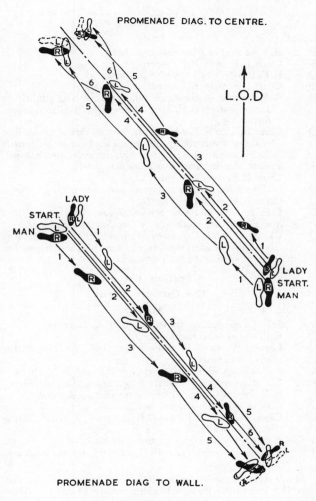

PROMENADE DIAG. TO CENTRE.

L.O.D

PROMENADE DIAG TO WALL.

LOLA TANGO. PROMENADE

Count	Lady	Bars
S	R.F. to side in *promenade pos.* (heel).	
S	Cross L.F. over R.F. (heel).	5
Q	R.F. to side in *promenade pos.* (heel).	
Q	Cross L.F. over R.F. (heel).	
Q	R.F. to side in *promenade pos.* (heel), swivel slightly to L. on flat of R.F. after the weight has been transferred.	
Q	Close L.F. to R.F. *parallel pos.* inside edge of whole foot without transferring weight. Finish in *contra position* facing against L.O.D. (see also notes on man's steps).	6
S	L.F. to side in *contra promenade pos.* (heel).	
S	Cross R.F. over L.F. (heel).	
Q	L.F. to side in *contra promenade pos.* (heel).	
Q	Cross R.F. over L.F. (heel).	
Q	L.F. to side in *contra promenade pos.* (heel). Swivelling very slightly to R. on flat of L.F.	
Q	Close R.F. to L.F. *parallel pos.* inside edge of whole foot without transferring weight. Finish square to partner backing diag. to wall down L.O.D.	8

Section Three
The Quarter Turns
Man

S	L.F. forward diag. to wall turning to L. (heel).	
Q	R.F. to side still turning (w.f.).	
Q	Close L.F. to R.F. *parallel pos.* (w.f.). Finish facing diag. to centre.	9
S	R.F. back with slight overswing of body to L. check.	
S	L.F. forward very slightly lengthening the step (heel).	10
S	R.F. forward diag. to centre turning to R. (heel).	
Q	L.F. to side still turning (w.f.).	
Q	Close R.F. to L.F. *parallel pos.* (w.f.). Finish facing diag. to wall.	11
S	L.F. back with slight L. shoulder lead.	
S	R.F. forward diag. to wall (heel) very slightly lengthening the step.	12

Many dancers use slight continuation of turn to R. on the last step, R.F., until the body is backing square to centre. Although this assists the entry in to the promenade pivot turn this method is *not* correct. The first two steps of the promenade pivot turn should have a diagonal inclination in relation to the L.O.D.

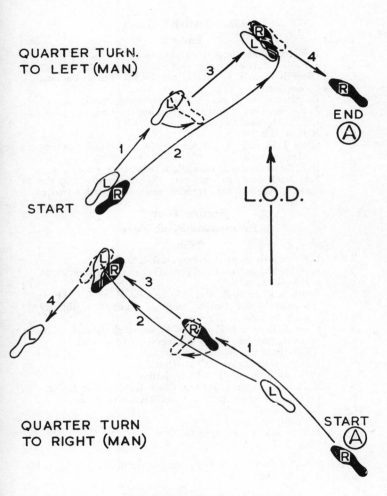

QUARTER TURN.
TO LEFT (MAN)

START

L.O.D.

END
Ⓐ

QUARTER TURN
TO RIGHT (MAN)

START
Ⓐ

LOLA TANGO. QUARTER TURNS (MAN)

49

LOLA TANGO (contd.)

Count	Lady	Bars
S	R.F. back diag. to wall turning to L.	9
Q	L.F. to side still turning (w.f.).	
Q	Close R.F. to L.F. *parallel pos.* (w.f.). Finish backing diag. centre.	
S	L. forward (heel) note slight overswing, check.	
S	R.F. back very slightly lengthening the step.	10
S	L.F. back diag. to centre turning to R.	
Q	R.F. to side (w.f.).	
Q	Close L.F. to R.F. *parallel pos.* (w.f.). Finish backing diag. to wall.	11
S	R.F. forward (heel) note slight overswing, check.	
S	L.F. back diag. to wall very slightly lengthening the step. Keep R. leg extended and underneath partner.	12

Section Four
Promenade Pivot Turn
Man

S	L.F. back diag. to centre against L.O.D.	
S	R.F. back diag. to centre preparing to turn partner into *promenade pos.*	13
S	Brush L.F. to R.F. and step to side along L.O.D. in *promenade pos.* (inside edge of foot) face slightly diag. to wall.	
S	Cross R.F. over L.F. turn to R. to nearly back L.O.D. (heel, turn on b.o.f.) partner square at end. Continue turning strongly to R.	14
S	L.F. to side across L.O.D. (b.o.f.). Continue turning to R. on ball of L.F.	15
S	R.F. forward down L.O.D. (heel) finish facing L.O.D. Nearly a whole turn to R. on last three steps.	
Q	L.F. forward (heel).	
Q	R.F. forward (heel).	
Q	L.F. to side a short step (w.f.).	
Q	Close R.F. to L.F. (w.f.).	16

Keep R. leg in front of body and underneath partner while pivoting on the sixth step.

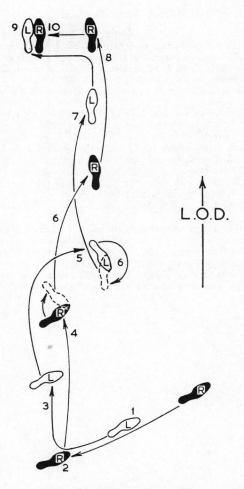

LOLA TANGO. PROMENADE TURN (MAN)

LOLA TANGO (*contd.*)

Count	Lady	Bars
S	R.F. forward diag. to centre against L.O.D. (heel).	
S	L.F. forward preparing to turn into *promenade pos.* heel.	13
S	Brush R.F. to L.F. and step to side along L.O.D. in *promenade pos.* (inside edge of foot).	
S	Cross L.F. over R.F. commencing to turn body to R. (heel).	14
S	R.F. forward down L.O.D. partner now square (heel), R.F. will be underneath partner. Turning strongly to R. on ball of R.F.	
S	L.F. back down L.O.D., finish backing L.O.D. half turn to R. on the last two steps.	15
Q	R.F. back.	
Q	L.F. back.	
Q	R.F. to side, a short step (w.f.).	
Q	Close L.F. to R.F. *parallel pos.* (w.f.).	16

Note. The tango movement is frequently elusive. Try to dance with a slight staccato action ("catlike" is the term sometimes used to describe this style): step the feet rather sharply and lightly into position—do not glide as in the waltz.

Endeavour to keep a light hip contact with your partner, the inside hips touching also in the *promenade* and *contra promenade positions.*

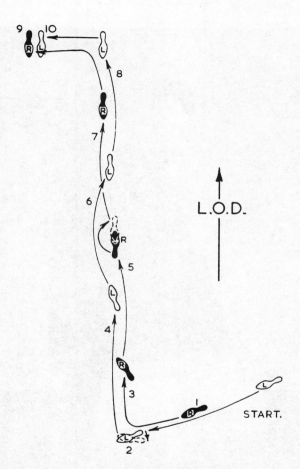

LOLA TANGO. PROMENADE TURN (LADY)

53

LOLA TANGO. SECOND STEP IN THE PROMENADE

54

MOONLIGHT SAUNTER

CHARLES J. DANIELS, P.P.N.A.T.D. TIME 4/4—TEMPO 28

Music published by Messrs. Darewski, c/o Feldman & Co., Ltd.

A DANCE that is aptly named—try to saunter leisurely and smoothly, gliding the feet and the body.

The description is in four sections, each section is repeated while dancing: total sequence 32 bars.

Commencing position—Man facing L.O.D., lady backing L.O.D. The hold is similar to a modern waltz hold, forward steps are heel led immediately lowering to the flat of the foot, the exceptions are noted (Hold No. 1).

Section One
Walks and Outside Movement

Count	Man	Bars
SSS	Forward L.F., R.F., L.F. down L.O.D.	
S	R.F. forward, turning eighth turn to R. on ball of R.F.	1–2
S	L.F. forward outside partner on her L. side.	
Q	R.F. to side, without weight *2nd pos.* (toe).	
Q	Swivel quarter turn to L. on ball of L.F. with a pivoting action keeping R. toe in place. Finish facing almost diag. to centre.	3
S	R.F. forward outside partner on her R. side.	
Q	L.F. to side, without weight *2nd pos.* (toe).	
Q	Swivel eighth turn to R. on ball of R.F. with a pivoting action keeping L. toe in place. Finish facing L.O.D. square to partner.	4
	Brush L.F. towards R.F. and continue forward down L.O.D. repeating these four bars.	5–8

55

MOONLIGHT SAUNTER (contd.)

Count	Lady	Bars
SSS	Back R.F., L.F., R.F. down L.O.D.	
S	L.F. back, turning eighth turn to R. on ball of L.F.	1–2
S	R.F. back, partner outside on L. side.	
Q	L.F. to side, without weight 2nd pos. (toe).	
Q	Swivel quarter turn to L. on ball of R.F. with a pivoting action keeping L. toe in place. Finish backing almost diag. to centre.	3
S	L.F. back partner outside on R. side.	
Q	R.F. to side, without weight 2nd pos. (toe).	
Q	Swivel eighth turn to R. on ball of L.F. with a pivoting action keeping R. toe in place. Finish back to L.O.D. partner square.	4
	Brush R.F. towards L.F. and continue backward down L.O.D. repeating these four bars.	5–8

Section Two

The Square

Man

SS	Forward L.F. R.F. down L.O.D.	9
S	L.F. forward, check.	
S	R.F. back.	10
Q	Brush L.F. to R.F. and step L.F. to side (w.f.).	
Q	Close R.F. to L.F. parallel pos. (w.f.).	
S	L.F. back against L.O.D.	11
Q	Brush R.F. to L.F. and step R.F. to side (w.f.).	
Q	Close L.F. to R.F. parallel pos. (w.f.).	
S	R.F. forward down L.O.D.	12
	Face L.O.D. throughout this section.	
	Repeat the Square, but on last step open partner into promenade pos.	13–16
	Man R.F. forward turning an eighth turn to R. to face diag. to wall brushing L.F. towards R.F.	

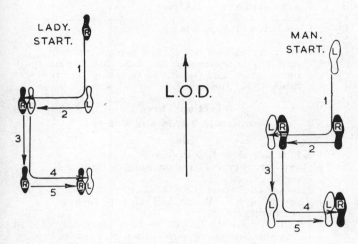

MOONLIGHT SAUNTER. THE SQUARES, BARS 10 TO 12

Count	Lady	Bars
SS	Back R.F., L.F. down L.O.D.	9
S	R.F. back, check.	
S	L.F. forward.	10
Q	Brush R.F. to L.F. and step R.F. to side (w.f.).	
Q	Close L.F. to R.F. *parallel pos.* (w.f.).	
S	R.F. forward against L.O.D.	11
Q	Brush L.F. to R.F. and step L.F. to side (w.f.).	
Q	Close R.F. to L.F. *parallel pos.* (w.f.).	
S	L.F. back.	12
	Repeat the Square, but on last step partner will turn lady in to *promenade pos.* L.F. back turning three-eighths turn to R. to face diag. centre brushing R.F. towards L.F.	13–16

Section Three
Promenade Turns and Points
Man

S	L.F. to side along L.O.D. (heel).	
S	Cross R.F. over L.F. commencing to turn to R. (heel).	17
S	L.F. to side across L.O.D. (ball then w.f.). Turn strongly to R. on ball of L.F. to face centre diagonally.	
S	*Point* R.F. down the L.O.D. (toe) opposite *3rd pos.* A little over three-quarter turn to R. is made on the last three steps. Finish in *contra promenade pos.*, retain the hold but slightly loosen the R. arm, bring L. hand in and over the shoulder. The body inclines over the pointed foot. Man has now changed position with lady.	18
S	Extend R.F. forward down L.O.D.	
S	L.F. forward turning body slightly to R.	19
S	R.F. forward down L.O.D. square to partner.	
S	*Point* L.F. down L.O.D. (toe) opposite *3rd pos.* About a quarter turn to R. is made on the last two steps, turning partner into *promenade pos.*	20
	L.F. to side along L.O.D. and repeat this section.	21–24

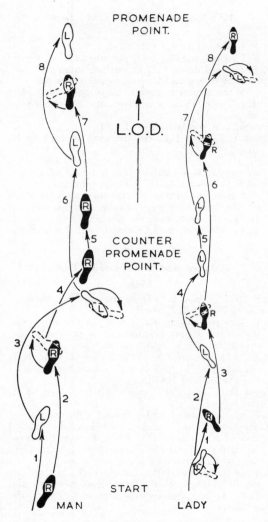

PROMENADE
POINT.

L.O.D.

COUNTER
PROMENADE
POINT.

START

MAN

LADY

MOONLIGHT SAUNTER. PROMENADE TURN AND POINT, BARS 17 TO 20

Count	Lady	Bars
S	R.F. to side along L.O.D. (heel).	
S	L.F. forward, turning body slightly to R.	17
S	R.F. forward down L.O.D. partner square.	
S	*Point* L.F. down L.O.D. (toe) opposite *3rd pos.*	18

About a quarter turn to R. is made on the last three steps. Partner will turn into a *contra promenade pos.*

S	Extend L.F. forward down L.O.D.	
S	Cross R.F. over L.F. commencing to turn to R. (heel).	19
S	L.F. to side across L.O.D. (ball then w.f.). Turn strongly to R. on ball of L.F. to face diag. centre.	
S	*Point* R.F. down L.O.D. (toe) opposite *3rd pos.*	20

A little over three-quarter turn to R. is made on the last three steps. Finish in *promenade pos.* Incline the body over the pointed foot.

	R.F. to side along L.O.D. and repeat this section.	21–24

Section Four

Balancé and Promenade Turn

Man

S	L.F. to side along L.O.D. in *promenade pos.* (heel).	
S	Cross R.F. over L.F. (heel).	25
S	L.F. forward closing R.F. to a *3rd pos. rear*, close with a lilt, slight pressure on ball of closing foot, do not transfer weight, *promenade pos.*	
S	R.F. back against L.O.D. and close L.F. to R.F. *5th pos. point* L. heel over R. toe *promenade pos.*	26
S	L.F. to side along L.O.D. (heel).	
S	Cross R.F. over L.F. commencing to turn to R. (heel–b.o.f.).	27
S	L.F. to side across L.O.D. (b.o.f.), still turning.	
S	Turn strongly to R. on ball of L.F. R.F. forward down L.O.D. finish brushing L.F. to R.F. almost facing diag. to wall in *promenade pos.* A complete turn to R. is made on last three steps.	28

Repeat balancé and promenade turn, but on last step R.F. do not turn partner into *promenade pos.* Face L.O.D. partner square to repeat the sequence.   29–32

Count	Lady	Bars
S	R.F. to side along L.O.D. in *promenade pos.* (heel).	
S	Cross L.F. over R.F.	25
S	R.F. forward closing L.F. to a 3*rd pos. rear*, close with a lilt, slight pressure on ball of closing foot do not transfer weight, *promenade pos.*	
S	L.F. back against L.O.D. and close R.F. to L.F. 5*th pos. point* R. heel over L. toe, *promenade pos.*	26
S	R.F. to side along L.O.D. in *promenade pos.*	
S	Cross L.F. over R.F. (heel).	27
S	Turning to R. to face L.O.D., R.F. forward a strong step between partner's feet (heel then b.o.f.).	
S	L.F. to side and slightly back, across L.O.D. continuing to turn to R. on ball of L.F. brush R.F. to L.F. Finish facing diag. to centre in *promenade pos.* A full turn to R. is made on the last two steps.	28
	Repeat the forward balancé and promenade turn, but on last step partner will not turn into *promenade pos.*, the L.F. will move to side and slightly back across L.O.D., the body finishing backing the L.O.D. to repeat the sequence.	29-32

ROYAL EMPRESS TANGO. FOURTH POINT

ROYAL EMPRESS TANGO

PRIZE DANCE 1922 by H. A. CLIFTON
2/4 TIME—16 BAR SEQUENCE—TEMPO 30/32
Music published by Feldman & Co., Ltd.

6 Bars introduction: Lady curtsy—Man acknowledge.

The hold is similar to that in the waltz, except that the palm of man's L. hand is facing forward and downward instead of upward, holding the fingers of the lady's R. hand between his thumb and fingers; the lady should hold the man's L. thumb in a comfortable manner. The man's R. arm is placed a little more round partner, rather towards the small of the back than under the shoulder blade as in the waltz. Bring the raised hands inwards by bending the elbows slightly.

The lady will poise slightly back from the hips, the body will not be upright as in the waltz; this must not, however, affect the balance of the body. Although it is a matter of individual style, it is considered to be more in keeping with the character of the tangos to retain hip contact, and for the lady to adopt a slightly backward poise.

The technique of this dance is based on natural footwork: forward steps are led with the heel meeting the floor first, immediately lowering to the whole of the foot; closed positions are made with the feet parallel, not 3rd or 5th pos.

Step into position with the foot leaving the floor, with a knee action similar to a normal walking step—the gliding style of the waltz is not the correct interpretation of the Royal Empress Tango.

Start facing the L.O.D. (lady back to L.O.D.), the man holds the lady in front of him, and she should avoid the common tendency to move towards her partner's R. side.

Described in six sections—a competition lead in is given at end.

Section One
Walks

Count		Man	Bars
1	S	L.F. forward.	
2	S	R.F. forward taking the weight of body well over the foot relax the R. knee (plié) do not bend the body over the leg, keep the trunk upright.	1
3	S	Transfer weight back to L.F. straightening R. knee.	

4   S   R.F. back a short step on b.o.f. lightly lower heel to the   2
floor relax the knee and straighten again when the
following step moves forward.

Diagonal Chassés

1   Q   L.F. forward and leftwards (heel) (toe pointing diag.
to centre),

and   Q   Close R.F. to L.F. *parallel pos.* (w.f.).

2   S   L.F. forward (heel) at end of step brush R.F. to L.F.
parallel pos. with slight body turn to right. Body is
facing towards diag. centre during 3rd bar.   3

3   Q   R.F. forward (heel) (toe pointing diag. to wall down
L.O.D.),

and   Q   Close L.F. to R.F. *parallel pos.* (w.f.).

4   S   R.F. forward (heel), bring the L. hip and shoulder
back slightly, swivelling leftwards on flat of foot
at end of step and opening into *promenade pos.* L.F.
will veer towards R.F. whilst opening into *promenade*   4
pos. (inside edge of ball of foot without weight).
Body is facing diag. to wall during 4th bar.
Finish facing diag. to centre down L.O.D.

Walks
Lady

1   S   R.F. back.

2   S   L.F. back relaxing knee (plié).   1

3   S   Transfer weight forward to R.F. (heel w.f.).

4   S   L.F. forward (heel w.f.).   2

Diagonal Chassés

1   Q   R.F. back and rightwards (ball w.f.),

and   Q   Close L.F. to R.F. *parallel pos.* (w.f.).

2   S   R.F. back (ball w.f.) at end of step brush L.F. to R.F.   3
parallel pos. with slight body turn to right. Body is
backing diag. to centre down L.O.D. during 3rd bar.

3   Q   L.F. back (ball w.f.) (toe pointing diag. to centre
against L.O.D.),

and   Q   Close R.F. to L.F. *parallel pos.* (w.f.).

4   S   L.F. back (ball w.f.) with very slight body turn to   4
right as man turns into *promenade pos.* Veer R.F.
towards L.F. at end of step. Body is backing
diag. to wall down L.O.D. during 4th bar.

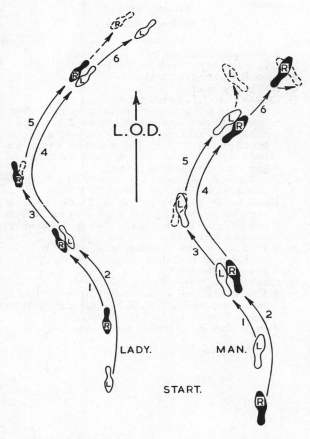

L.O.D.

LADY.

MAN.

START.

ROYAL EMPRESS TANGO. DIAGONAL CHASSÉS, BARS 3 TO 4

Section Two
The Promenades

Count		Man	Bars

Promenade and Chassé to centre of room.

1	S	L.F. to side in *promenade pos.* (heel–w.f.).	
2	S	Cross R.F. over L.F. (heel–w.f.).	5
3	Q	L.F. to side (heel–w.f.).	
and	Q	Close R.F. to L.F. *parallel pos.* (w.f.).	
4	S	L.F. to side taking the weight firmly on to the foot	6

(heel–w.f.) then turn inwards (to the R.).

Most dancers begin to turn as the weight is being transferred to the L.F. This makes for a smoother turn, but it is better style to delay the turn and give more expression to the step.

The R.F. will move a little towards L.F. as the turn is made (inside edge of ball of R.F.).

Finish facing diag. to wall down L.O.D. in *contra promenade pos.* swaying over slightly to the R. This will bring the L. hand in and over the L. shoulder.

Promenade and Chassé to the wall.

1	S	R.F. to side in *contra promenade pos.* (heel–w.f.).	
2	S	Cross L.F. over R.F. (heel–w.f.).	7
3	Q	R.F. to side (heel–w.f.),	
and	Q	Close L.F. to R.F. *parallel pos.* (w.f.).	
4	S	R.F. forward to wall, a medium length step (heel w.f.);	8

and nearly close L.F. to R.F. without transferring weight (inside edge b.o.f.).

Turn partner into *promenade pos.* at end of step.

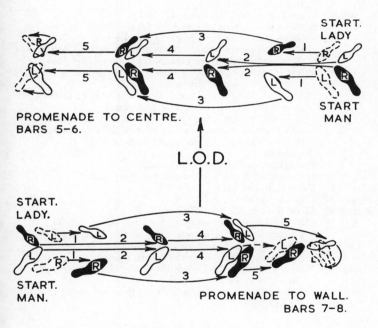

PROMENADE TO CENTRE.
BARS 5-6.

L.O.D.

PROMENADE TO WALL.
BARS 7-8.

ROYAL EMPRESS TANGO. BARS 5 TO 8

Section Two
The Promenades

Count		Lady	Bars

Promenade and Chassé to centre of room.

1	S	R.F. to side in *promenade pos.* (heel–w.f.).	
2	S	Cross L.F. over R.F. (heel–w.f.).	5
3	Q	R.F. to side (heel–w.f.),	
and	Q	Close L.F. to R.F. *parallel pos.* (w.f.).	
4	S	R.F. to side taking the weight firmly on to the foot (heel–w.f.) then turn inwards (to the L.).	6

Most dancers begin to turn as the weight is being transferred to the R.F. This makes the turn smoother, but it is better style to delay the turn, and gives more expression to the step.

The L.F. will move a little towards R.F. as the turn is made (inside edge of ball of L.F.).

Finish facing diag. to wall against L.O.D. in *contra promenade pos.* swaying over slightly to the L.; this will bring the R. hand in and over the R. shoulder.

Promenade and Chassé to the wall.

1	S	L.F. to side in *contra promenade pos.* (heel–w.f.).	
2	S	Cross R.F. over L.F. (heel–w.f.)	7
3	Q	L.F. to side (heel–w.f.),	
and	Q	Close R.F. to L.F. *parallel pos.* (w.f.).	
4	S	L.F. forward and to side, turning to R. (b.o.f.), partner's R.F. will move under the body as the *promenade pos.* is lost, partner square; continue to turn to R. until facing the centre diag.;	8
and		Nearly close R.F. to L.F. without transferring weight (inside edge of foot).	

Finish in *promenade pos.*, preparing to move along the L.O.D.

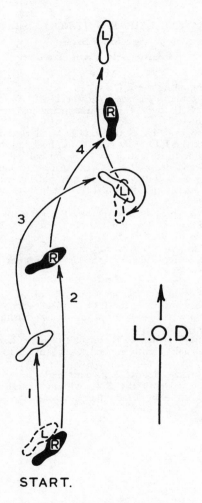

START.

L.O.D.

ROYAL EMPRESS TANGO. PROMENADE PIVOT TURN (MAN)

ROYAL EMPRESS TANGO (*contd.*)
Section Three
Promenade Pivot Turn

Count		Man	Bars
		Moving along the L.O.D.	
1	S	L.F. to side in *promenade pos.* (heel–w.f.).	
2	S	Cross R.F. over L.F. commencing to turn to R. (heel–w.f.).	9
3	S	L.F. to side across the L.O.D. well round partner back the L.O.D. at end (b.o.f., heel can lower).	
4	S	Continue to turn strongly to R. on ball of L.F. R.F. forward down the L.O.D. turning to face almost diag. to wall down L.O.D. turn partner into *promenade pos.* at end of step, L.F. brushing towards R.F. (heel–w.f.).	10

Note partner loses *promenade pos.* on the 3rd step and regains it at the end of 4th step. Keep the R. leg in front of the body and underneath partner as the 4th step moves into position. Nearly a whole turn to R. is made on the last three steps.

Lady

1	S	R.F. to side in *promenade pos.* (heel–w.f.).	
2	S	L.F. forward down the L.O.D. (heel–w.f.).	9
3	S	R.F. forward between partner's feet turning to R. (heel).	
4	S	Continue turning to R. on ball of R.F. L.F. to side and back (slightly across L.O.D.) turn in to *promenade pos.*,	10
and		Nearly close R.F. to L.F. with slight pressure on the inside edge of the R.F. without transferring the weight. Note: lady has a whole turn to R. on 3rd and 4th steps.	

70

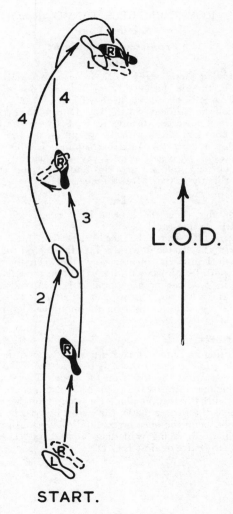

START.

ROYAL EMPRESS TANGO. PROMENADE PIVOT TURN (LADY)

ROYAL EMPRESS TANGO (*contd.*)
Section Four
Promenade and Point

Count		Man	Bars
		Moving along the L.O.D. in *promenade pos.*	
1	S	L.F. to side (heel–w.f.).	
2	S	Cross R.F. over L.F. (heel–w.f.).	11
3	S	*Point* the L. toe down the L.O.D. (toe on the floor).	
4	S	Swivel inwards, turning to R. between the balls of both feet, finish with the weight on the L.F., R. toe in a *point pos.* pointing against L.O.D. and in *contra promenade pos.* Sway over slightly to R., curving the L. arm in and over the shoulder slightly as the swivel is made.	12

Lady

		Moving along the L.O.D. in *promenade pos.*	
1	S	R.F. to side (heel–w.f.).	
2	S	Cross L.F. over R.F. (heel–w.f.).	11
3	S	*Point* the R. toe down the L.O.D. (toe on the floor).	
4	S	Swivel inwards, turning to L. between the balls of both feet, finish with the weight on the R.F., L. toe in *point pos.* pointing against L.O.D. and in *contra promenade pos.* Sway over slightly to L., curving the R. arm in and over the shoulder slightly as the swivel is made.	12

General Notes

The pointing foot moves forward passing beyond the stationary foot a little (*short 4th pos.*), knee is bent as the toe of the foot is pointed downwards, the toe is on the floor. The upper part of the body inclines towards the pointing foot (sway). The swivels are made with the feet in place the weight of the body being transferred as the turn is made, the swivel inverts the *point* to the opposite foot, bend the knee on the 2nd *point pos.* 4th count.

Man will finish facing wall diag. against L.O.D. Lady will finish diag. to centre against L.O.D.

ROYAL EMPRESS TANGO *(contd.)*
Section Five
Contra Promenade and Point

Count		Man	Bar
1	S	R.F. to side against the L.O.D. in *contra promenade pos.* (heel–w.f.).	
2	S	Cross L.F. over R.F. (heel–w.f.).	13
3	S	*Point* the R. toe against L.O.D., sway R.	
4	S	Swivel inwards, turning to L. between the balls of both feet almost to a *promenade pos.* Finish with the weight on the R.F. facing slightly diag. to wall down the L.O.D. L. toe pointing diag. to wall in a *point pos.*	14

Note: there is slightly less turn on this swivel than in the previous movement, which facilitates the dancing of the rotary chassés that follow.

Lady

1	S	L.F. to side against the L.O.D. in *contra promenade pos.*	
2	S	Cross R.F. over L.F. (heel–w.f.).	13
3	S	*Point* the L. toe against L.O.D. sway L.	
4	S	Swivel inwards turning to R. between the balls of both feet almost to a *promenade pos.* Finish with the weight on the L.F. facing slightly diag. to centre down the L.O.D. R. toe pointing diag. to centre in a *point pos.*	14

Section Six
Rotary Chassés

Count		Man	Bars
		Turning to R.	
1	Q	L.F. to side across L.O.D. (b.o.f.),	
and	Q	Close R.F. to L.F. *parallel pos.* partner square (b.o.f.).	
2	S	L.F. back down the L.O.D. turning to R.	15
3	Q	R.F. to side along the L.O.D. still turning (b.o.f.),	
and	Q	Close L.F. to R.F. *parallel pos.* (b.o.f.).	
4	S	R.F. forward down the L.O.D. (heel).	16

A little under a whole turn to R. is made on the chassés.

Section Six
Rotary Chassés

Count		Lady	Bars
1	Q	R.F. diag. forward (b.o.f.).	
and	Q	Close L.F. to R.F. *parallel pos.* square to partner (b.o.f.).	
2	S	R.F. forward down L.O.D. turning to R. (heel).	15
3	Q	L.F. to side across L.O.D. (b.o.f.).	
and	Q	Close R.F. to L.F. *parallel pos.* (b.o.f.).	
4	S	L.F. back down the L.O.D.	16

About five-eighths of a turn to R. is made on the chassés.

An attractive "lead in" for the competition dancer and medallist during the six-bar introduction is as follows—

Face L.O.D. with veleta hold, hesitate for 1st bar.

Count	Man
S	L.F. to side turning inwards to face partner, release hold.
S	Close R.F. to L.F. *3rd pos. front.*
S	Hesitate, bowing to partner.
S	Replace R.F. towards partner turn to face L.O.D. Hold hand again.
S	L.F. back against L.O.D.
S	R.F. back against L.O.D. and close L.F. to R.F. *parallel pos.* Hesitate for 2 bars, leading lady forward with R. hand. Assume normal tango hold at end.

	Lady
S	R.F. to side turning inwards to face man.
SS	L.F. *back 4th pos.* and curtsy.
S	L.F. forward towards partner turn to face L.O.D.
S	R.F. back against L.O.D.
S	L.F. back against L.O.D. and close R.F. to L.F. without weight. Four steps forward curving to L. (half turn) to face partner.
SS	R.F., L.F. forward.
SS	R.F., L.F. forward, closing R.F. to L.F. with a brushing action.

74

IMPERIAL WALTZ

J. POWELL, P.P.B.A.T.D. 3/4 TIME—TEMPO 42
Music published by Francis Day & Hunter, Ltd.

ONE of the most charming of the old time waltz sequences, it is the first dance in the book that includes solo waltzing, generally referred to in textbooks as Inwards and Outwards Waltz.

It is described in three sections. Commencing position as in the Veleta.

Section One
Outwards Waltz and Point

Count	Man	Bars
1, 2, 3	Progressive reverse turn. L.F., R.F., L.F.	1
1, 2, 3	Rotary reverse turn. R.F., L.F., R.F.	2

The 1st step of the rotary turn is taken with back to L.O.D., the R.F. moves *back* and slightly to the side, not to the side as in a normal rotary turn; this prevents the partners from moving too far apart—the complete turn will form an elliptical pattern. Finish in a normal 5*th pos.*, facing L.O.D. Release R. hand, but retain the hand in position in the air, at the completion of the turn the hand is ready to take the lady's L. hand again.

Count	Man	Bars
1, 2, 3	L.F. forward down L.O.D. (b.o.f. then w.f.) 4*th pos.*	3
1, 2, 3	*Point* R.F. forward (toe) look at partner (head to R.).	4

Lady

Count	Lady	Bars
1, 2, 3	Progressive natural turn. R.F., L.F., R.F.	1
1, 2, 3	Rotary natural turn—note remarks on the man's steps.	2
1, 2, 3	R.F. forward down L.O.D. (b.o.f. then w.f.) 4*th pos.*	3
1, 2, 3	*Point* L.F. forward (toe) look inwards (head to L.).	4

Note that in the first bar partners turn away from each other, an outward waltz turn.

The forward steps on the 3rd bar are stepped moving slightly towards each other, the *point* is made with the toes in line.

75

IMPERIAL WALTZ (*contd.*)
Section Two
Inwards Waltz and Point

Count	Man	Bars
1, 2, 3	Progressive natural turn. R.F., L.F., R.F.	5
1, 2, 3	Rotary natural turn. L.F., R.F., L.F.	6
	An elliptical pattern danced in similar manner to the outwards waltz turn.	
	Release the R. hand, and regain the hold at end.	
1, 2, 3	R.F. forward down L.O.D. (b.o.f. then w.f.) *4th pos.*	7
1, 2, 3	*Point* L.F. forward (toe) look down L.O.D.	8

Lady

1, 2, 3	Progressive reverse turn. L.F., R.F., L.F.	5
1, 2, 3	Rotary reverse turn. R.F., L.F., R.F.	6
	An elliptical pattern danced in similar manner to the outwards waltz turn.	
1, 2, 3	L.F. forward down L.O.D. (b.o.f. then w.f.) *4th pos.*	7
1, 2, 3	*Point* R.F. forward (toe) look outwards (head to R.).	8

Man and lady should note that on the 4th bar the point is made with the "inside" foot, and on the 8th bar with the "outside" foot.

Point the foot with the toes turned slightly outward.

Section Three
Pas de Valse and Balancés, etc.
Man

1	L.F. forward (heel) lead the R. hand forward slightly.	
2	R.F. forward, toe pointing down the L.O.D. (b.o.f.).	
3	Close L.F. to R.F. *3rd pos. rear* (b.o.f. then w.f.). Finish facing diag. to centre with the raised arms forward and obliquely backing partner.	9
	This movement is sometimes called an outwards pas de valse. The forward steps are more travelled than the pas de valse used in normal waltzing.	
1	R.F. forward (heel, then b.o.f.).	
2, 3	Close L.F. to R.F. *3rd pos. rear* (forward balancé), still backing partner obliquely.	10

IMPERIAL WALTZ (contd.)

Count	Man	Bars
1	L.F. back against L.O.D. turning to R.	
2	Close R.F. to L.F. *5th pos. rear* (b.o.f.)	
3	Pivot to R. (inwards) similar to Nat. Rotary Waltz turn, to face partner, finish *3rd pos. front.*	11
1	R.F. to side against L.O.D. (b.o.f.w.f.) toe pointing towards wall. Both hands joined (Double Hold No. 5).	
2, 3	Close L.F. to R.F. *3rd pos. front* (W.W.).	12
	Assume normal waltz hold—Waltz Nat. Turns similar to last four bars Veleta.	13–16

Lady

1	R.F. forward (heel) partner leads raised hands forward.	
2	L.F. forward, toe pointing down the L.O.D. (b.o.f.).	
3	Close R.F. to L.F. *3rd pos. rear* (b.o.f. then w.f.). Finish facing diag. to wall, back to partner obliquely.	9
1	L.F. forward (heel then b.o.f.).	
2, 3	Close R.F. *5th pos. rear* (forward balancé), still backing partner obliquely.	10
1	R.F. back against L.O.D. turning to L.	
2	Close L.F. to R.F. *5th pos. rear* (b.o.f.)	
3	Pivot to L. (inwards) similar to Rev. Rotary Waltz turn, to face partner, finish *3rd pos. front.*	11
1	L.F. to side against L.O.D. (b.o.f.w.f.) toe pointing towards centre. Both hands joined (Double Hold No. 5).	
2, 3	Close R.F. to L.F. *3rd pos. front* (W.W.).	12
	Partner will take normal waltz hold and dance four bars natural waltz, opening out on last bar, similar to Veleta.	13–16

Notes. Some dancers prefer to dance a Backward Pas de Valse on the 11th bar, instead of the Rotary Waltz action.

Teachers should note that this dance is an excellent one for class teaching—it contains many fine features technically, the sequence being quickly assimilated by the beginner and improver.

MILITARY TWO STEP

JAMES FINNIGAN

TIME 6/8 or 2/4—TEMPO 48—16 BAR SEQUENCE

Music published by Francis Day & Hunter, Ltd.

A CHAMPIONSHIP dance. Commence as in the Veleta—facing L.O.D. (Hold No. 2.)

Count	Man	Bars
1	*Point* L.F. forward down L.O.D. *4th pos.*	
2	Pause with the foot still pointed, weight on R.F.	1
3, 4	Turn quarter turn to R. to face partner (b.o.f. R.F.). *Point* L.F. behind R. heel *5th pos. rear.* Bring the raised arms back.	2
1, 2	Turn quarter turn to L. to face L.O.D. March (pas allé) L.F., R.F. forward down L.O.D.	3
3	L.F. forward a medium length step (feet turned slightly outward).	
4	Turn to R. weight mainly on ball of L.F. to face nearly against L.O.D. Release R. hand and take partner's R. hand in L. hand. Finish with L.F. pointing to wall, R.F. pointing against L.O.D., do not lower R. heel.	4
1	*Point* R.F. against L.O.D. *4th pos.*	
2	Pause with the foot still pointed, weight on L.F.	5
3	Turn smartly quarter turn to L. to face partner on ball of L.F. and close R.F. to L.F. *parallel pos.* (w.f.). Bring the raised arms back, salute partner with R. hand, the R. arm moving outwards and upwards.	
4	Bring the R. arm sharply to the side but do not swing the arm outwards. The hand moves straight down.	6
1, 2, 3	Turn to face against L.O.D. quarter turn to R. March (pas allé) R.F., L.F., R.F. against L.O.D. (heel) (feet turned slightly outward).	
4	Turn quarter turn to L. to face partner (b.o.f. R.F.). Close L.F. to R.F. *parallel pos.* without weight, and assume normal waltz hold.	7–8
	Dance eight bars natural waltz commencing rotary turn. Open out on last bar to commencing position as in the Veleta.	9–16

78

MILITARY TWO STEP (*contd.*)

Count	**Lady**	Bars
1	*Point* R.F. forward down L.O.D. *4th pos.*	
2	Pause with the foot still pointed.	1
3	Turn quarter turn to L. to face partner and step R.F. to short *4th pos. rear* and "Bob" curtsy to partner. Bend L. knee.	
4	Straighten L. knee bringing body upright.	2
1, 2	Turn quarter turn to R. to face L.O.D. March (pas allé) R.F., L.F. forward down L.O.D.	3
3	R.F. forward a medium length step (feet turned slightly outward).	
4	Turn to L., weight mainly on ball of R.F., to face nearly against L.O.D. Finish with R.F. pointing to centre L.F. pointing against L.O.D., do not lower heel.	4
1	*Point* L.F. against L.O.D. *4th pos.*	
2	Pause with the foot still pointed, weight on R.F.	5
3	Turn to R. (b.o.f. R.F.) to face centre and partner and step L.F. with a semi-rondé action to *4th pos. rear*, bend R. knee and curtsy to partner. The curtsy should be more emphasized than the preceding one.	
4	Straighten R. knee and bring the body towards upright position.	6
	Turn to L. (quarter turn) to face against L.O.D. March (pas allé) (feet turned slightly outward).	
1, 2, 3	L.F., R.F., L.F. against L.O.D. (heel).	
4	Turn to R. quarter turn (b.o.f. L.F.). Close R.F. to L.F. *parallel pos.* without weight. Partner will assume normal waltz hold.	7–8
	Dance eight bars natural waltz commencing progressive turn, open out to commencing position on last bar.	9–16

Note. Dance smartly in a military manner. Although this is a championship dance it is not likely to appeal to those dancers who prefer the more flowing type of dance.

MAXINA. COMMENCING POSITION (HOLD No. 3)

MAXINA

MADAME LOW-HURNDALL
TIME 2/4—TEMPO 30/32—24 BAR SEQUENCE
Music published by Francis Day & Hunter, Ltd.

THIS is a clever dance which introduces movements reminiscent of the Brazilian Maxiste. Partners commence L.F. facing L.O.D. (see illustration opposite). The dance is described in five sections.

Section One
Pas Marches and Chassés

Count		Man and Lady	Bars
1	S	L.F. diag. forward to the L. (b.o.f. then w.f.) (toe pointing diag. to centre) the R.F. will move towards the L.F. a loose *3rd pos. rear* as the L.F. takes the weight. Turn the shoulders and the raised hands leftwards with a swaying action.	
2	S	R.F. diag. forward to the R. (b.o.f. then w.f.) (toe pointing diag. to wall) the L.F. will move towards the R.F. a loose *3rd pos. rear* as the R.F. takes the weight. Turn the shoulders and the raised hands rightwards with a swaying action.	1
3, 4		Repeat these two steps.	2
1	Q	L.F. diag. forward to the L. (toe pointing diag. centre) (b.o.f. then w.f.).	
and	Q	Close R.F. to L.F. *3rd pos. rear* (b.o.f. then w.f.).	Chassé 3
2	S	L.F. diag. forward to centre (b.o.f. then w.f.) the R.F. will move towards the L.F. (a loose *3rd pos. rear*). Sway arms and shoulders to L.	
3	Q	R.F. diag. forward to wall (toe pointing diag. wall) (b.o.f. then w.f.).	
and	Q	Close L.F. to R.F. *3rd pos. rear* (b.o.f. then w.f.).	Chassé 4
4	S	R.F. diag. forward to wall (b.o.f. then w.f.). Sway arms and shoulders to R.	

MAXINA (contd.)
Section Two
The Pivots and Points

Lady in front and towards R. side of partner.

1   S   L.F. forward down L.O.D. facing slightly diag. to wall (b.o.f. then w.f.).

2   S   R.F. forward down L.O.D. (b.o.f. then w.f.). Turn   5 to R. on ball of R.F. to face against L.O.D. Finish with lady on L. side of man, lady's R. hip in front on man's L. hip. Do not release the hold.

3   S   L.F. forward against L.O.D. (b.o.f. then w.f.).

4   S   *Point* R.F. forward against L.O.D. *short 4th pos.* (toe).   6

1   S   R.F. forward against L.O.D. (b.o.f. then w.f.).

2   S   L.F. forward against L.O.D. (b.o.f. then w.f.).   7 Turn to L. on ball of L.F. to face L.O.D. Finish with lady in front and towards R. side of man.

3   S   R.F. forward down L.O.D. (b.o.f. then w.f.).

4   S   *Point* L.F. forward down L.O.D. *short 4th pos.* (toe).   8

Section Three
The Piqué Movement

As the first step is taken raise the R. arms and lower L. arms.

1   Move L.F. very slightly leftwards, with the heel only on the floor, toe pointing upward,

and   Transfer the weight back to R.F.

Repeat for a count of 2 "and" 3 "and" 4 "and" 5 "and" 6 "and" 7 "and" 8 "and" (sixteen quick steps). Turn to L. gradually throughout, finish facing L.O.D. having made a complete turn and regaining upright position of body at end. Man rotates in place, the lady being on the outside of the turn. She will take very small steps forward and leftwards with the L.F. closing R.F. to the L.F. *3rd pos. rear.*   9–12

The man's R.F. is the axis of the movement.
The lady remains in front of partner's R. hip throughout.

MAXINA. PIQUÉ MOVEMENT

83

Section Four
The Heel and Toe Movement

Count			Bar
1	S	L.F. forward down L.O.D. turn L. toe outward (b.o.f. then w.f.).	
2	S	R.F. forward, R. toe outward, plié (b.o.f. then w.f.). Turn shoulders to R. slightly but keep head facing down L.O.D. Lady will turn head and shoulders to R.	13
3	Q	L.F. forward a short step, heel only in contact with the floor, toe pointing upward. Shoulders straight.	
and	Q	Close R.F. to L.F. a loose 3rd pos. rear (w.f.).	14
4	S	L.F. back against L.O.D. toe closing to R. heel 5th pos. rear knee bent, the toe pointing downwards do not transfer the weight to the L.F.	
1–4		Repeat exactly above two bars.	15–16

Section Five
Allemande and Chassés
Man

			Bar
1	S	L.F. forward down L.O.D. (b.o.f. then w.f.).	
2	S	R.F. forward down L.O.D. (b.o.f. then w.f.).	17
3	S	L.F. forward down L.O.D. Release R. hands, raise L. hands, turning partner to R.	
4	S	Turning to face wall on ball of L.F. (quarter turn to R.). Close R.F. to L.F. parallel pos. (w.f.). Release L. hand as partner turns under the raised hand and assume normal waltz hold, and dance slow natural rotary chassé turns, opening out on last bar to commencing position, see note at end.	18 — 19–24

An alternative ending is danced in substitution of the 19th and 20th bars which has the advantage of phrasing to the music better than the original ending.

Count			Bars
1	Q	L.F. to side along L.O.D. (b.o.f. then w.f.).	} Chassé 19
and	Q	Close R.F. to L.F. parallel pos. (w.f.).	
2	S	L.F. to side, brushing R.F. toward L.F.	
3	Q	R.F. to side against L.O.D. (b.o.f. then w.f.).	} Chassé 20
and	Q	Close L.F. to R.F. parallel pos. (w.f.).	
4	S	R.F. to side along L.O.D. (b.o.f. then w.f.) brushing L.F. towards R.F.	

Natural rotary chassé turn. 4 bars.

Section Five

Count		Lady	Bars
1	S	L.F. forward down the L.O.D. (b.o.f. then w.f.).	
2	S	R.F. forward down L.O.D. commencing to turn to R.	17
3	S	L.F. to side and back still turning to R. (b.o.f.).	
and	Q	R.F. to side along the L.O.D. (b.o.f. then w.f.).	
4	Q	Close L.F. to R.F. *parallel pos.* (w.f.)	18

Three-quarters of a turn to R. is made on the last four steps (allemande) finish facing centre and square to partner, with normal waltz hold.

Slow rotary chassé turn, opening out on last bar. 19–24
Man on last bar—

R.F. to side and forward, release L. hand.

L.F. forward down L.O.D. a short step, this would normally be a closed step.

Close R.F. to L.F. *3rd pos. rear* assuming hold as at commencement.

Lady, turning very strongly to R.

L.F. to side across L.O.D. (b.o.f.).

R.F. short step to side still turning (b.o.f. then w.f.).

Turn three-quarter turn to R. approximately on the last two steps.

Finish facing almost down the L.O.D.

Close L.F. to R.F. *3rd pos. front* without weight.

Alternative ending (see note at end of man's steps)—

1	Q	R.F. to side along the L.O.D. (b.o.f. then w.f.).	
and	Q	Close L.F. to R.F. *parallel pos.* (w.f.).	Chassé 19
2	S	R.F. to side along the L.O.D. (b.o.f. then w.f.). The L.F. will brush towards R.F. but do not close.	
3	Q	L.F. to side against L.O.D. (b.o.f. then w.f.).	
and	Q	Close R.F. to L.F. *parallel pos.* (w.f.).	Chassé 20
4	S	L.F. to side against L.O.D. (b.o.f. then w.f.). The R.F. will brush towards L.F. but do not close.	

CROWN AND CORONET

TIME 3/4—TEMPO 46/48—16 BAR SEQUENCE

A DAINTY dance with a real old time atmosphere.

Commencing position the same as La Rinka—but man L.F. *3rd pos. front*, lady R.F. *3rd pos. front* (see illustration, page 92).

Count	Man	Bars
1	L.F. forward down L.O.D. (heel).	
2	R.F. forward (b.o.f.) toe pointing down L.O.D.	Pas de valse 1
3	Close L.F. to R.F. *3rd pos. rear.* Finish facing slightly towards centre down L.O.D.	
1	R.F. forward down L.O.D. *4th pos.* (heel).	
2, 3	Close L.F. to R.F. *5th pos. rear.* Take the close with a body rise, rising to the ball of the R.F. A balancé.	2
1	L.F. back against L.O.D. (lower R. heel).	
2	R.F. back, toe pointing diag. to wall.	Pas de valse 3
3	Close L.F. to R.F. *3rd pos. front* (b.o.f. then w.f.). Finish facing slightly diag. to wall.	
1	R.F. back against L.O.D.	
2, 3	Close L.F. to R.F. *5th pos. front* (b.o.f.).	4
	Repeat 1st bar.	5
1	R.F. forward down L.O.D. (heel–b.o.f.) turn to R. to face wall and partner.	
2, 3	Close L.F. to R.F. *5th pos. rear* (toe). Finish facing partner with arms crossed across body.	6
1	L.F. to side along L.O.D. (b.o.f. then w.f.) toe pointing to wall.	
2, 3	Close R.F. to L.F. *3rd pos. front* (b.o.f. then w.f.). Finish backing slightly diag. to centre.	7
	Repeat last bar.	8
1	L.F. to side across L.O.D. a short step (b.o.f. then w.f.) commence to raise the joined hands moving R. hand rightwards, and L. hand leftwards.	
2, 3	Close R.F. to L.F. *3rd pos. front* (b.o.f. then w.f.), lady will now have her back to man.	9
1	L.F. to side towards the wall a short step (b.o.f. then w.f.), toe pointing diag. to wall against L.O.D.	
2, 3	Close R.F. to L.F. *3rd pos. front* (b.o.f.). Finish with partner toward man's R. side, her head "framed" by the joined R. arms which are raised with the hands over her head. *Bower position.*	10

86

CROWN AND CORONET (*contd.*)

Count	Man	Bars
1	R.F. to side moving rightward behind lady (b.o.f. then w.f.), toe pointing against L.O.D.	
2, 3	Close L.F. to R.F. 3*rd pos. front* (b.o.f. then w.f.), lady will now have her back to man.	11
1	R.F. to side (b.o.f. then w.f.) lower the arms.	
2, 3	Close L.F. to R.F. 3*rd pos. front* (b.o.f.). Finish facing wall and partner release the hands and assume normal waltz hold.	12
	Dance four bars natural waltz turns opening out to commencing position on last bar.	13-16

Lady

	Normal opposite to the end of the fifth bar, then—	
1	L.F. forward down L.O.D. (heel–b.o.f.), turn to L. to face partner.	
2, 3	Close R.F. to L.F. 5*th pos. rear* (toe), now facing partner arms crossed across body.	6
1	R.F. to side along L.O.D. (b.o.f. then w.f.) toe pointing to centre.	
2, 3	Close L.F. to R.F. 3*rd pos. front*. Finish backing slightly diag. to wall down L.O.D.	7
	Repeat last bar.	8
1	R.F. forward and rightwards in front of partner, toe pointing against L.O.D. (b.o.f. then w.f.).	
2, 3	Close L.F. to R.F. 3*rd pos. front*.	9
1	R.F. to side against L.O.D. a short step (b.o.f. then w.f.), toe pointing to wall.	
2, 3	Close L.F. to R.F. 3*rd pos. front* (b.o.f.). On the last two bars approximately three-eighths turn to L. is made, finish facing wall, partner now on L. side, arms raised over the head. *Bower position.*	10
1	L.F. forward and leftwards towards wall (b.o.f. then w.f.) moving in front of partner.	
2, 3	Close R.F. to L.F. 3*rd pos. front* (b.o.f. then w.f.).	11
1	L.F. to side (b.o.f. then w.f.), slight turn to R. Turning on ball of L.F. to face diag, centre down L.O.D.	
2, 3	Close R.F. to L.F. 3*rd pos. front* (b.o.f.). On last two bars a little over half turn to R. is made. Finish partner taking waltz hold.	12
	Dance four bars natural waltz turns opening out on last bar to commencing position.	13-16

DOUBLE HOLD (HOLD NO. 5)

88

DORIS WALTZ

J. BICKERSTAFFE

TIME 3/4—TEMPO 44/48—16 BAR SEQUENCE

Music published by Paxton & Co., Ltd.

COMMENCING hold is similar to Maxina, but partners face towards wall diagonally down L.O.D.

Man L.F. *3rd pos. front,* lady L.F. *3rd pos. rear.*

It is described in two sections.

Section One

Count	Man and Lady	Bars
1	L.F. along L.O.D. (b.o.f. then w.f.).	
2, 3	Close R.F. to L.F. *3rd pos. rear* (b.o.f.).	1
	Turn the bodies to the R. to face wall as the close is made with a lilting action, the heel of the L.F. can leave the floor very slightly using a foot rise as the lilting action is made.	
1	R.F. back against L.O.D. (replace to starting position).	
2, 3	Close L.F. to R.F. *3rd pos. front* (b.o.f.). Turn slightly to L. to face wall diag.	2
1	L.F. along L.O.D. (b.o.f. then w.f.).	
2, 3	Close R.F. to L.F. *3rd pos. rear* (b.o.f. then w.f.).	3
1	L.F. along L.O.D. toe pointing diag. to wall (b.o.f. then w.f.).	
2, 3	Close R.F. to L.F. *3rd pos. front.* Finish facing diag. to wall against L.O.D.	4
	Lady now towards L. side of man, L. foot pointing to wall, R.F. pointing against L.O.D.	
1	R.F. against L.O.D. (b.o.f. then w.f.).	
2, 3	Close L.F. to R.F. *3rd pos. rear.* Lilt. Turn the bodies to L. to face wall.	5
1	L.F. back against L.O.D.	
2, 3	Close R.F. to L.F. *3rd pos. front* (b.o.f.). Turn slightly to R. to face wall diag. against L.O.D.	6
1	R.F. against L.O.D.	
2, 3	Close L.F. to R.F. *3rd pos. rear* (b.o.f. then w.f.). Transfer weight to the foot, turn to L. very slightly.	7

89

DORIS WALTZ (*contd.*)

Man's and lady's steps are different in the next bar—

Count	**Man**	Bars
1	R.F. against L.O.D. (b.o.f. then w.f.). Release L. hand and commence to turn partner under the raised R. hands. Allemande.	
2, 3	Close L.F. to R.F. 3rd *pos. rear* (b.o.f.), turn to L. to face wall. Finish facing partner R. hands joined L. hand on hip.	8

Lady

1	R.F. against L.O.D. Turn strongly to L. on ball of R.F. (approx. a half turn).	
2, 3	Close L.F. to R.F. 3rd *pos. rear* without weight (toe). Keep the balance of the body firmly over the ball of the R.F., finish facing partner and centre, R. hands joined.	8

Section Two
Man

1	L.F. back to centre, toe pointing diag. to wall down L.O.D.	
2, 3	Close R.F. to L.F. 3rd *pos. front* (b.o.f.).	9
1	R.F. forward towards partner raising the joined hands (b.o.f. then w.f.).	
2, 3	Close L.F. to R.F. 3rd *pos. rear* lilt.	10
	Repeat the last two bars, but on last step assume waltz hold and dance four bars natural waltz turns opening but on last bar to commencing position in similar manner to the Maxina.	11–12 13–16

Lady

1	L.F. back to wall, toe pointing diag. to centre against L.O.D.	
2, 3	Close R.F. to L.F. 3rd *pos. front* (b.o.f.).	9
1	R.F. forward towards partner (b.o.f. then w.f.).	
2, 3	Close L.F. to R.F. 3rd *pos. rear*, lilt.	10
	Repeat last two bars, but on last step transfer the weight to the L.F. Partner will take normal waltz hold and dance four bars of natural waltz turns, opening out on last bar to commencing position. Note that lady on the last step of the rotary turn will finish with the L.F. in a 3rd *pos. rear*, do not transfer the weight to the L.F.	13–16

Doris Waltz. Allemande

91

LA RINKA. THE HOLD (HOLD No. 6)

92

LA RINKA

W. F. HURNDALL
TIME 3/4—TEMPO 44/46—24 BAR SEQUENCE
Music published by Paxton & Co., Ltd.

THE commencing hold and position is illustrated on page 92. Partners commence on the right foot.

It is described in three sections.

Section One

Count	**Man and Lady**	Bars
1	R.F. forward diag. to R. (b.o.f. then w.f.).	
2, 3	Close L.F. to R.F. *3rd pos. rear* (b.o.f. then w.f.).	1
1, 3	Repeat above.	2
1	L.F. forward diag. to L. (b.o.f. then w.f.).	
2, 3	Close R.F. to L.F. *3rd pos. rear* (b.o.f. then w.f.).	3
1, 3	Repeat last bar.	4
1	R.F. forward diag. to R. (b.o.f. then w.f.).	
2, 3	Close L.F. towards R.F., a loose *3rd pos. rear*, with slight pressure on the b.o.f., do not transfer weight.	5
1	L.F. forward diag. to L. (b.o.f. then w.f.).	
2, 3	Close R.F. towards L.F., a loose *3rd pos. rear*, with slight pressure on the b.o.f., do not transfer weight.	6

Partner's steps on next two bars are different—

Lady

1, 2, 3	R.F. forward turning to L. to face partner.	7
1, 2	L.F. back, towards wall, bend R. knee and curtsy.	8
3	Recover upright position, preparing to step forward with L.F. into next movement.	

Man

1	R.F. forward diag. to R. (b.o.f. then w.f.).	
2, 3	Close L.F. towards R.F., a loose *3rd pos. rear*, commencing to turn body to the R.	7
1	L.F. to side and back turning to face wall and partner, move away from lady, release L. hand but retain R. hand.	
2, 3	Close R.F. to L.F. *3rd pos. front* and bow to lady.	8

93

Section Two
The Allemande

Count	Man	Bars

Elevate the joined R. hands.

L. hand on L. hip.

1, 2, 3 Dance progressive natural waltz turn, R.F., L.F., R.F. 5*th pos. front.*   9

    Take the 1st step towards R. side of partner, on the 2nd step man will be facing towards his partner's back, finish backing wall completing half turn to R.

1   L.F. back towards wall.

2, 3   Close R.F. to L.F. 3*rd pos. front* (b.o.f.). Do not transfer weight.   10

Repeat these two bars, finishing in the commencing position, but on the last step (the close) release R.   11–12
hand, take partner's L. hand in R. hand, and partner's R. hand in L. hand (double hold).

Lady

Partner will elevate joined R. hands.

1, 2, 3 Dance progressive reverse waltz turn, L.F., R.F., L.F. 5*th pos. front.*   9

    Take the 1st step towards R. side of partner, on 2nd step back will be towards man, finish facing wall completing half turn to L.

1   R.F. back towards centre.

2, 3   Close L.F. to R.F. 3*rd pos. front* (b.o.f.). Do not transfer weight.   10

Repeat these two bars, finishing in the commencing position, partner retains R. hand in his R. hand   11–12
on both the Allemandes, but on last step will take double hold.

    The 10th and 12th bars are similar to a pas glissé, they can be danced with a lilting action and many dancers prefer this style, which is rather like a balancé.

LA RINKA (*contd.*)
Section Three
Pas Glissade—Pas Glissé—8 Bars Natural Waltz Turns

Count	Man	Bars
1	R.F. to side against L.O.D.	
2, 3	Close L.F. to R.F. *3rd pos. front* (b.o.f.).	13
1	R.F. to side against L.O.D. (lower L. heel).	
2, 3	Close L.F. to R.F. *3rd pos. front* (b.o.f.). Raise R. hand lower L. hand swaying over slightly to L.	14
1	L.F. to side along L.O.D.	
2, 3	Close R.F. to L.F. *3rd pos. front* (b.o.f.).	15
1	L.F. to side along L.O.D.	
2, 3	Close R.F. to L.F. *3rd pos. front* (b.o.f. then w.f.). Raise L. hand, lower R. hand swaying over slightly to R.	16
	Recover upright position of body, assume normal waltz hold and dance eight bars natural waltz turns (commencing rotary part of turn) opening out on last bar to commencing position. See note at end.	17–24

Lady

Count	Lady	Bars
1	L.F. to side against L.O.D.	
2, 3	Close R.F. to L.F. *3rd pos. front* (b.o.f.).	13
1	L.F. to side against L.O.D. (lower R. heel).	
2, 3	Close R.F. to L.F. *3rd pos. front* (b.o.f.).	14
1	R.F. to side along L.O.D.	
2, 3	Close L.F. to R.F. *3rd pos. front* (b.o.f.).	15
1	R.F. to side along L.O.D.	
2, 3	Close L.F. to R.F. *3rd pos. front* (b.o.f.). Note sways and holds in man's steps.	16
	Waltz, commencing progressive turn.	17–24

To regain commencing position on last bar—

Man will dance a pas de valse with very little turn. R., L., R. closing *3rd pos. front*. Release L. hand and lower R. hand on 2nd step.

Lady will finish rotary turn in a *3rd pos.* Release L. arm on 2nd step moving it forward.

Partners take commencing hold on 3rd step.

FYLDE WALTZ

T. ALMOND
TIME 3/4—TEMPO 40—16 BAR SEQUENCE
Music published by Francis Day & Hunter, Ltd.

A CLEVER dance with unusual features and expression. It is one of the most popular competition dances.

It is described in three sections. Commencing position is the same as in the Veleta (Hold No. 2).

Section One

Count	Man	Bars
1	L.F. forward down L.O.D.	
2	R.F. forward down L.O.D. } Pas de valse.	1
3	Close L.F. to R.F. *3rd pos. rear.*	

Lead the raised arms forward as in the Veleta.

Count	Man	Bars
1	R.F. forward down L.O.D. (heel–b.o.f.)	
2, 3	Close L.F. to R.F. *3rd pos. rear* (b.o.f.) } Balancé.	2

Keep the L. shoulder back as the R. shoulder takes a strong forward and upward swing on the first step of the balancé, when closing rise on to the ball of R.F. Body facing diag. centre, down L.O.D.

Count	Man	Bars
1	L.F. back against L.O.D. (lower R. heel).	
2, 3	Close R.F. to L.F. *3rd pos. front* (b.o.f.–w.f.), retain the head and shoulder line, finish preparing to turn the body to the R.	3
1	L.F. back against L.O.D. turning inwards to the R. and commencing to bring the raised arms back.	
2	Close R.F. to L.F. *5th pos. rear* (toe).	
3	Pivot to R. on the balls of both feet to face about against L.O.D., finish *5th pos. front* having released R. hand and now holding partner's R. hand in L. hand, weight on L.F. The last three steps are a rotary waltz turn.	4

Note that first and second bars move forward along the L.O.D., the third and fourth backward and against L.O.D.

FYLDE WALTZ. END OF SECOND BAR

Section One

Count	Lady	Bars

1   R.F. forward down L.O.D.
2   L.F. forward down L.O.D.   } Pas de valse.   1
3   Close R.F. to L.F. *3rd pos. rear*,
    partner will lead the raised arms forward.

1   L.F. forward down L.O.D. (heel–b.o.f.)   } Balancé.   2
2, 3   Close R.F. to L.F. *3rd pos. rear* (b.o.f.)
    Keep the R. shoulder back as the L. shoulder takes a strong forward and upward swing on the first step of the balancé, when closing rise on to the ball of the L.F. Body facing diag. wall, down L.O.D. The elbow of the R. arm which is holding the gown will be pointing against L.O.D.

1   R.F. back against L.O.D. (lower L. heel).
2, 3   Close L.F. to R.F. *3rd pos. front* (b.o.f. then w.f.).   3
1   R.F. back against L.O.D. turning inwards to the L.
2   Close L.F. to R.F. *5th pos. rear* (toe).
3   Pivot to L. on the balls of both feet to face almost against   4
    L.O.D., finish *5th pos. front*, weight on R.F.
    Partner will change the hold on last step, lady will take gown in L. hand.

Section Two
Inversion of First Section
Man

1   R.F. forward against L.O.D.
2   L.F. forward against L.O.D.   } Pas de valse.   5
3   Close R.F. to L.F. *3rd pos. rear*,
    lead the raised arms forward.

1   L.F. forward against L.O.D. (heel-b.o.f.)   } Balancé.   6
2, 3   Close R.F. to L.F. *3rd pos. rear* (toe)
    Keep the R. shoulder back as the L. shoulder takes a strong forward and upward swing on the first step of the balancé, when closing rise on to the ball of the L.F. Body facing diag. centre, against L.O.D.

FYLDE WALTZ (contd.)

Count	**Man**	Bars
1	R.F. back down L.O.D.	
2, 3	Close L.F. to R.F. 3rd pos. front (b.o.f. then w.f.), retain the head and shoulder line, finish preparing to turn the body to the L.	7
1	R.F. back down L.O.D. turning inwards to the L. and beginning to bring the raised arms back.	
2	Close L.F. to R.F. 5th pos. rear (toe).	
3	Pivot to L. on the balls of both feet to face almost down L.O.D., finish 5th pos. front having released L. hand and now holding partner's L. hand as at the commencing position, weight on R.F.	8

The last three steps are a rotary waltz turn.

Lady

1	L.F. forward against L.O.D.	
2	R.F. forward against L.O.D. } Pas de valse.	5
3	Close L.F. to R.F. 3rd pos. rear,	

partner will lead the raised arms forward.

1	R.F. forward against L.O.D. } Balancé.	6
2, 3	Close L.F. to R.F. 3rd pos. rear	

Keep the L. shoulder back as the R. shoulder takes a strong forward and upward swing on the first step of the balancé, when closing rise on to the ball of the R.F. Body facing diag. wall, against L.O.D.

1	L.F. back down L.O.D.	
2, 3	Close R.F. to L.F. 3rd pos. front (b.o.f. then w.f.) retain the head and shoulder line, finish preparing to turn the body to the R.	7
1	L.F. back down L.O.D., turning inwards to the R.	
2	Close R.F. to L.F. 5th pos. rear (toe).	
3	Pivot to R. on the balls of both feet to face almost down L.O.D., finish 5th pos. front, weight on L.F.	8

Partner will regain hold as at commencement.

FYLDE WALTZ (contd.)

Section Three

Count	Man	Bars
1, 2, 3	Progressive L. turn (outwards), L.F., R.F., L.F. Lead R. arm forward.	9
	Note that 8th and 9th bars constitute an inwards and outwards reverse waltz turn. Finish with R. toe pointing to centre, L. toe pointing against L.O.D., body almost facing diag. centre against L.O.D.	
	Release R. hand and place on R. hip.	
1	R.F. to side along L.O.D., toe pointing to centre. Take partner's R. hand in L. hand.	
2, 3	Close L.F. to R.F. 3rd pos. front (b.o.f. then w.f.), facing diag. centre against L.O.D., L. toe pointing against L.O.D.	10
1	R.F. back down L.O.D., turning body to L.	
2	Close L.F. to R.F. 5th pos. rear (toe).	
3	Pivot on the balls of both feet to face partner and wall. Hold lady's R. hand in L. hand, and L. hand in R. hand.	11
	Last three steps are a reverse rotary waltz turn.	
1	L.F. to side along L.O.D. (double hold).	
2, 3	Close R.F. to L.F. 3rd pos. front; pas glissade.	12
	Assume normal waltz hold and dance four bars waltz, opening out to commencing position as in Veleta.	13–16

Lady

Count		Bars
1, 2, 3	Progressive R. turn (outwards), R.F., L.F., R.F.	9
1	L.F. to side along L.O.D., toe pointing to wall.	
2, 3	Close R.F. to L.F. 3rd pos. front (b.o.f. then w.f.).	10
1	L.F. back down L.O.D., turning body to R.	
2	Close R.F. to L.F. 5th pos. rear (toe).	
3	Pivot to R. to face partner; finish with weight on L.F. 5th pos.	11
	Last three steps are a natural rotary turn.	
1	R.F. to side along L.O.D. (double hold).	
2, 3	Close L.F. to R.F. 3rd pos. front; pas glissade.	12
	Waltz opening out as in the Veleta.	13–16
	Note arm changes in man's description.	

WALTZ COQUETTE

TIME 3/4—TEMPO 42/44

*Music composed by Maurice Smart and published by
Francis Day & Hunter, Ltd.*

AN excellent dance that has movement, atmosphere, a lilting melody and delightful phrasing happily wedded to the dance.

A 24 bar sequence, described in three sections. Commence in open position as in the Veleta.

Section One

Man

Count		Bars
1, 2, 3	Pas de valse L.F., R.F., L.F., body turn outwards (to L.) head line inwards looking towards partner.	1
1	R.F. forward down L.O.D. (heel) turning inwards (to R.) to face partner.	
2, 3	Close L.F. to R.F. 5*th pos. rear* without weight. Dance this step with a lilting action rising well on to the ball of R.F. with strong body rise. Continue body turn to R. Nat. rotary turn.	2
1, 2, 3	L.F., R.F., L.F.—first step will be to side and back moving along L.O.D. Finish facing towards L.O.D. release R. hand on first step but retain hand in position in the air.	3
1, 2, 3	R.F. forward down L.O.D. (heel), rejoin inside hands on the first beat of the bar.	4
1, 2, 3	Rondé L.F. forward with a wide outwards sweeping action to 4*th pos.* (toe) slight *plié* on R. leg. Finish with body facing diag. to wall down L.O.D. and towards partner. Look at your partner.	5
1	L.F. back against L.O.D., foot turned well outward (to L.) toe pointing slightly diag. to centre against L.O.D.	
2, 3	Close R.F. to L.F. 5*th pos. point* head line to left against L.O.D.—partners back to back. Release R. hand and take partner's R. hand in L. hand. Look at the joined hands.	6

WALTZ COQUETTE (*contd.*)

Man

Moving along L.O.D.—Reverse Rotary Turn.

Count   Bars

1, 2, 3   R.F., L.F., R.F. finish 5*th pos*. L. toe almost pointing   7
           down L.O.D., body and head facing towards partner.
              The first step of the rotary turn will move along
              L.O.D. almost backwards.

1   L.F. to side along L.O.D. (b.o.f. then w.f.) toe pointing   8
           to wall.

2, 3   Close R.F. to L.F. (b.o.f.) without weight (*pas glissé*).
              Incline body slightly over the closing foot. Body
           will be facing diag. to wall against L.O.D. Look
           at your partner.

Note. There is only one change of hold, the disengaged hand
being placed on the hip. Do not force the raised hands forward
and backward—you do nothing with the hands when holding,
the flowing action is created by the turning of the shoulders and
body.
            1st bar: hands move forward along L.O.D.
            2nd bar: against L.O.D.
            3rd bar: release turning outwards.
            4th and 5th bars: regain hold and continue the outwards
            swing into an inwards swing, the hands on the Rondé
            moving slightly against L.O.D.—do not obscure the
            lady's face.
            6th bar: hands move forward along L.O.D.—then release.
            7th bar: hands flow inward.
            8th bar: hands to side along L.O.D.

Lady

Count   Bars

1, 2, 3   Pas de valse R.F., L.F., R.F., turn outwards (to R.).   1
           Swing R. hand and gown outwards and backwards
           with a sweeping action.
              Head line inwards looking towards partner.

1   L.F. forward along L.O.D. (heel) turning inwards
           (to L.) to face partner.

2, 3   Close R.F. to L.F. 5*th pos. rear* without weight.   2
              Dance with a lilting action rising to ball of L.F.
           with strong body rise, sweep the gown forward and
           slightly upward.
           Continuing to turn body to left—Rev. rotary turn.

WALTZ COQUETTE (*contd.*)

Lady

Count		Bars
1, 2, 3	R.F., L.F., R.F.—first step will be to side and back moving along L.O.D. Finish facing towards L.O.D., partner will release hold. Hold gown away from the body flowing inward and then outward.	3
1, 2, 3	L.F. forward down L.O.D. (heel) rejoin inside hands.	4
1, 2, 3	Rondé R.F. forward down L.O.D. with a wide sweeping action to *4th pos.* (toe) with slight plié on L. leg. Finish with body facing diag. to centre down L.O.D. and towards partner. Look at your partner. Flow the gown outwards and then forward following the foot line of the R.F.	5
1	R.F. back against L.O.D. foot turned well outward (to R.) toe pointing slightly diag. to wall against L.O.D. Swing gown outwards and rightwards against L.O.D.	
2, 3	Close L.F. to R.F. *5th pos. point* head line to right against L.O.D.—partners back to back. Partners will release L. hand and take R. hand in his L. hand. Look at the joined hands. Moving along L.O.D.—Nat. Rotary turn.	6
1, 2, 3	L.F. R.F., L.F., finish *5th pos.* R. toe pointing almost down L.O.D. body and head facing towards partner. The first step of the rotary turn will move along L.O.D. almost backwards. Flow the gown inwards (gown now in L. hand).	7
1	R.F. to side along L.O.D. (b.o.f. then w.f.) toe pointing to centre.	
2, 3	Close L.F. to R.F (b.o.f.) without weight (*pas glissé*). Incline body slightly over the closing foot. Body will be facing diag. to centre against L.O.D. Look at your partner. Continue the inwards flow of the gown rightwards and slightly upwards. See notes on change of hold given with man's steps.	8

WALTZ COQUETTE (*contd.*)

Section Two

Inversion of first section but moving against L.O.D. Man commence R.F.—Lady L.F.

Man will dance the steps of lady's 1st section. Lady will dance the steps of man's 1st section. Finish facing each other on the Pas Glissé; 16th bar—looking at your partner.

Man: Pas de valse—lilt L.F.—Rev. rotary rondé R.F.—5*th point* L.F.—Nat. rotary—Glissé.

Lady: Pas de valse L.F.—lilt R.F.—Nat. rotary rondé L.F.—5*th point* R.F.—Rev. rotary—Glissé.

Section Three

8 bars waltzing danced in the following manner.

Count			Bars
1, 2, 3	Man:	Pas de valse forward down L.O.D., L.F., R.F., L.F., turning lady to right (allemande) under the raised R. hand.	
	Lady:	Nat. prog. turn R.F., L.F., R.F.	17
1, 2, 3	Man:	Nat. prog. turn R.F., L.F., R.F.	
	Lady:	Nat. rotary turn L.F., R.F., L.F.	18
		Partners assume normal waltz hold.	
1–9	Man:	Nat. rotary turn L.F., R.F., L.F.	
		Nat. prog. turn R.F., L.F., R.F.	
		Nat. rotary turn L.F., R.F., L.F.	
	Lady:	Nat. prog. turn R.F., L.F., R.F.	
		Nat. rotary turn L.F., R.F., L.F.	
		Nat. prog. turn R.F., L.F., R.F.	19–21
1–3	Man:	Pas de valse forward down L.O.D., R.F., L.F., R.F.	
	Lady:	Pas de valse backward L.F., R.F., L.F.	22
1–6	Man:	Rev. prog. turn L.F., R.F., L.F.	
		Rev. rotary turn R.F., L.F., R.F.	
	Lady:	Rev. rotary turn R.F., L.F., R.F.	23–24
		Pas de valse forward down L.O.D. moving slightly rightwards towards commencing position. L.F., R.F., L.F. 3*rd pos. rear.*	
		Disengage R. hand during the last bar.	

LA MASCOTTE

BY THE OFFICIAL BOARD OF BALLROOM DANCING

TIME 4/4—TEMPO 24—16 BAR SEQUENCE

COMMENCING position similar to Veleta—Hold No. 2. **Man** commences L.F.—Lady commences R.F.

Count	**Man**	Bars
1	L.F. forward down L.O.D.	
2	Close R.F. to L.F. *3rd pos. rear* (b o.f., w.f.)	
3	L.F. forward down L.O.D. (b.o.f., w.f.)	
4	R.F. forward to *low 4th front aerial pos.*	1
1	R.F. forward down L.O.D.	
2	Close L.F. to R.F. *3rd pos. rear* (b.o.f., w.f.).	
3	R.F. forward down L.O.D. (b.o.f., w.f.)	
4	L.F. forward to *low 4th aerial pos.* (Lady dances normal opposite).	2
1, 2	L.F. forward down L.O.D. face diag. wall down L.O.D. Assume Double Hold—No. 5.	
3, 4	Cross R.F. forward over L.F., turn to R. to face diag. wall against L.O.D.	3
1, 2	L.F. sideways along L.O.D. (b.o.f., w.f.).	
3, 4	R.F. back (b.o.f., w.f.).	4
1	L.F. to side along L.O.D. (b.o.f., w.f.) toe pointing to wall.	
2	Close R.F. to L.F. *3rd pos. front* (b.o.f., w.f.).	
3	L.F. to side along L.O.D. (b.o.f., w.f.).	
4	Close R.F. to L.F. *5th pos.* point (toe).	5
1	R.F. to side against L.O.D. (b.o.f., w.f.) toe pointing to wall.	
2	Close L.F. to R.F. *3rd pos. front* (b.o.f., w.f.).	
3	R.F. to side against L.O.D. (b.o.f., w.f.).	
4	Close L.F. to R.F. *5th pos.* point. (toe)	6
1–8	Assume normal waltz hold. Waltz Nat. Turns Rotary, Prog. Rotary, Pas de Valse down L.O.D. R.F., L.F., R.F., finish facing diag. wall down L.O.D., Lady's R. hand in R. hand.	7–8
1–16	Partners dance bars 1 and 2 twice. Once round to the R. (clockwise) (similar action to a Tour de Main). Man finishes facing wall and partner releasing the hold.	9–12
1, 2	L.F. back towards centre of room (b.o.f., w.f.).	
3, 4	R.F. back (b.o.f., w.f.) raising L.F. to low *4th front aerial pos.* with a Bowing action.	13

LA MASCOTTE (*contd.*)

Count	**Man**	Bars
1, 2	L.F. forward (heel) towards partner.	
3, 4	R.F. forward (heel) towards partner. Finish closing L.F. to R.F. 3rd *pos. rear* (W.W.) assuming normal waltz hold with partner.	14
1–8	Nat. Waltzing—Rotary L.F., R.F., L.F.—Prog. R.F., L.F., R.F.—Rotary L.F., R.F., L.F.—Pas de Valse R.F., L.F., R.F. (as last two bars Latchford Schottische).	15–16

Lady

1–8	R.F. forward down L.O.D. normal opposite to man.	1–2
1, 2	R.F. forward down L.O.D., turn to L. to face diag. centre against L.O.D. Double Hold.	
3, 4	L.F. back (b.o.f., w.f.) behind R.F. turn to R. to face diag. centre down L.O.D.	
1–2	R.F. sideways along L.O.D. (b.o.f., w.f.).	
3–4	L.F. forward diag. to centre down L.O.D. body turn to L. at end of step.	4
1	R.F. to side along L.O.D. (b.o.f., w.f.) toe pointing to centre of room.	
2	Close L.F. to R.F. 3rd *pos. front* (b.o.f., w.f.).	
3	R.F. to side along L.O.D. (b.o.f., w.f.).	
4	Close L.F. to R.F. 5th *pos.* point. (toe).	5
1	L.F. to side against L.O.D. (b.o.f., w.f.) toe pointing to centre of room.	
2	Close R.F. to L.F. 3rd *pos. front* (b.o.f., w.f.).	
3	L.F. to side against L.O.D. (b.o.f., w.f.).	
4	Close R.F. to L.F. 5th *pos.* point (toe).	6
1–8	Waltz Nat. Turns—Prog. Rotary, Prog. L.F. back, Close R.F. to L.F. 3rd *pos. front* (W.W.) facing diag. centre against L.O.D. (R. hands joined).	7–8
1–16	Dance bars 1 and 2, twice, once round to the R.	9–12
1, 2	R.F. back towards wall (b.o.f., w.f.).	
3, 4	L.F. back (b.o.f., w.f.) raising R.F. to low 4th front *aerial pos.*	13
1, 2	R.F. forward (heel) towards partner.	
3, 4	L.F. forward (heel) towards partner, closing R.F. to L.F. 3rd *pos. front* (W.W.) assuming waltz hold.	14
1–8	Nat. Waltzing—Prog. R.F., L.F., R.F., Rotary L.F., R.F., L.F. Prog. R.F., L.F., R.F. Rotary L.F., R.F., L.F. (as last two bars Latchford Schottische).	15–16

GAINSBOROUGH GLIDE

MARJORIE FAIRLEY, U.K.A.
TIME 4/4—TEMPO 24
Music published by Francis Day & Hunter, Ltd.

A CHAMPIONSHIP dance described in 3 sections: sequence 16 bars.

Lady and man commence L.F. 3rd pos. front facing down L.O.D. Open position Hold No. 2 similar to Veleta.

Man and Lady

Count	Section One	Bars
	Forward Chassé—Pas de Basque—Zephyr "Tap"	
1	L.F. forward down L.O.D. (b.o.f. w.f.) toe pointing diag. centre.	
2	Close R.F. to L.F. 3rd pos. rear (b.o.f. w.f.) toe pointing diag. to wall down L.O.D., body facing L.O.D.	
3–4	Repeat the above two steps.	1
1, 2	Pas de Basque to left, L.F., R.F., L.F., 5th pos.	
3, 4	Pas de Basque to right, R.F., L.F., R.F. 5th pos. Headline for partners is rightwards on Pas de Basque to L., leftwards on Pas de Basque to R.	2
1	L.F. forward down L.O.D. (b.o.f. w.f.)	
2	R.F. forward, Zephyr action to 4th front pos. (low aerial) touch floor with toe of foot when R.F. is level with L.F. (touch on 2nd beat).	
3	Commence to move R.F. towards body. Touch floor with toe of R.F. immediately in front of L.F. moving into a crossed position.	
4	Tap floor with toe of R.F. (foot line pointing downwards to the floor—outside edges of feet almost touching, head line leftwards). Dance last three beats with a continuous action of the R. leg.	3
1	R.F. forward down L.O.D. (b.o.f. w.f.)	
2	Zephyr L.F. forward, skimming floor as L.F. passes R.F.	
3	Move L.F. towards the body, passing towards a crossed position.	
4	Tap floor with toe of L.F. (head line rightwards, foot line downwards).	

Repeat above 4 bars, but on 2nd beat of eighth bar transfer lady's L. hand to man's L. hand—on 3rd beat man places R. hand on lady's R. hip (rather round lady's waist). Lady retains gown in R. hand. Gown is held away from the body. There is no swinging action. 5–8

Section Two

Skating—Diagonal Chassés
Natural Pivot and "Swing"

Count		Bars
1	L.F. forward diag. to centre down L.O.D. (b.o.f. w.f.). Head line leftwards, body facing L.O.D.	
2	Close R.F. to L.F. *3rd pos. rear* (b.o.f. w.f.).	
3	L.F. forward diag. to centre down L.O.D. (b.o.f. w.f.).	
4	Brush R.F. to L.F. (*3rd pos. rear*) without weight	9
1	R.F. forward diag. to wall down L.O.D. (b.o.f. w.f.). Man's R.F. slightly in front of lady, man's hip behind, not in front of lady's L. hip. Head line rightwards, body facing L.O.D.	
2	Close L.F. to R.F. *3rd pos. rear* (b.o.f. w.f.).	
3, 4	R.F. forward diag. to wall down L.O.D. (b.o.f. w.f.). Finish brushing L.F. towards *3rd pos. rear*.	10
	Partners face down L.O.D. in 9th and 10th bars.	
1	L.F. forward (heel) down L.O.D.	
2	Swing R.F. forward to *4th front aerial pos.* toe pointed downward. Do *not* touch floor as foot passes L.F.	
3, 4	Turn to right on ball of L.F. to face against L.O.D. (half turn) at the same time swing R.F. against L.O.D. (toes of R.F. will lower towards floor as R.F. passes L.F. but do *not* touch the floor). Finish *4th aerial pos.* against L.O.D.	11
	During 3rd and 4th counts of 11th bar, change the arm positions. Lady's R. hand in man's R. hand—L. hand on lady's L. hip (round waist). Lady holds gown in L. hand.	
1, 2, 3	R.F., L.F., R.F., back down L.O.D.—facing against L.O.D.	12
	Close L.F. to R.F. *parallel pos.* with weight, man with L. hip slightly behind lady's R. hip.	

GAINSBOROUGH GLIDE. FIRST STEP OF TENTH BAR

Section Three

Skating—Diagonal Chassés

Count	Natural Waltz	Bars
1	R.F. forward diag. to centre against L.O.D. (b.o.f. w.f.). Head line rightwards, body facing against L.O.D.	
2	Close L.F. to R.F. 3rd pos. rear (b.o.f. w.f.).	
3	R.F. forward diag. to centre against L.O.D. (b.o.f. w.f.).	
4	Brush L.F. to R.F. (*3rd pos. rear*).	13
1	L.F. forward diag. to wall against L.O.D. (b.o.f. w.f.). Head line leftwards, body facing against L.O.D.	
2	Close R.F. to L.F. 3rd pos. rear (b.o.f. w.f.).	
3	L.F. forward diag. to wall against L.O.D. (b.o.f. w.f.).	
4	Close R.F. to L.F. *parallel pos.* (slight turn to L. as man). Lady turns to R. on ball of L.F. to face centre of room (three-eighths turn approx.). Close *parallel pos.* without weight.	14

Assume waltz hold during last two beats.

Man: Rotary L.F., R.F., L.F., *5th pos.* Prog. R.F., L.F., R.F., *5th pos.* Rotary L.F., R.F., L.F., *5th pos.* Pas de valse forward and diag. to left releasing hold. R.F. L.F., R.F., *3rd pos. rear.*   15–16

Lady: Prog. R.F. L.F., R.F., *5th pos.* Rotary L.F., R.F., L.F. *5th pos.* Prog. R.F., L.F., R.F., In the last bar, lady is *not* to dance a normal rotary dance but a pivoting action on ball of L.F. turning approx. five-eighths turn to R. to face L.O.D. and closes R.F. to L.F. *3rd pos. rear* with weight.

Note on Footwork, *1st and 5th Bars*. Footwork of the leading step L.F. is given as danced by Competition Dancers. It is a standardized heel lead, *toe being released from the floor at end of step.* Very few dancers succeed in dancing this footwork with expression and soft movement.

MAGENTA MODERN WALTZ

TIME 3/4—TEMPO 32

THE most popular of the Modern Waltz Sequences. Included in the Medal Tests of several dancing societies.

Normal ballroom hold throughout. This dance has the advantage that it can be danced in any size studio or ballroom, without distorting the pattern.

Forward Changes—Whisk—Whisk Wing

Count	Man	Bars
1	L.F. forward down L.O.D. (heel).	
2	R.F. to side (b.o.f.) fairly wide step.	
3	Close L.F. to R.F. *parallel pos.* (rise to toes).	1
1	R.F. forward down L.O.D. (heel).	
2	L.F. to side (b.o.f.) fairly wide step.	
3	Close R.F. to L.F. *parallel pos.* (rise to toes).	2
1	L.F. forward down L.O.D. (heel) slight body turn to L.	
2	R.F. to side and slightly back (b.o.f.) towards wall—preparing to turn lady to *promenade pos.*	
3	Whisk (cross) L.F. in behind R.F. (toes) *promenade pos.* Face diag. to centre down L.O.D.	3
1	R.F. forward towards centre (heel) leading lady forward towards LEFT SIDE—medium length step.	
2	L.F. diag. forward (b.o.f.) towards centre—short step.	
3	Cross R.F. in behind L.F. (rising to toes) lady now on L. side of man—man's L. hip in contact with lady's L. hip. Man still facing diag. to centre—lady's back diag. to centre down L.O.D.	4

Telemark—Natural Spin Turn

1	L.F. forward (heel) diag. to centre down L.O.D.—on L. side of lady turning body strongly to L.	
2	R.F. to side across L.O.D. (b.o.f.) body backing L.O.D.—finish with partner square.	
	Continue to turn body to L.	
3	L.F. to side (and slightly forward) (b.o.f.). Face diag. to wall down L.O.D. preparing to step outside partner on R. side—¾ turn to L. on last 3 steps.	5

Count		Bars
1	R.F. forward (diag. to wall) turning to R. (heel).	
2	L.F. to side (b.o.f.) across L.O.D. a wide step.	
3	Close R.F. to L.F. *parallel pos.* (rising to toes).	
	Finish backing L.O.D.—partner square.	6
1	L.F. back down L.O.D. (b.o.f.) a medium length step turning body strongly to R. with a pivoting action.	
2	R.F. forward down L.O.D. (heel) continuing turn to R.	
3	L.F. to side (slightly back) (b.o.f.) on same line as previous step. Face diag. to wall against L.O.D.	
	Approx. ⅞ turn to R. on last three steps.	7
1	R.F. back (diag. to centre) turning to L.	
2	L.F. to side (b.o.f.), facing diag. to wall down L.O.D.	
3	Close R.F. to L.F. (toes) *parallel pos.* (¼ turn to L.).	8
1	L.F. forward (heel) turn to L.	
2	R.F. to side (b.o.f.) a wide step.	
3	Close L.F. to R.F. *parallel pos.* (rising to toes)—facing L.O.D. (⅛ turn approx.).	9
1	R.F. back against L.O.D. (b.o.f., w.f.) slight turn to L.	
2	L.F. to side (towards centre) (b.o.f.), toe pointing diag. to centre down L.O.D.	
3	Close R.F. to L.F. *parallel pos.* (rise to toes) facing diag. to centre down L.O.D. (⅛ turn approx.).	10
1	L.F. forward diag. to centre (heel) turning to L.	
2	R.F. to side across L.O.D. (b.o.f.).	
3	Close L.F. to R.F. *parallel pos.* back L.O.D.	11
1	R.F. back down L.O.D. (turning to L.) (b.o.f., w.f.).	
2	Close L.F. to R.F. *parallel pos.* (b.o.f.) body facing wall.	
3	Rise to toes—hesitate—body turning to face diag. wall down L.O.D. (⅜ turn on last three steps). Finish preparing to lead partner forward towards R. side.	12

Back Whisk—Chassé—Hesitation Change

1	L.F. back diag. to centre against L.O.D. (b.o.f., w.f.).	
2	R.F. to side (b.o.f.) leading lady into promenade pos.	
3	Cross L.F. in behind R.F. (toes), body still facing diag. to wall down L.O.D.—lady facing diag. to centre down L.O.D.—promenade pos.	13
1	R.F. forward down L.O.D. (heel) preparing to turn lady square.	
2	L.F. to side along L.O.D. (b.o.f.).	
and	Close R.F. to L.F. *parallel pos.* (toes) partner square.	
3	L.F. to side along L.O.D. (b.o.f.) preparing to step outside partner on R. side.	

Count		Bars
	Face diag. to wall down L.O.D. on last 2 bars.	14
1–3	Dance 3 steps of Natural Turn as bar 6—R.F., L.F., R.F.	15
1	L.F. back down L.O.D. (b.o.f., w.f.) turning to R.	
2–3	Close R.F. to L.F. *parallel pos.*, knees slightly relaxed —hesitation action. Face down L.O.D.—half turn to R. on last three steps.	16

Lady
Changes—Whisk—Wing

1	R.F. back down L.O.D. (b.o.f., w.f.).	
2	L.F. to side (b.o.f.) a fairly wide step.	
3	Close R.F. to L.F. *parallel pos.* rise to toes.	1
1	L.F. back down L.O.D. (b.o.f., w.f.).	
2	R.F. to side (b.o.f.) a wide step.	
3	Close L.F. to R.F. *parallel pos.* (rise to toes).	2
1	R.F. back down L.O.D. (b.o.f., w.f.).	
2	L.F. to side (b.o.f.) swivelling to R. to face diag. to centre against L.O.D.	
3	Cross (Whisk) R.F. in behind L.F. (toes) *promenade pos.* Headline to R.	3
1	L.F. forward (heel) towards centre.	
2	R.F. forward (b.o.f.) curving to L.—body facing against L.O.D.	
3	L.F. forward (toes) curving to L.—body facing diag. wall against L.O.D.	4
	Curve ¼ to L. on last bar—finish on LEFT side of man.	

Lady
Telemark—Natural Spin Turn

1	R.F. back turning to L. (b.o.f., w.f.) diag. to centre down L.O.D.	
2	Close L.F. to R.F. (heel turn) body facing down L.O.D.	
3	R.F. to side—continuing turn to L. on ball of L.F.— Finish backing diag. to wall down L.O.D.	5
1	L.F. back (b.o.f., w.f.) turning to R.	
2	R.F. to side across L.O.D. (b.o.f.).	
3	Close L.F. to R.F. *parallel pos.* (rise to toes) body facing down L.O.D.—partner square—⅜ turn on 6th bar.	6
1	R.F. forward down L.O.D. (heel b.o.f.) turning strongly to R. (half turn).	
2	L.F. back down L.O.D.—slightly across L.O.D.— continue to turn to R. on ball of L.F. (⅜ turn).	

MAGENTA MODERN WALTZ (*contd.*)

Count		Bars
3	Brush R.F. to L.F. (*parallel pos.*) and step R.F. forward between man's feet (b.o.f.)—finish facing diag. to centre down L.O.D.	7
1	L.F. forward (heel) turning to L.	
2	R.F. to side (b.o.f.) a wide step—backing towards wall.	
3	Close L.F. to R.F. *parallel pos.* (toes).	8

Reverse Turn—Reverse Corte

1	R.F. back towards diag. wall down L.O.D. (b.o.f., w.f.) turning to L.	
2	L.F. to side (b.o.f.).	
3	Close R.F. to L.F. *parallel pos.*, rising on toes ($\frac{1}{8}$ turn).	9
1–2	L.F. forward (heel) turning to L.—R.F. to side (b.o.f.).	
3	Close L.F. to R.F. *parallel pos.*, rising to toes ($\frac{1}{8}$ turn). Finish backing diag. to centre down L.O.D.	10
1	R.F. back (b.o.f., w.f.) turning to L.	
2	L.F. across L.O.D. (b.o.f.), toe pointing down L.O.D.	
3	Close R.F. to L.F. *parallel pos.* (toes), facing down L.O.D. $\frac{3}{8}$ turn to L. on last bar.	11
1	L.F. foward down L.O.D. (heel) turning to L.	
2	R.F. to side along L.O.D.	
3	Close L.F. to R.F. *parallel pos.* face diag. centre against L.O.D. ($\frac{3}{8}$ turn).	12

Whisk—Chassé—Hesitation Change

1	R.F. forward diag. to centre against L.O.D. (heel) on R. side of man turning to R.	
2	L.F. to side (b.o.f.) (against L.O.D.)—face centre.	
3	Cross (Whisk) R.F. in behind R.F.—swivelling on ball of L.F. to face almost down L.O.D.—headline to R. —$\frac{3}{8}$ turn—*promenade pos.*	13
1	L.F. forward down L.O.D. (heel), body turn to L.— *promenade pos.*	
2	R.F. to side along L.O.D. (b.o.f.).	
and	Close L.F. to R.F. (toes), face centre—square to man.	
3	R.F. to side (b.o.f.), body backing wall diag. down L.O.D. ($\frac{3}{8}$ turn).	14
1–3	Dance three steps of Nat. Turn as bar 6 L.F., R.F., L.F.	15
1	R.F. forward down L.O.D. (heel b.o.f.) turning to R.	
2	L.F. to side across L.O.D. (b.o.f., w.f.).	
3	Brush R.F. to L.F. *parallel pos.*—L. knee slightly relaxed. Finish back to L.O.D.—half turn on last bar.	16

114

MANHATTAN BLUES

TIME 4/4—TEMPO 46/48—16 BAR SEQUENCE

TRY this to "12th Street Rag." An easy dance with a swing.

Commencing position as in Foxtrot. Man facing L.O.D., lady backing L.O.D.

Count	Man	Bars
SSS	L.F., R.F., L.F. forward down L.O.D. (heel leads).	
S	*Point* R.F. forward (toe) turn head and shoulder forward towards the point, check.	1–2
SSS	R.F., L.F., R.F. back against L.O.D.	
S	*Point* (or tap) L.F. back, turn head to L., check.	3–4
S	L.F. forward down L.O.D. commencing to turn body to R.	
S	R.F. forward diag. to wall down L.O.D. turning to R. for rotary chassé.	5
QQ	L.F. to side, close R.F. to L.F. *parallel pos.* back L.O.D.	
S	L.F. back down L.O.D., preparing to lead lady outside.	6
S	R.F. back diag. to wall.	
S	L.F. back partner outside on R. side, turning to R. for turning chassé.	7
Q	R.F. to side along L.O.D. facing diag. to centre.	
Q	Close L.F. to R.F. *parallel pos.* almost facing L.O.D.	
S	R.F. forward down L.O.D.	8
S	L.F. forward down L.O.D. square to partner.	
S	*Point* R.F. to side 2nd pos. slight body turn to R. Turn on ball of L.F. to L. to face diag. centre and	9
S	R.F. towards centre in *promenade pos.*	
S	*Point* L.F. to side towards centre.	10
S	Restep L.F. towards centre.	
S	Swing R.F. through *low aerial promenade pos.*	11
S	R.F. to side towards wall turn to face diag. wall.	
S	Swing L.F. through *low aerial contra promenade pos.*	12
S	L.F. to side towards centre body facing L.O.D.	
S	Close R.F. to L.F. without weight, partner square.	13
S	R.F. to side.	
S	Close L.F. to R.F., without weight, partner square.	14
	Use a Charleston action on 13th and 14th bars.	
QQS	Diag. chassé forwards and leftwards, L.F., R.F., L.F.	15
QQS	Diag. chassé forwards and rightwards, R.F., L.F., R.F.	16

115

Count	Lady	Bars
SSS	R.F., L.F., R.F. back down L.O.D.	
S	*Point* L.F. back (or tap), check, turn head and shoulder towards L.F. (leftwards).	1–2
SSS	L.F., R.F., L.F. forward against L.O.D.	
S	*Point* R.F. forward against L.O.D., check, turn head and shoulder towards R.F. (rightwards).	3–4
S	R.F. back, commencing to turn body to R.	
S	L.F. back towards diag. wall turning to R. for Rotary chassé.	5
QQ	R.F. to side and forward—close L.F. to R.F. *parallel pos.* face L.O.D.	
S	R.F. forward down L.O.D.	6
S	L.F. forward body facing slightly diag. to wall.	
S	R.F. forward outside partner on R. side. Turning to R. for turning chassé.	7
Q	L.F. to side across L.O.D.	
Q	Close R.F. to L.F. *parallel pos.* backing L.O.D.	
S	L.F. back down L.O.D.	8
S	R.F. back down L.O.D. partner square.	
S	*Point* L.F. to side *2nd pos.* slight body turn to L. Turn on ball of R.F. to R. to face diag. centre against the L.O.D. and	9
S	L.F. towards centre in *promenade pos.*	
S	*Point* R.F. to side towards centre.	10
S	Restep R.F. towards centre in *promenade pos.*	
S	Swing L.F. through *low aerial promenade pos.*	11
S	L.F. to side towards wall turn to face diag. wall against L.O.D.	
S	Swing R.F. through *low aerial contra promenade pos.*	12
S	R.F. to side towards centre body facing against L.O.D.	
S	Close L.F. to R.F. without weight, square to partner.	13
S	L.F. to side.	
S	Close R.F. to L.F. without weight, partner square.	14
	Use a Charleston action on 13th and 14th bars.	
QQS	Diag. chassé backward and rightwards, R.F., L.F., R.F.	15
QQS	Diag. chassé backward and leftwards, L.F., R.F., L.F.	16

MIDNIGHT TANGO

GILBERT DANIELS, P.P.N.C.D.T.A.

TIME 2/4—TEMPO 30/32—16 BAR SEQUENCE

Commence normal Tango Hold (No. 4)—Man facing, Lady backing, L.O.D.

Count	**Man**	Bars
	Half Squares—Promenade Chassé and Run	
Q	L.F. to side (w.f.).	
Q	Close R.F. to L.F. *parallel pos.* (w.f.).	
S	L.F. forward down L.O.D. (heel).	1
Q	R.F. to side (w.f.).	
Q	Close L.F. to R.F. *parallel pos.* (w.f.).	
S	R.F. forward down L.O.D. (heel) turn ⅛ turn R. to face diag. wall down L.O.D. brushing L.F. to R.F. turn partner to *promenade pos.*	2
Q	L.F. to side along L.O.D. in *promenade pos.* (heel, w.f.).	
Q	Close R.F. to L.F. *parallel pos.* (w.f.).	
S	L.F. to side along L.O.D. in *promenade pos.* (heel, w.f.).	3
Q	Cross R.F. over L.F. moving along L.O.D. (heel, w.f.).	
Q	L.F. to side (w.f.).	
S	Close R.F. to L.F. *parallel pos.* (w.f.).	4

Double Allemande (under left hand)

Count	Man	Bars
Q	L.F. to side along L.O.D. (heel, w.f.) turn partner to R. under L. hand—R. hand on R. hip.	
Q	Cross R.F. over L.F. (heel w.f.).	
S	L.F. to side along L.O.D. (b.o.f., w.f.).	5
	As L.F. takes weight of body turn slightly rightwards on ball of L.F. to almost face diag. wall against L.O.D. Finish feet apart—ball of R.F. in contact with the floor, preparing to move against L.O.D.	
Q	R.F. to side against L.O.D. (heel, w.f.) turn partner to L. under L. hand—R. hand on R. hip.	
Q	Cross L.F. over R.F. (heel, w.f.).	
S	R.F. to side against L.O.D. (b.o.f., w.f.).	6
	Slight turn to L. on last step. Finish facing square to partner (and wall) assuming a loose normal tango hold.	

Count	Man	Bars

Double Fan (Points to left and right)

S — Point L.F. to side (to centre) (toe) turn body to face L.O.D. partners in very open *promenade pos.*

S — Close L.F. to R.F. *parallel pos.* (w.f.), ¼ turn R. to face partner.   7

S — Point R.F. to side (to centre) (toe) release R. hand from partner, opening out to *con. promenade pos.* (¼ to R.), Lady's R. hand still in Man's L. hand— Man's R. hand at side.

S — Close R.F. to L.F. (w.f.) turn L. on L.F. to face down L.O.D. (½ turn to L.). Partners finish both facing down L.O.D., Lady towards Man's R. side, L. hands joined—R. hands joined at approx. shoulder height (Hold No. 3).   8

Man and Lady
The Slow Rock (partners on "same" leg)

SS — L.F., R.F. forward down L.O.D. (heel) Check   9

S — Transfer weight back to L.F. with body turn to R.

Q — R.F. to side (against L.O.D.) (w.f.) toe pointing to wall, Man dancing a slightly longer step than Lady.

Q — Close L.F. to R.F. *parallel pos.* (w.f.) ¼ turn R. last 3 steps. Finish facing square to wall, Lady now towards L. side of man, Lady's R. hip almost in contact with Man's hip.   10

SS — R.F., L.F. forward (heel) to wall, Check.   11

S — Transfer weight back to R.F. with body turn to L.

Q — L.F. to side across L.O.D. (w.f.) toe pointing down L.O.D., Man's dancing a slightly longer step than Lady.

Q — Close R.F. to L.F. *parallel pos.* (w.f.), ¼ turn L. on last 3 steps. Finish as at commencement of this section.   12

Man
The "Lunge Curtsy" (4 steps)

SSS — L.F., R.F., L.F., forward down L.O.D. (heel) on last step release the hands, Lady turning to L. preparing to face square to man. Man finishes taking Lady's R. hand in his L. hand (not an Allemande).

S — R.F. forward down L.O.D.—plié (bend R. knee)

Count	**Man**	Bars
	with a Lunge action (strong R. shoulder lead), R. hand "pointing" forward and downwards.	13–14
S	L.F. back against L.O.D. (b.of., w.f.) body facing L.O.D., assuming normal Tango hold.	
S	R.F. back against L.O.D. (b.o.f.), Check.	15
SS	L.F., R.F., forward down L.O.D. (heel). Finish brushing L.F. to R.F.	16

Lady

Half Squares—Promenade Chassé and Run

Q	R.F. to side (w.f.).	
Q	Close L.F. to R.F. *parallel pos.* (w.f.).	
S	R.F. back down L.O.D.	1
Q	L.F. to side (w.f.).	
Q	Close R.F. to L.F. *parallel pos.* (w.f.).	
S	L.F. back down L.O.D. (b.o.f., w.f.) turn approx. ⅜ turn R. to face diag. centre. Finish in *promenade pos.* down L.O.D. brushing R.F. towards L.F. *parallel pos.*	2
Q	R.F. to side along L.O.D. in *promenade pos.* (heel).	
Q	Close L.F. to R.F. *parallel pos.* (w.f.).	
S	R.F. to side along L.O.D. (heel, w.f.).	3
Q	Cross L.F. over R.F. moving along L.O.D. (heel).	
Q	R.F. to side (w.f.).	
S	Close L.F. to R.F. *parallel pos.* (w.f.).	4

The Double Allemande

Q	R.F. forward (heel, b.o.f.) down L.O.D. turn R. to face diag. wall against L.O.D. (under Man's L. hand), gown in L. hand.	
Q	L.F. diag. back moving along L.O.D. (b.o.f., w.f.). Still turning to R. to face against L.O.D.	
S	Continue body turn to R.—R.F. diag. back down L.O.D. (b.o.f., w.f.).	5
	Approx. ¾ turn R. last 3 steps. Finish facing diag. to centre against L.O.D.	
Q	L.F. forward against L.O.D. turn L. to face diag. wall down L.O.D. (heel, b.o.f.).	
Q	R.F. diag. back moving against L.O.D. (b.o.f., w.f.).	
S	Continue body turn to L.—L.F. to side against L.O.D. Finish facing centre of room—square to partner. Approx. ⅞ turn to L. on last 3 steps. Partners assume a loose Tango hold.	6

Count	Lady	Bars

Double Fan (Points to Right and Left)

S   Point R.F. to side—towards wall (toe) opening out to a very open *promenade pos.* body almost facing down L.O.D.—¼ turn R.—headline to R.

S   Close R.F. to L.F. *parallel pos.* turn ¼ to L. to face square to partner and centre.   7

S   Point L.F. to side—towards wall (toe), opening out to *con. promenade pos.* and facing against L.O.D. (¼ turn to L.)—headline to L. Man releases hand from lady's waist—Lady holds gown in L. hand.

S   Swivel strongly to R. on heel of R.F.—½ turn—to face down L.O.D. Close L.F. to R.F. *parallel pos.* (W.W.). Lady releases L. hand from gown and raises both arms towards end of step.   8

   Face down L.O.D. assuming hold as in Doris Waltz.

The Slow Rock

See Man's steps, Bars 9/12.

Note that lady dances a short step R.F. to side (Q) 10th bar, also a short step L.F. to side (Q) 12th bar.

The "Lunge Curtsy" (5 steps)

SS   L.F., R.F. forward down L.O.D. (heel) preparing to turn to L. at end of 2nd step.   13

Q   L.F. forward (heel, b.o.f.) turn L. to almost back L.O.D. Dance this step very lightly across front of Man, release R. hand at end of step, Lady retaining arm position in the air.

Q   R.F. diag. back down L.O.D. now square to Man having danced a ½ turn to L. on last two steps.

   Man releases L. hands, and takes Lady's R. hand in his L. hand, Lady holds gown in her L. hand.

S   L.F. back down L.O.D. (b.o.f., w.f.) with a strong L. shoulder lead. body almost backing centre of room. Headline well to L. over L. shoulder.   14

S   R.F. forward against L.O.D. (heel) correcting over-swing of body and assuming normal Tango hold.   15

S   L.F. forward against L.O.D. (heel), Check.

SS   R.F., L.F. back down L.O.D.

   Finish brushing R.F. towards L.F. (*parallel pos.*).   16

POLKA

Music published by Reynolds & Co., Ltd.

AN old dance to music written in 2/4 time. It is better to count 4 beats to a bar, the rhythm of the steps is better expressed as "and" "a" 1, 2, 3, pausing on the 3rd beat for the duration of almost the whole of the 4th beat.

To commence stand with the weight on R.F. with the toe of L.F. behind the R. heel, R. knee very slightly bent.

Count	
"and"	Brace the R. knee and the waist muscles the body moving upwards. The action is taken in such a manner that the foot will leave the floor.
"a"	The hopping foot meets the floor (R.F.).
1	L.F. forward (b.o.f.).
2	Close R.F. to L.F. *3rd pos. rear* knee very slightly bent.
3	Spring from the R.F. to the L.F. moving L.F. forward and at the same time move R. toe behind L. heel (jeté).
"and"	Brace the L. knee and the waist muscles, the body moving upwards. The action is taken in such a manner that the foot will leave the floor.
"a"	The hopping foot meets the floor (L.F.).
1	R.F. forward (b.o.f.).
2	Close L.F. to R.F. *3rd pos. rear*, knee very slightly bent.
3	Spring from the L.F. to the R.F. moving R.F. forward and at the same time move L. toe behind R. heel (jeté).

When dancing as a couple commence on opposite feet, when turning the movement of the body is rather diag., most of the turn is made during the temps levé (rise and hop). Turn the R. knee outwards on 3rd step (jeté). Remember to hop before the 1st beat *not* on the beat.

Dance the movement twice (2 bars) to make a complete turn and at the same time turn the heads to *promenade and contra promenade pos.*

Technical description: Temps Levé—Chassé—Coupé—Jeté.

A useful teaching method: Hop—Step—Underneath—Spring.

SCHOTTISCHE

COMMENCING position. Waltz hold, man facing diag. to wall.

Count	**Man**	Bars
1	L.F. along L.O.D.	
2	Close R.F. to L.F. *3rd pos. rear.*	
3	L.F. along L.O.D. bend knee slightly.	
4	Temps levé on L.F. turning body slightly to L. to face towards L.O.D., head rightwards. Close R.F. to L.F. *5th rear aerial pos.* R.F. pointing towards inside edge of foot against inside of L. calf.	1
1	R.F. towards wall diag. down L.O.D.	
2	Close L.F. to R.F. *3rd pos. rear.*	
3	R.F. towards wall diag. knee slightly bent.	
4	Temps levé R.F. bring L.F. to *5th rear aerial pos.* turn slightly to R. to face diag. to wall.	2
1–8	Waltz rotary, progressive, rotary, pas de valse. Finish in commencing position and repeat.	3-4

Note: step hop can be used instead of waltzing—
L.F. to side hop on L.F. turning to R.
R.F. to side hop on R.F. turning to R.

	Lady	
1	R.F. back.	
2	Close L.F. to R.F. *3rd pos. front.*	
3	R.F. back bend knee slightly	
4	Temps levé on R.F. and close L.F. to R.F. *5th aerial pos.* slight body turn to L.	1
1	L.F. back.	
2	Close R.F. to L.F. *3rd pos. front.*	
3	L.F. back, bend knee slightly.	
4	Temps levé on L.F., bring R.F. to *5th aerial pos.*, turn slightly to R.	2
1–8	Waltz progressive, rotary, progressive, curving pas de valse (L.F. back—R.F. back—close L. to R. *3rd pos. front*).	3-4

VARSOVIANA

Music published by Messrs. Herman Darewski

AN old round dance in waltz rhythm with a 16 bar sequence. It consists of two distinct movements, the mazurka step, and a turn with a point. These movements are amalgamated by dancing two mazurka steps, turn-point, two mazurka steps, turn-point, then the turn-point four times.

Commencing position: waltz hold, man facing diag. to wall, lady diag. to centre, both man and lady turn the heads to face down the L.O.D. the forward foot pointing down L.O.D.

It assists the dancing of the mazurka step if the inside hips are lightly in contact.

The Mazurka Movement

Count	Man	Bars
1	L.F. along L.O.D. (toe pointing down L.O.D.), dance this step with first the toe in contact with the floor, the L. shoulder inclined over the foot, then slide the foot along the floor with a pushing action, lowering to the ball of the foot and at end of step to the flat of the foot. As the foot becomes horizontal let the shoulder become level.	
2	Close R.F. to L.F. *3rd pos. rear* (toe pointing to wall), R. knee very slightly bent, the L. shoulder rising.	
3	Hop very lightly on the R.F. and at the same time whip (fouetté) the L.F. forward off the floor, then continue by bringing the foot back to the calf of R. leg, the L. toe pointed to the floor.	1
	The track of the L.F. is downwards and forwards, then upwards and inwards—an elliptical action.	
	Technically the mazurka movement comprises: a demi glissé—coupé—pas sauté with fouetté.	
	Repeat the first bar—	
1	L.F., L. shoulder down.	
2	R.F., L. shoulder up.	
3	L.F., finish L. shoulder downward.	2
	The upper part of the body has a rocking action from the waist upwards.	

VARSOVIANA *(contd.)*

The Turn (Into Contra Promenade Position)

Count	Man	Bars
1	L.F. forward and to side commencing to turn body to the R. (b.o.f. then w.f.).	
2	Close R.F. to L.F. *3rd pos. rear* (b.o.f.).	
3	L.F. short step to side still turning (lady will step R.F. forward between man's feet). Continue turning on ball of L.F. until body is facing diag. to centre, approximately three-quarters turn to R. on these steps.	3
1, 2, 3	*Point* R.F. along L.O.D. toe pointing down L.O.D. Finish in *contra promenade pos.*, retaining the hold. Incline the body forward over the pointed foot.	4
1, 2, 3	Mazurka movement commencing on opposite foot—R.F. close, L.F. *3rd rear*, fouetté R.F. repeat R.F., L.F., R.F., still in *contra promenade pos.*	5 6

The Turn (Into Promenade Position)

Man

Count	Man	Bars
1	R.F. down L.O.D. (b.o.f. then w.f.).	
2	Close L.F. to R.F. *3rd pos. rear* (b.o.f. then w.f.).	
3	R.F. forward a short step between partner's feet, leading partner into *promenade pos.* Turn to R. on last step to face diag. to wall approximately a quarter turn.	7
1, 2, 3	*Point* L.F. along L.O.D., toe pointing down L.O.D. Continue by dancing the turns four times—	8
	L.F., R.F., L.F., *Point* R.F., three-quarters turn R.	9–10
	R.F., L.F., R.F., *Point* L.F., quarter turn R.	11–12
	L.F., R.F., L.F., *Point* R.F., three-quarters turn R.	13–14
	R.F., L.F., R.F., *Point* L.F., quarter turn R.	15–16
	Repeat from the beginning.	

The lady's steps are the normal opposite throughout, whilst man is dancing the 1st and 2nd bars, lady dances 5th and 6th, and whilst man is dancing the 3rd and 4th bars, lady dances 7th and 8th.

It should be noted that when dancing the turns, the person on the inside of the room turns three-quarters of a turn to R., whilst the person on the outside of the room turns slightly to R. (approximately a quarter turn).

LILAC WALTZ

ALFRED HALFORD, F.E.S.T.D.
TIME 3/4—TEMPO 44—16 BAR SEQUENCE

COMMENCING position similar to Veleta (Hold No. 2). Throughout this dance endeavour to dance with a foot and body rise on the 2nd beat of each bar—rise from the ball of the foot to the toes with a lilting action.

Zephyrs and Backward Locks

Count	Man	Bars
1	L.F. forward down L.O.D. (heel).	
2	Zephyr (swing) R.F. forward to 4*th front aerial pos.* rising on ball of L.F.	
3	Swing R.F. across front of L.F.	1
1	R.F. toe on floor (*crossed* 5*th front pos.*) lowering to whole of L.F.	
2	Zephyr (swing) R.F. forward to 4*th front aerial pos.* rising to ball. of L.F.	
3	Swing R.F. back against L.O.D., lower to whole of L.F.	2
1	R.F. back against L.O.D. (b.o.f.) foot straight (toe pointing down L.O.D.).	
2, 3	Cross L.F. in front of R.F. rising to toes of both feet.	3
1	R.F. back against L.O.D. (b.o.f.) lower L. heel.	
2, 3	Cross L.F. in front of R.F. (W.W.) rising to toes of both feet.	4

Solo Turns (Outwards)

1	L.F. forward down L.O.D. turning to L. (heel).	
2	R.F. to side (along L.O.D. on same line as previous step) toe—facing diag. centre against L.O.D.	
3	Continue turning on ball of R.F. to face against L.O.D. Man releases hands between 2nd and 3rd beats.	5
1	L.F. back down L.O.D. (b.o.f., w.f.) (lower R. heel).	

LILAC WALTZ (*contd.*)

Count	**Man**	Bars
2, 3	Hesitate for 2nd and 3rd beats with feet in place, body facing diag. to wall against L.O.D.—headline towards partner. Rise to toe of L.F. on 2nd beat, although R.F. is in place the foot will *very* slightly veer towards L.F. as the rise is taken on L. toe (b.o.f. remaining in contact with the floor). Man takes Lady's R. hand in his L. hand on first beat. Approx. ⅝ turn to L. on last two bars.	6
1	R.F. forward against L.O.D. turning to R. (heel).	
2	L.F. to side (against L.O.D. on same line as previous step) toe—facing towards centre of room	
3	Continue turning on ball of L.F. to face diag. centre down L.O.D. Man release hands between 2nd and 3rd beats.	7
1	R.F. back against L.O.D. (b.o.f., w.f.) (lower L. heel).	
2, 3	Hesitate with feet in place, body facing diag. to wall down L.O.D.—headline towards partner. Rise to toe of R.F. on 2nd beat. Man takes Lady's R. hand in his L. hand as he steps backwards on the first beat.	8

Points and Balancés

1	L.F. forward down L.O.D. (heel).	
2, 3	Point R.F. forward (toe) rise to ball of L.F. on 2nd beat as the R.F. passes L.F., then lower to whole of L.F. when pointing—headline down L.O.D., body almost facing L.O.D.	9
1	R.F. forward down L.O.D. (heel).	
2, 3	Point L.F. forward (toe) rise to ball of R.F. on 2nd beat as the L.F. passes R.F. then lower to whole of R.F. when pointing—headline inwards towards partner, body almost diag. to wall down L.O.D.	10
	With body turn rightwards to face partner (and wall).	
1	L.F. back towards centre of room (b.o.f., w.f.).	
2, 3	Close R.F. to L.F. *3rd pos.* (b.o.f.) (W.W.) rising to ball of L.F.—man releases hands but hands remains in the air—do not lower.	11

LILAC WALTZ (*contd.*)

Count	Man	Bars
1	R.F. forward towards partner (heel).	
2, 3	Close L.F. to R.F. *3rd pos. rear* (b.o.f.) (W.W.), rising to ball of R.F. and assuming waltz hold.	12
	Waltz natural turns as in Veleta, etc.	
1, 6	Natural rotary turn L.F R.F. L.F.—Natural progressive turn R.F. L.F. R.F.	13–14
1, 6	Natural rotary turn L.F. R.F. L.R.—Forward Pas de Valse R.F. L.F. R.F.	15–16
	Finish in commencing position.	

Zephyrs and Backward Locks
Lady

1	R.F. forward down L.O.D. (heel).	
2	Zephyr (swing) L.F. forward to *4th front aerial pos.* rising to ball of R.F.	
3	Swing L.F. across front of R.F.	1
1	L.F. toe on floor *crossed 5th front pos.* lowering to whole of R.F.	
2	Zephyr (swing) L.F. forward to *4th front pos.* rising to ball of R.F.	
3	Swing L.F. back against L.O.D., lower to whole of R.F.	2
1	L.F. back against L.O.D. (b.o.f.) foot straight (toe pointing down L.O.D.).	
2, 3	Cross R.F. in front of L.F. rising to toes of both feet.	3
1	L.F. back against L.O.D. (b.o.f.) lower R. heel.	
2, 3	Cross R.F. in front of L.F. (W.W.) rising to toes of both feet.	4

Solo Turns (Outwards)

1	R.F. forward down L.O.D. turning to R. (heel).	
2	L.F. to side (along L.O.D. on same line as previous step) toe facing diag. to wall against L.O.D.	
3	Continue turning on ball of L.F. to face against L.O.D. Man releases hold between 2nd and 3rd steps.	5
1	R.F. back down L.O.D. (b.o.f., w.f.) (lower L. heel).	

127

Count	**Lady**	Bars
2, 3	Hesitate for 2nd and 3rd beats with feet in place, body facing diag. to centre against L.O.D.—headline inwards towards partner. Rise to toe of R.F. 2nd beat, although L.F. is in place the foot will *very* slightly veer towards R.F. as the rise is taken on R. toe (b.o.f. remains in contact with the floor).	6
	Rejoin inside hands on 1st beat—approx. ⅝ turn to R. on last two bars.	
1	L.F. forward against L.O.D. turning to L. (heel).	
2	R.F. to side (against L.O.D. on same line as previous step) toe—facing towards wall.	
3	Continue turning on ball of R.F. to face diag wall down L.O.D. Hands are released between 2nd and 3rd beats.	7
1	L.F. back against L.O.D. (b.o.f., w.f.) lower R. heel).	
2, 3	Hesitate with feet in place, body facing diag. to centre down L.O.D.—headline towards partner. Rise to toe of L.F. on 2nd beat. Partners rejoin inside hands as the step backward on the first beat is taken.	8

Points and Balancés

1	R.F. forward down L.O.D. (heel).	
2, 3	Point L.F. forward (toe) rise to ball of R.F. on 2nd beat as the L.F. passes R.F., then lower to whole of R.F. when pointing—headline down L.O.D.	9
1	L.F. forward down L.O.D. (heel).	
2, 3	Point R.F. forward (toe) rise to ball of L.F. on 2nd beat as the R.F. passes L.F., then lower to whole of L.F. when pointing—headline inwards towards partner, body almost facing diag. to centre down L.O.D.	10
	With body turn leftwards to face partner (and centre).	
1	R.F. back towards wall (b.o.f., w.f.).	
2, 3	Close L.F. to R.F. *3rd pos. front* (b.o.f.) (W.W.) rising to ball of R.F.—inside hands are released but both partners retain hands in the air—do not lower.	11

LILAC WALTZ (*contd.*)

Count	Lady	Bars
1	L.F. forward towards partner (heel).	
2, 3	Close R.F. to L.F. *3rd pos. rear* (b.o.f.) (W.W.) rising to ball of L.F. Partners assume waltz hold.	12
	Waltz natural turns as in Veleta, etc.	
1, 6	Natural progressive turn R.F. L.F. R.F.—natural rotary turn L.F. R.F. L.F.	13–14
1, 6	Natural progressive turn R.F. L.F. R.F.—natural rotary turn L.F. R.F. L.F. *3rd pos.*	15–16
	Release hold during last bar and assume commencing position.	

This dance can be made Progressive by Man's moving towards a new partner on 12th bar, in similar style to Progressive Barn Dance.

CAMELLIA TANGO

ERIC STONEHOUSE, F.E.S.T.D.
TEMPO 30/32—16 BAR SEQUENCE

COMMENCE both partners facing down L.O.D. L. hands joined at approximately shoulder height, man's R. hand on lady's R. hip, lady holds gown in R. hand away from the body (to side). Hold No. 7.

Count	**Man and Lady**	Bars
S	L.F. forward (heel) and diag. to R., dance this step well across front of body in modern style (strong C.B.M.P.).	
S	R.F. diag. forward (diag. to wall down L.O.D.) (heel). Plié (relax). In front of lady. Check. Headline to right, bodies still facing down L.O.D.	1
S	Transfer weight back to L.F.	
Q	R.F. back, short step very slightly across the body.	
Q	Close L.F. to R.F. *parallel pos.* (w.f.) with weight, preparing to move forward diag. to centre of room. Headline down L.O.D.—footline pointing down L.O.D.	2
SS	R.F L.F. (heel) forward and diag. to L. Plié. Check. Headline to L.	3
S	L.F. back, a short step.	
Q	L.F. back, a short step.	
Q	Close R.F. to L.F. *parallel pos.* with weight (w.f.). Finish preparing to move diag. to centre down L.O.D., footline pointing diag. centre down L.O.D.	4
SS	L.F. R.F. forward diag. to centre down L.O.D. (heel), body facing diag. to centre.	5
Q	L.F. forward diag. centre (heel).	
Q	Close R.F. to L.F. *parallel pos.* (w.f.).	
Q	L.F. forward (heel) diag. centre (man dances a slightly longer step than lady) at end of step swivel (pivot) to face diag. wall down L.O.D. ($\frac{1}{4}$ turn to right).	
Q	Brush (close) R.F. to L.F. *parallel pos.* without weight.	6

CAMELLIA TANGO (*contd.*)

Count	**Man and Lady**	Bars
SS	R.F. L.F. forward diag. to wall down L.O.D. body facing diag. wall down L.O.D.—Lady towards R. side of man (heel).	7
Q	R.F. forward (heel) diag. to wall.	
Q	Close L.F. to R.F. *parallel pos.* (w.f.).	
	Man at end of step prepares to release the hold.	
Q	R.F. forward diag. to wall (heel), short step.	
Q	Close L.F. to R.F. *parallel pos.*—man without weight.	8
	Lady on last two steps turns to L. to face diag. centre down L.O.D.—R.F. forward turning $\frac{1}{4}$ turn to L.—close L.F. to R.F. *parallel pos.* WITH WEIGHT. Finish with normal tango hold in *promenade pos.*, preparing to move along the L.O.D.	
	Last 4 bars are similar to man's steps, Royal Empress Tango.	

Man

S	L.F. to side along L.O.D. in *promenade pos.* (heel w.f.).	
Q	R.F. forward and across L.F. (heel) *promenade pos.*	
Q	Swivel to R. ($\frac{1}{8}$ turn) on flat of R.F. to face square to lady (and wall).	9
	Close L.F. to R.F. *parallel pos.* feet slightly apart without weight. This bar is the promenade link from Modern Tango.	
S	L.F. forward (heel) to wall, headline to R. slightly over partner's L. shoulder, plié, similar action to contra check in Modern Tango—weight of body partially carried into the step.	
Q	Transfer weight back to R.F.	
Q	Close L.F. to R.F. *parallel pos.* (W.W.), with slight left-wards turn to face diag. wall down L.O.D. Finish in *promenade pos.*	10
	Repeat 9th bar. Promenade link. SQQ.	11
S	L.F. back to centre with slight oversway of body—slight plié.	
Q	Transfer weight forward to R.F. (heel).	
Q	Close L.F. to R.F. *parallel pos.* (W.W.).	12
	Finish in *promenade pos.* preparing to move along L.O.D.	
S	L.F. to side along L.O.D. in *promenade pos.* (heel).	

131

CAMELLIA TANGO (*contd.*)

Count	**Man**	Bars
S	R.F. forward in *promenade pos.* commencing to turn body to R.	13
S	L.F. across L.O.D. (b.o.f., w.f.) lady steps R.F. forward between man's feet.	
S	Continue body to R. to face diag. centre down L.O.D. R.F. forward down L.O.D. (heel), ¾ turn to R. approximately on last 3 steps. Finish in *contra promenade pos.* Man on outside of room. Lady on inside of room. Last 4 steps are similar to bars 17–18 Moonlight Saunter, except for omission of Point.	14
S	L.F. forward down L.O.D. (heel) (across R.F. in C.B.M.P.).	
Q	R.F. forward down L.O.D. (heel), a short step, body facing down L.O.D., Lady steps across front of man.	
Q	Close L.F. to R.F. (W.W.) *promenade pos.* Man facing slightly diag. to wall down L.O.D.—¼ turn to R. approximately on last 3 steps.	15
S	L.F. to side moving towards centre of room—partners opening out to face down L.O.D.—slight body turn to L.—Man releases hold and takes lady's R. hand in his L. hand.	
Q	Transfer weight back to R.F. still facing down L.O.D.	
Q	Close L.F. to R.F. *parallel pos.* (W.W.)—assuming hold as at commencement of dance.	16

Lady

S	R.F. to side along L.O.D. in *promenade pos.* (heel, w.f.).	
Q	L.F. forward and across R.F. (heel) *promenade pos.*	
Q	Swivel to L. (⅛ turn) on flat of L.F. to face centre and man. Close R.F. to L.F. *parallel pos.* feet slightly apart without weight.	9
S	R.F. back towards wall—plié—headline to left.	
Q	Transfer weight forward to L.F. (heel).	
Q	Close R.F. to L.F. *parallel pos.* (W.W.)—finish in *promenade pos.*	10
	Repeat 9th bar. Promenade link. SQQ.	11
S	R.F. forward towards centre with slight oversway of body—plié.	
Q	Transfer weight back to L.F.	
Q	Close R.F. to L.F. *parallel pos.* (W.W.)—in *promenade pos.*	12
S	R.F. to side along L.O.D. in *promenade pos.* (heel).	

CAMELLIA TANGO (*contd.*)

Count	Lady	Bars
S	L.F. forward and across R.F. (heel) with body turn to R. at end of step.	13
S	R.F. forward down L.O.D. (heel) between man's feet, body facing L.O.D.	
S	L.F. forward down L.O.D. (heel) facing diag. wall down L.O.D. *contra promenade pos.* (Lady on inside of room—¼ turn to R. approximately on last 3 steps.)	14
S	R.F. forward (and across L.F.) preparing to turn to R.	
Q	L.F. to side across L.O.D. (b.o.f., w.f.) continuing to turn to R.	
Q	Pivot strongly to R. on ball of L.F. to almost face down L.O.D. Close R.F. to L.F. *parallel pos.* without weight. ¾ turn to R. on last 3 steps.	15
S	R.F. to side moving towards wall—body facing down L.O.D.—L. hand in man's R. hand—R. hand holding gown.	
Q	Transfer weight to L.F.	
Q	Close R.F. to L.F. *parallel pos.* with weight.	16

LIBERTY TWO STEP

RAYMOND BAILEY, M.N.A.T.D., M.I.D.M.A.
TIME 6/8—TEMPO 48—16 BAR SEQUENCE

COMMENCING position similar to Military Two Step (Hold No. 2).
Man's Steps described—Lady's Contra except where stated.

Count		Bars
1, 2	L.F. forward, Point R.F. to 4*th pos.* front	1
3, 4	Close R.F. to 5*th pos. rear*, Pivot inwards to face against L.O.D., end with R.F. 5*th pos. front*— Change hands at end of bar 2.	2
1, 4	Dance bars 1–2 commencing R.F.	3–4
	At end of 4th bar man changes to L. hand on hip R. hand shoulder level—Lady dress held in L. hand R. hand shoulder level.	
1, 4	Solo waltz turn (outwards). Man reverse turn L.F. R.F. L.F. R.F. L.F. R.F. Lady natural turn R.F. L.F. R.F. L.F. R.F. L.F. Partners finish facing each other R. hands joined.	5–6
1, 4	Pas de Basque to left and right (R. hands held). Man L.F. R.F. L.F.—R.F. L.F. R.F. Lady R.F. L.F. R.F.—L.F. R.F. L.F.	7–8
1, 4	Clockwise circling walks to opposite places. Man L.F. R.F. L.F. Close 5*th pos.* Lady R.F. L.F. R.F. Close 5*th pos.* (R. hands held—L. hand holding gown and on hip respectively.)	9–10
1, 4	Pas de Basque to right and left. Man R.F. L.F. R.F.—L.F. R.F. L.F. Lady L.F. R.F. L.F.—R.F. L.F. R.F.	11–12
1, 4	Clockwise circling walks to original places. Man R.F. L.F. R.F. Close 3*rd pos. rear.* Lady L.F. R.F. L.F. Close 3*rd pos. front.* Partners assume normal waltz hold.	13–14
1, 4	Man rotary natural waltz turn L.F. R.F. L.F. Pas de Valse R.F. L.F. R.F. Lady dances one natural turn (Progressive—Rotary).	15–16

134

TANGO MAGENTA

JACK CROSSLEY, F.I.S.T.D.
TEMPO 30/32—16 BAR SEQUENCE

COMMENCE with normal Tango hold (No. 4). Man facing, lady backing, L.O.D.

Forward Walks—Swivel to Parallel Close

Count	Man	Bars
S	L.F. forward down L.O.D. (heel).	
S	R.F. forward down L.O.D. (heel) at end of step swivel to R. to face diag. wall down L.O.D. (⅛th turn). Headline leftwards over lady's R. shoulder.	1
Q	L.F. forward (heel) diag. to wall down L.O.D., on partner's L. side (L. hip to L. hip) body turn to L. at end of step (⅛th).	
Q	R.F. to side across L.O.D. (b.o.f., w.f.) toe pointing down L.O.D.	
S	Close L.F. to R.F. *parallel pos.* (w.f.) square to partner— facing L.O.D.	2

Repeat pattern of last 2 bars commencing R.F. finish in *promenade pos.*

S	R.F. forward down L.O.D. (heel).	
S	L.F. forward down L.O.D. (heel) at end of step swivel to L. to face diag. centre down L.O.D. (⅛th turn.)	3
Q	R.F. forward (heel) diag. to centre, on partner's R. side (R. hip to R. hip) at end of step swivel on ball of foot (foot flat) to face almost diag. to wall down L.O.D.	
Q	L.F. sideways along L.O.D. (b.o.f., w.f.) a short step in line with partner (¼ turn to R. last two steps) toe pointing diag. wall down L.O.D.	
S	R.F. sideways (diag. back against L.O.D. in relation to the body) turn partner to R. *promenade pos.*, action is similar to a short step in *fallaway pos.* (Toe pointing diag. to wall down L.O.D.) (b.o.f., w.f.).	4

Promenade Walks—Swivel to Contra Check—Rock

Count	Man	Bars
S	L.F. to side and forward along L.O.D. in *promenade pos.* (heel).	
S	R.F. forward in *promenade pos.* (heel) toe pointing almost down L.O.D. (C.B.M.P.). Body turn to L. at end.	5
QQ	With feet in place swivel to L. to face almost diag. to centre against L.O.D. (⅜ths turn approximately) turn with feet flat weight of the body being over sole of R.F. (toe of L.F.)	
S	L.F. forward (b.o.f., w.f.) diag. to centre against L.O.D. knee slightly bent (plié). L. shoulder is held back as shoulder line tends to turn slightly leftwards (⅛th turn approximately).	
	Dance this step across the body in C.B.M.P. lady's R. thigh in contact with man's L. thigh. R. shoulder leads at end of this contra check action.	6
S	Replace weight of body back to R.E. (b.o.f., w.f.).	
Q	L.F. back (b.o.f. w.f.) diag, to wall down L.O.D., L. shoulder lead retained, weight of body mainly on inside edge of foot (toe of foot points almost against L.O.D.).	
Q	Transfer weight of body forward to R.F. (inside edge of foot—w.f.) R. shoulder lead retained.	7
S	L.F. back diag. to wall down L.O.D. (b.o.f. w.f.) slightly lengthen the foot travel.	
S	R.F. diag. back (b.o.f. w.f.) foot moves slightly sideways along L.O.D. Finish turning partner to *promenade pos.* Closing L.F. to R.F. *parallel pos.* (w.f.) without weight (brush).	8
	Repeat bars 5–8 moving against L.O.D.	
S	L.F. to side and forward against L.O.D. in *promenade pos.* (heel).	
S	R.F. forward in *promenade pos.* (heel) toe pointing almost against L.O.D. (C.B.M.P.).	9
QQ	Swivel to L. with feet in place to face almost diag. to wall down L.O.D. Feet flat.	
S	L.F. forward (b.o.f., w.f.) diag. to wall down L.O.D. (contra check).	10
S	Replace weight back to R.F. (b.o.f., w.f.).	
Q	L.F. back (b.o.f., w.f.) diag. to centre against L.O.D. (toe of foot points almost down L.O.D.).	

Count	Man	Bars
Q	Transfer weight of body forward to R.F. (w.f.) R. shoulder lead.	11
S	L.F. back diag. to centre against L.O.D. (b.o.f., w.f.) lengthen foot travel slightly.	
S	Brush R.F. to L.F. and then sideways against L.O.D. (b.o.f., w.f.) turning partner to R. to *promenade pos.* Man has very slight body turn to R. Finish closing L.F. to R.F. *parallel pos.* without weight (w.f.).	12

Promenade Link—Promenade Turn—Progressive Side Step Brush Tap

S	L.F. to side and forward along L.O.D. in *promenade pos.* (heel) (toe pointing diag. to wall down L.O.D.) headline to L.	
Q	R.F. forward (heel) *promenade pos.* (Lady turns slightly inwards.)	
Q	Close L.F. to R.F. (inside edge b.o.f.) without weight. Dance this step with a Tap action, L.F. placed a few inches slightly forward from R.F. (Man has no body turn.)	13

Next four steps are similar to the Promenade Turn, Lola Tango 14th and 15th bars.

S	L.F. to side and forward along L.O.D. (heel) *promenade pos.*	
S	R.F. forward (heel) preparing to turn to R.	14
S	L.F. to side across L.O.D. (b.o.f. w.f.) (back to L.O.D.).	
S	Continue to turn to R. on ball of L.F.—R.F. forward down L.O.D. (heel) $\frac{7}{8}$th turn to R. on last 3 steps. Partner square at end.	15
Q	L.F. forward down L.O.D. (heel).	
Q	R.F. to side across L.O.D. (w.f.).	
&	Sharply close L.F. to R.F. *parallel pos.* without weight (inside edge b.o.f.).	
S	Place L.F. a few inches to the side of R.F. (inside edge of foot) without weight—footline still parallel.	16

Rearward Walks—Swivel to Parallel Close

Count	Lady	Bars
S	R.F. back down L.O.D. (b.o.f. w.f.).	
S	L.F. back down L.O.D. (b.o.f., w.f.) at end of step Swivel to R. to face diag. centre against L.O.D. (b.o.f.—foot flat) ⅛th turn.	1
Q	R.F. back (b.o.f. w.f.) diag. to wall down L.O.D. (man steps forward towards L. side of lady). Headline to L.	
Q	L.F. so side across L.O.D. (w.f.) toe pointing against L.O.D. ⅛th turn R.	
S	Close R.F. to L.F. *parallel pos.* (w.f.) square to man facing against L.O.D.	2

Repeat pattern of last two bars commencing L.F. finish in *promenade pos.*

S	L.F. back down L.O.D. (b.o.f. w.f.).	
S	R.F. back down L.O.D. (b.o.f., w.f.) at end of step Swivel to L. to face diag. wall against L.O.D. (b.o.f.-foot flat ⅛th turn).	3
Q	L.F. back (b.o.f., w.f.) diag. to centre down L.O.D. (man steps forward towards R. side of lady) body turn to R. at end.	
Q	R.F. to side along L.O.D. (w.f.) toe pointing approximately square to centre of room. Very short step, body backing diag. to wall down L.O.D.	
S	With body turn to R. to face diag. centre down L.O.D., Move L.F. diag. back against L.O.D. (b.o.f. w.f.) toe pointing diag. centre down L.O.D. (½ turn to R. approximately last 3 steps).	4

L. hip in contact with man's R. hip—*Promenade pos.*

Promenade Walks—Reverse Lock Turn to Contra Check—Rock

S	R.F. to side and forward down L.O.D. in *promenade pos.* (heel).	
S	L.F. forward down L.O.D. (heel) toe pointing towards centre of room commencing to turn to LEFT (headline leftwards at end).	5
Q	R.F. to side across L.O.D.—foot moving against L.O.D. (b.o.f.) body is almost backing diag. to centre down L.O.D. at end of step.	

Count	**Lady**	Bars
Q	Continue body turn to L.—Cross L.F. in front of R.F. (b.o.f. w.f.) body almost backing diag. to centre against L.O.D.	
S	R.F. back diag. to centre against L.O.D. (toe), heel very lightly lowers at end of step. Body backing diag. to centre against L.O.D. Headline leftwards. ¾ turn to L. on last 3 steps. Most of the turn is felt on the ball of the R.F.	6
S	Replace weight forward to L.F. (heel).	
Q	R.F. forward (heel) R. shoulder leading, weight of body mainly on inside edge of foot.	
Q	Transfer weight of body back to L.F. (b.o.f. w.f.) L. shoulder lead retained.	7
S	R.F. forward diag. to wall down L.O.D. (heel) slightly lengthen the foot travel.	
S	With body turn to R. to face diag. wall against L.O.D. (¼ turn). L.F. sideways down L.O.D. (b.o.f., w.f.). Finish brushing (closing) R.F. to L.F. *parallel pos.* without weight. *promenade pos.*	8

Repeat last 4 bars moving against L.O.D.

S	R.F. to side and forward against L.O.D. in *promenade pos.* (heel).	
S	L.F. forward (heel) *promenade pos.* toe pointing towards wall, commencing to turn to Left.	9
Q	R.F. to side across L.O.D.—foot moving towards L.O.D. body almost backing diag. to wall against L.O.D. at end of step.	
Q	Continue body turn to L.—Cross L.F. in front of R.F. (b.o.f., w.f.) body almost backing diag. to wall down L.O.D. at end.	
S	R.F. back diag. to wall down L.O.D. (toe-heel) body backing diag. wall—headline to L. ¾ turn to L.	10
S	Replace weight forward to L.F. (heel).	
Q	R.F. forward (heel) R. shoulder lead.	
Q	Transfer weight of body back to L.F. (b.o.f., w.f.) L. shoulder lead retained.	11
S	R.F. forward (heel) diag to centre against L.O.D.	
S	With body turn to R. to face diag. centre down L.O.D. (¼ turn). L.F. sideways against L.O.D. (b.o.f., w.f.). Brush R.F. to L.F. at end, *promenade pos.*	12

TANGO MAGENTA (*contd.*)

Promenade Link—Slow Promenade Turn—
Progressive Brush Tap
Lady

S   R.F. to side along L.O.D. in *promenade pos.* (heel).

Q   L.F. forward and slightly across R.F. (heel) turning R. hip (and body) sharply towards partner (very slight swivel on L.F.).

Q   Close R.F. to L.F. *parallel pos.* (w.f.) without weight. Headline still towards L.O.D.   ·13

S   R.F. to side along L.O.D. (heel) in *promenade pos.*

S   L.F. forward (heel) slightly across R.F.—toe pointing almost down L.O.D.   14

S   R.F. forward down L.O.D. (heel) between partner's feet, ⅛th turn to R. on last two steps.

S   With strong pivot action on ball of R.F. (½ turn) L.F. back down L.O.D. (b.o.f., w.f.).   15

Q   R.F. back down L.O.D. (b.o.f., w.f.).

Q   L.F. to side across L.O.D. (w.f.) toes in line.

&   Sharply close R.F. to L.F. *parallel pos.* without weight.

S   Place (tap) R.F. a few inches to side of L.F. (inside edge of foot without weight).   16

BRITANNIA SAUNTER

TIME 4/4—TEMPO 28—16 BAR SEQUENCE

ARRANGED by the Official Board of Ballroom Dancing for the purpose of Competitive Dancing. It is popular with those dancers who prefer modern sequence dancing to orthodox old time dancing. Partners commence with normal ballroom hold—Man facing—Lady backing L.O.D.

Walks—Open Twinkles—Promenade Walks—Parallel Close

Count	Man	Bars
SSS	L.F., R.F., L.F., forward down L.O.D. (heel).	
S	R.F., forward down L.O.D. (heel), turn to R. to face diag. wall down L.O.D., ⅛ turn.	1–2
S	L.F., forward (heel) diag. to wall down L.O.D. Check on L. side of partner.	
Q	R.F. back diag. to centre against L.O.D. turn to L. (b.o.f. then w.f.).	
Q	L.F. to side (b.o.f.).	3
S	R.F. forward (heel) diag. to centre down L.O.D. on R. side of partner—Check. ¼ turn to L. on last three steps.	
Q	L.F. back diag. wall against L.O.D. (b.o.f. then w.f.) turn to R.	
Q	R.F. sideways against L.O.D. (b.o.f.).	4
S	L.F. to side along L.O.D. in *promenade pos.* (b.o.f. then w.f.), ¼ turn to R. on last three steps.	
S	R.F. forward down L.O.D. (heel) *promenade pos.*	5
Q	L.F. to side along L.O.D. *promenade pos.* (heel).	
Q	Close R.F. to L.F. *parallel pos.* (w.f.).	½

Rev. Telemark—Parallel Close—Promenade Walks —Point

Full turn to L. is danced on next four steps—

S	L.F. forward down L.O.D., turn to L. Hold released (heel).	6
S	R.F. to side along L.O.D., face centre of room (b.o.f.).	
Q	Continue turn to L. to face wall (ball of R.F.). L.F. to side along L.O.D. (b.o.f. then w.f.).	
Q	Close R.F. to L.F., *parallel pos.* (w.f.). Facing diag. wall down L.O.D., normal ballroom hold in *promenade pos.*	7

Count	**Man**	Bars
S	L.F. to side along L.O.D., in *promenade pos.* (heel).	
S	R.F. forward down L.O.D. (heel).	8
S	L.F. to side along L.O.D. (heel).	
S	*Point* R.F. forward (toe) in *promenade pos.*	9

Nat. Turn—Rock—Rev. Fourstep—Promenade Pos.

Q	R.F. forward down L.O.D., turn to R. (heel).	
Q	L.F. to side along L.O.D. (b.o.f. then w.f.) square to partner.	
S	R.F. back diag. to centre down L.O.D. (b.o.f. then w.f.). ¼ turn to R. on last three steps.	10
Q	Transfer weight forward to L.F. (heel).	
Q	Transfer weight back to R.F. (b.o.f. then w.f.).	
S	L.F. forward (heel) diag. wall against L.O.D., turn to L.	11
Q	R.F. to side against L.O.D. (b.o.f. then w.f.).	
Q	L.F. back (b.o.f. then w.f.) diag. to centre against L.O.D. partner towards R. side.	
S	R.F. to side against L.O.D. (b.o.f. then w.f.). Face diag. wall down L.O.D., partners in *promenade pos.* ¼ turn to L. on last 4 steps.	12

Promenade Walk—Nat. Chassé and Pivot Turn—Twinkles

S	L.F. to side along L.O.D. *promenade pos.* (heel).	
S	R.F. forward diag. to wall down L.O.D., on partner's R. side. Turn to R. (heel).	13
Q	L.F. to side across L.O.D. (b.o.f.).	
Q	Close R.F. to L.F. *parallel pos.* (b.o.f. then w.f.) square to partner. Backing L.O.D. ⅜ turn to R.	
S	L.F. back down L.O.D., (b.o.f. then w.f.) strong turn to R. to face down L.O.D. Pivot action dancing ½ turn.	14
Q	R.F. forward down L.O.D., (heel) strong turn to R., to back down L.O.D. Forward Pivot action dancing ½ turn.	
Q	L.F. diagonally back down L.O.D. (b.o.f. then w.f.). continuing to turn strongly to R. to face down L.O.D. ½ turn to R.	
S	R.F. forward down L.O.D. (heel).	15
Q	L.F. forward down L.O.D. (heel-toe).	
Q	Close R.F. to L.F. *parallel pos.* (toe-heel).	

BRITANNIA SAUNTER (*contd.*)

Count	**Man**	Bars
Q	L.F. back against L.O.D. (toe-heel).	
Q	Close R.F. to L.F. *parallel pos.* (toe-heel).	16

Walks—Open Twinkles—Promenade Walks—Parallel Close

Lady

SSS	R.F., L.F., R.F., back down L.O.D. (b.o.f. then w.f.).	
S	L.F. back down L.O.D. turn to R. to back diag. wall down L.O.D. $\frac{1}{8}$ turn.	1–2
S	R.F. back (b.o.f. then w.f.) diag. to wall down L.O.D. Check with partner towards L. side.	
Q	L.F. forward (heel) diag. to centre against L.O.D. turn to L.	
Q	R.F. to side (b.o.f. then w.f.).	3
S	L.F. back (b.o.f. then w.f.) diag. to centre down L.O.D. Check with partner towards R. side. $\frac{1}{4}$ turn to L.	
Q	R.F. forward (heel) diag. to wall against L.O.D. turn to R.	
Q	L.F. to side against L.O.D. (b.o.f.) face centre of room.	4
S	R.F. to side along L.O.D. (b.o.f. then w.f.) face diag. centre down L.O.D. *promenade pos.* $\frac{1}{2}$ turn to R. on last three steps.	
S	L.F. forward down L.O.D. (heel) *promenade pos.*	5
Q	R.F. to side along L.O.D. (heel) *promenade pos.*	
Q	Close L.F. to R.F. *parallel pos.* (w.f.).	$\frac{1}{2}$

Nat. Telemark—Parallel Close—Promenade Walks —Point

	Full turn to R. is danced on next four steps—	
S	R.F. forward down L.O.D. turn to R. Hold released (heel).	6
S	L.F. to side along L.O.D. face towards wall (b.o.f.).	
Q	Continue turn to R. to face centre of room (ball of L.F.), R.F. to side along L.O.D. (b.o.f. then w.f.).	
Q	Close L.F. to R.F. *parallel pos.* (w.f.). Facing diag. centre down L.O.D., normal ballroom hold in *promenade pos.*	7
S	R.F. to side along L.O.D. in *promenade pos.* (heel).	
S	L.F. forward down L.O.D. (heel).	8

Count	Lady	Bars
S	R.F. to side along L.O.D. (heel).	
S	*Point* L.F. forward (toe) in *promenade pos.*	9

Rock—Rev. Fourstep—Promenade Pos.

Q	L.F. forward down L.O.D. (heel).	
Q	R.F. forward towards diag. centre down L.O.D. (b.o.f. then w.f.).	
S	L.F. forward (heel) diag. to centre down L.O.D. square to partner.	10
Q	Transfer weight back to R.F. (b.o.f. then w.f.).	
Q	Transfer weight forward to L.F. (heel).	
S	R.F. diag. wall against L.O.D., turn to L. (b.o.f. then w.f.).	11
Q	L.F. to side against L.O.D. (b.o.f. then w.f.) face centre of room.	
Q	R.F. forward diag. to centre against L.O.D. (heel) on R. side of partner ¼ turn to L. on last three steps.	
S	With body turn to R. to face diag. centre down L.O.D. L.F. to side against L.O.D. (b.o.f. then w.f.) *promenade pos.* ¼ turn to R.	12

Rev. Swivel—Nat. Chassé and Pivot Turn—Twinkles

S	R.F. to side along L.O.D., *promenade pos.* (heel). Swivel to L. to back diag. wall down L.O.D. ¼ turn.	
S	L.F. back diag. to wall down L.O.D. (b.o.f. then w.f.) turn to R. at end of step.	13
Q	R.F. to side (b.o.f.) towards wall.	
Q	Close L.F. to R.F. *parallel pos.* (b.o.f. then w.f.). Face down L.O.D., ⅜ turn to R. on last three steps.	
S	R.F. forward down L.O.D. (heel) turn strongly to R. to back L.O.D. ½ turn Pivot action.	14
Q	L.F. sideways along L.O.D. (b.o.f. then w.f.) diag. back in relation to the body. Turn strongly to R. to face down L.O.D. ½ turn Pivot action.	
Q	R.F. forward down L.O.D. (heel). Turn strongly to R. to back down L.O.D. ½ turn Pivot.	
S	L.F. back down L.O.D. (b.o.f. then w.f.).	15
Q	R.F. back down L.O.D. (b.o.f. then w.f.).	
Q	Close L.F. to R.F. *parallel pos.* (toes).	
Q	R.F. forward against L.O.D. (heel—b.o.f.).	
Q	Close L.F. to R.F. *parallel pos.* (toes—w.f.).	16

PREMIER TWO STEP

TIME 6/8—TEMPO 44—16 BAR SEQUENCE

ARRANGED by the Official Board of Ballroom Dancing for the purpose of Competitive Dancing. Partners commence with No. 2 Hold (similar to Boston Two Step, etc.). Man facing diag. to wall down L.O.D. Lady facing diag. to centre down L.O.D.

Pas De Basque—Forward Glissade—Prog. Nat. Waltz Turn—Rear Glissade—Nat. Rotary Waltz Turn—Pas de Valse

Count	Man	Bars
1 and	Pas de basque L.F., R.F., L.F., similar to 1st. bar	
2	Boston Two Step. ⅛ turn to L.	1
3	R.F. forward down L.O.D. (heel) R. shoulder lead.	
4	Close L.F. to R.F. *3rd pos. rear* (b.o.f. then w.f.).	2
1	R.F. forward down L.O.D. (heel) turn to R.	
and	L.F. to side along L.O.D. (b.o.f.) release hold.	
2	Close R.F. to L.F. *5th pos. front* (b.o.f. then w.f.). Face diag. wall against L.O.D. Lady's R. hand in L. hand. ½ turn to R. on last three steps.	3
3	L.F. diag. back down L.O.D. (b.o.f. then w.f.).	
4	Close L.F. to L.F. *3rd pos. front* (b.o.f. then w.f.).	4
1	L.F. back down L.O.D. (b.o.f. then w.f.) turn to L.	
and	Close R.F. to L.F. *5th pos. rear* (b.o.f.) release hold.	
2	Turn to L. balls of both feet to face diag. centre down L.O.D. ½ turn to L. on last three steps.	5
3	R.F. forward down L.O.D. (heel) turn to R. Lady's L. hand in R. hand.	
and	L.F. forward down L.O.D. (b.o.f.) L. shoulder lead.	
4	Close R.F. to L.F. *3rd pos. rear* (b.o.f. then w.f.). Face diag. wall down L.O.D. ¼ turn to R. on last three steps.	6

Walks—Point—Rear Chassé—Forward Point—Rev. (Solo) Waltz Turn

1, 2, 3	L.F., R.F., L.F., forward down L.O.D. (heel).	
4	*Point* R.F. forward (toe).	7–8
1	R.F. back against L.O.D. (b.o.f.).	
and	Close L.F. to R.F. *3rd pos. front* (b.o.f.).	
2 and	Repeat last two steps—R.F., L.F.	9
3	R.F. back against L.O.D. (b.o.f. then w.f.).	
4	*Point* L.F. forward (toe) short step.	10

145

Count	Man	Bars
1	L.F. forward down L.O.D. (heel) turn to L. Hold	
and	released R.F. to side along L.O.D. (b.o.f.).	
2	Close L.F. to R.F. 5*th pos. front* (b.o.f. then w.f.). Face diag. centre against L.O.D. ½ turn to L.	11
3	R.F. back down L.O.D. (b.o.f. then w.f.) continue	
and	turn to L. Close L.F. to R.F. 5*th pos. rear* (b.o.f.).	
4	Pivot to L. (balls of both feet) to face diag. wall down L.O.D. ½ turn to L. Lady's L. hand in R. hand.	12

Pas de Basque—Forward Glissé—Nat. Rotary Waltz Turn—Pas de Valse

1 and	Pas de basque L.F., R.F., L.F., 5*th pos.* turn to R. to	
2	face wall—⅛ turn R. Lady's R. hand in L. hand (Double Hold No. 5).	13
3	R.F. forward (b.o.f. then w.f.).	
4	Close L.F. to R.F. 3*rd pos. front* (b.o.f.) without weight. Assume normal Ballroom Hold, facing diag. wall against L.O.D.	14
1	L.F. to side (b.o.f. then w.f.) turning to R. (across	
and	L.O.D.). Close R.F. to L.F. 5*th pos. rear* (b.o.f.).	
2	Pivot to R. (balls of both feet) to face diag. centre down L.O.D.	15
3	R.F. forward down L.O.D. (heel) continue turn to R. Hold released.	
and	L.F. forward (b.o.f.) towards diag. centre down L.O.D.	
4	Close R.F. to L.F. 3*rd pos. rear.* (b.o.f. then w.f.). Face diag. wall down L.O.D. commencing position and hold.	16

Pas de Basque—Forward Glissade—Rev. Prog. Waltz Turn—Rear Glissade—Rev. Rotary Waltz Turn—Pas de Valse

Lady

1 and	Pas de basque R.F., L.F., R.F., similar to 1st bar	
2	Boston Two Step. ⅛ turn to R.	1
3	L.F. forward down L.O.D. (heel) L. shoulder lead.	
4	Close R.F. to L.F. 3*rd pos. rear* (b.o.f. then w.f.).	2
1	L.F. forward down L.O.D. (heel) turn to L.	
and	R.F. to side along L.O.D. (b.o.f.) release hold.	
2	Close L.F. to R.F. 5*th pos. front* (b.o.f. then w.f.).	

Count	Lady	Bars
	Face diag. centre against L.O.D., R. hand in Man's L. hand. ½ turn to L. on last three steps.	3
3	R.F. diag. back down L.O.D. (b.o.f. then w.f.).	
4	Close L.F. to R.F. 3rd pos. front (b.o.f. then w.f.).	4
1	R.F. back down L.O.D. (b.o.f. then w.f.) turn to L.	
and	Close L.F. to R.F. 5th pos. rear (b.o.f.) release hold.	
2	Turn to L. (balls of both feet) to face diag. wall down L.O.D. ½ turn to L. on last three steps.	5
3	L.F. forward down L.O.D. (heel) turn to L. L. hand in Man's R. hand.	
and	R.F. forward down L.O.D. (b.o.f.) R. shoulder lead.	
4	Close L.F. to R.F. 3rd pos. rear (b.o.f. then w.f.). Face diag. centre down L.O.D. ¼ turn to L. on last three steps.	6

Walks—Point—Rear Chassé—Forward Point—Nat.
(Solo) Waltz Turn

1, 2, 3	R.F., L.F., R.F. forward down L.O.D. (heel).	
4	*Point* L.F. forward (toe).	7–8
1	L.F. back against L.O.D. (b.o.f.),	
and	Close R.F. to L.F. 3rd pos. front (b.o.f.),	
2 and	Repeat last two steps—L.F., R.F.,	9
3	L.F. back against L.O.D. (b.o.f. then w.f.).	
4	*Point* R.F. forward (toe) short step.	10
1	R.F. forward down L.O.D. (heel) turn to R. Hold	
and	released, L.F. to side along L.O.D. (b.o.f.).	
2	Close R.F. to L.F. 5th pos. front (b.o.f. then w.f.). Face diag. wall against L.O.D. ½ turn to R.	11
3	L.F. back down L.O.D. (b.o.f. then w.f.) continue	
and	turn to R. Close R.F. to L.F. 5th pos. rear (b.o.f.).	
4	Pivot to R. (balls of both feet) to face diag. centre down L.O.D. ½ turn to R. L. hand in Man's R. hand.	12

Pas de Basque—Forward Glissé—Nat. Waltz Turn

1	Pas de basque R.F., L.F., R.F., turn to L. to face	
and	centre of room — ⅛ turn L., R. hand in Man's L.	
2	hand. (Double Hold.)	13
3	L.F. forward towards partner (b.o.f. then w.f.).	

Count	Lady	Bars
4	Close R.F. to L.F. *3rd pos. front* (b.o.f.) without weight. Adopt normal waltz hold with partner.	14
1	R.F. forward (heel) down L.O.D. Turn to R.	
and	L.F. to side along L.O.D. (b.o.f.).	
2	Close R.F. to L.F. *5th pos. front* (b.o.f. then w.f.). Back diag. to centre down L.O.D.	15
3	L.F. to side and back down L.O.D. turning to R. (b.o.f. then w.f.).	
and	Close R.F. to L.F. *5th pos. rear* (b.o.f.).	
4	Pivot to R. to face diag. centre down L.O.D. Finish R.F. *3rd pos. front.* Assume commencing hold.	16

WAVERLEY TWO STEP

MAURICE FLETCHER, F.I.S.T.D.

TIME 6/8—TEMPO 48

PARTNERS commence facing down L.O.D. Hold No. 2
—Lady's L. hand in Man's R. hand—similar to Boston
Two Step.

Walks—Swivel to Point—Nat. Prog. Waltz Turn—Glissade

Count	Man	Bars
1, 2, 3	L.F., R.F., L.F. forward down L.O.D. (heel).	
4	Swivel on ball of L.F. to face wall and partner (quarter turn R.). *Point* R.F. forward (toe).	
1	R.F. forward (heel). Turn to R.—partners R. hip to R. hip. Hold released—R. hand en l'air (not an allemande).	
and	L.F. to side towards wall (b.o.f.).	1–2
2	Close R.F. to L.F. 5*th pos. front* (b.o.f., w.f.). Face against L.O.D.—quarter turn to R. Man now on outside of room (Lady inside).	3
3	L.F. to side (b.o.f., w.f.). Slightly forward against L.O.D. Partners in line.	
4	Close R.F. to L.F. 3*rd pos. rear* (b.o.f., w.f.). Glissade—finish both partners facing against L.O.D.—Lady's L. hand again in Man's R. hand.	4
	Repeat bars 1–4 moving against L.O.D.	
1, 2, 3	L.F., R.F., L.F. forward against L.O.D.	
4	Swivel to face centre of room. *Point* R.F. forward (quarter turn R.).	5–6
1 and 2	Natural Progressive Waltz Turn, R.F., L.F., R.F. Hold released (quarter turn R.).	7
3	L.F. to side and slightly forward down L.O.D.	
4	Close R.F. to L.F. 3*rd pos. rear* (b.o.f., w.f.). Glissade—partners again in commencing position.	8

Pas de Basque—Rev. Telemark to Zephyr—Nat. Prog. Waltz Turn—Glissade—Nat. Rotary Waltz Turn—Pas de Valse

Count	Man	Bars
1 and 2	Pas de Basque, L.F., R.F., L.F. 5*th pos.* towards centre of room. Headline towards partner.	9
3 and 4	Pas de Basque towards partner, R.F., L.F., R.F. 5*th pos.* Headline down L.O.D. Last two bars are similar to bars 1–2 Boston Two Step.	10
1	L.F. forward down L.O.D. (heel). Turn strongly to L.—Hold released at end of step (R. hand en l'air).	
2	R.F. sideways along L.O.D. (b.o.f., w.f.). Face diag. centre against L.O.D.	11
3	Continue turn to L. on ball of R.F. to face partner. L.F. sideways along L.O.D. (b.o.f., w.f.) toe pointing diag. wall down L.O.D. Rejoin inside hands (Lady's L. hand in Man's R. hand).	
4	Zephyr (swing) R.F. forward down L.O.D. to *low front aerial pos.* Slightly over three-quarter turn to L. on last 4 steps.	12
1	R.F. forward down L.O.D. (heel). Turn to R. (inwards).	
and	L.F. to side along L.O.D. (b.o.f.).	
2	Close R.F. to L.F. 5*th pos. front* (b.o.f., w.f.), quarter turn R.	13
3	L.F. to side along L.O.D. (b.o.f.). Lady's R. hand in L. hand (Double Hold No. 5).	
4	Close R.F. to L.F. 3*rd pos. front* (b.o.f., w.f.). Glissade. Finish assuming normal Waltz Hold.	14
1 and 2	Natural Rotary Waltz Turn, L.F., R.F., L.F.	15
3	R.F. forward down L.O.D. (heel). Slight turn to R.	
and	L.F. forward (b.o.f.). Slightly diag. centre down L.O.D. Hold released.	
4	Close R.F. to L.F. 3*rd pos. rear* (b.o.f., w.f.). Last two bars are similar to bars 15–16 Boston Two Step.	16

Walks—Swivel to Point—Rev. Prog. Waltz Turn—Glissade

Lady

1, 2, 3	R.F., L.F., R.F. forward down L.O.D. (heel).	
4	Swivel on ball of R.F. to face centre and partner (quarter turn L.). Point L.F. forward (toe).	1–2

Count	**Lady**	Bars
1	L.F. forward (heel). Turn to L.—partners R. hip to R. hip. Hold released—L. hand en l'air.	
and	R.F. to side towards centre of room (b.o.f.).	
2	Close L.F. to R.F. 5*th pos. front* (b.o.f., w.f.) quarter turn to L. Lady now on inside of room.	3
3	R.F. to side and very slightly backward (b.o.f., w.f.). In line with partner at end of step.	
4	Close L.F. to R.F. 3*rd pos. rear* (b.o.f., w.f.). Face against L.O.D., L. hand again in Man's R. hand.	4
	Repeat bars 1–4 moving against L.O.D.	
1, 2, 3	R.F., L.F., R.F. forward against L.O.D. (heel).	
4	Swivel to face wall—Point L.F. forward (quarter turn L.).	5–6
1 and 2	Reverse Progressive Waltz Turn—L.F., R.F., L.F. Hold released (quarter turn L.).	7
3	R.F. to side and slightly back.	
4	Close L.F. to R.F. 3*rd pos. rear*—Glissade—partners again with commencing position and hold.	8

Pas de Basque—Nat. Telemark Turn to Zephyr—Rev. Prog. Waltz Turn—Glissade—Nat. Waltz Turn

1 and 2	Pas de Basque towards wall—R.F., L.F., R.F. 5*th pos.* Headline towards partner.	9
3 and 4	Pas de Basque towards partner—L.F., R.F., L.F. 5*th pos.* Headline down L.O.D. Last two bars are similar to bars 1–2 Boston Two Step.	10
1	R.F. forward down L.O.D. (heel). Turn strongly to R. Hold released—L. hand en l'air.	
2	L.F. sideways along L.O.D. (b.o.f., w.f.). Face diag. wall against L.O.D.	11
3	Continue turn to R. on ball of L.F. to face partner— R.F. sideways along L.O.D. (b.o.f., w.f.) toe pointing diag. centre down L.O.D.—L. hand in Man's R. hand.	
4	Zephyr (swing) L.F. forward down L.O.D. *low front aerial pos.* Slightly over three-quarter turn to R. on last 4 steps.	12
1	L.F. forward down L.O.D. (heel). Turn to L. (inwards).	
and	R.F. to side along L.O.D. (b.o.f.).	
2	Close L.F. to R.F. 5*th pos. front* (b.o.f., w.f.). R. hand in Man's L. hand (Double Hold No. 5).	13

WAVERLEY TWO STEP (*contd.*)

Count	**Lady**	Bars
3	R.F. to side along L.O.D. (b.o.f., w.f.).	
4	Close L.F. to R.F. *3rd pos. front* (b.o.f., w.f.). At end of step Swivel to R. to face centre of room, preparing to assume normal Waltz Hold.	14
1 and 2	Natural Progressive Waltz Turn, R.F. L.F., R.F. *5th pos.*	15
3 and 4	Natural Rotary Waltz Turn, L.F., R.F., L.F. *3rd pos.* Last two bars are similar to bars 15–16 Boston Two Step.	16

RIALTO TWO STEP

DAVID ROLLINSON
TIME 6/8—TEMPO 48

PARTNERS commence Man facing diag. wall down
L.O.D.—Lady facing diag. centre down L.O.D. Lady's
L. hand in Man's R. hand. Hold No. 2 similar to
Boston Two Step.

Walks and Points—Rev. Waltz Turn (Solo)

Count	Man	Bars
1	L.F. forward down L.O.D. (heel).	
2	*Point* R.F. forward (toe). Slight R. shoulder lead.	1
3	R.F. forward down L.O.D. (heel).	
4	*Point* L.F. forward (toe). Slight L. shoulder lead.	2
1	L.F. forward down L.O.D. (heel). Turn to L. (outwards). Hold released.	
and	R.F. to side along L.O.D. (b.o.f.).	
2	Close L.F. to R.F. 5*th pos. front* (b.o.f., w.f.). Face diag. centre against L.O.D.—half turn to L.	3
3	R.F. back down L.O.D. (b.o.f., w.f.) continuing turn to L.	
and	Close L.F. to R.F. 5*th pos. rear* (b.o.f.).	
4	Levé Pivot to L. (balls of both feet). Face diag. wall down L.O.D. Lady's L. hand in R. hand as at commencement—half turn to L.	4

Walk and Zephyr—Nat. Swivel and Zephyr—Walks to Forward Glissade

1	L.F. forward down L.O.D. (heel). Partners R. hand in L. hand (Double Hold No. 5).	
2	Zephyr (swing) R.F. forward down L.O.D. to *low front aerial pos.*	5
3	Swivel to R. (inwards) on ball of L.F. to face diag. wall against L.O.D.—whilst turning close ball of R.F. to L. ankle.	
4	R.F. forward against L.O.D. to *low front aerial pos.* Release hold with R. hand.	6

153

Count	**Man**	Bars
1, 2	R.F., L.F. forward against L.O.D. (heel).	7
3	R.F. forward against L.O.D. (heel).	
4	Close L.F. to R.F. 3rd *pos. rear* (b.o.f., w.f.).	8

Pas de Basque—Forward Turning Glissé—Nat. Prog. Waltz Turn—Pas Glissade—Natural Waltzing

1	R.F. to side towards centre of room (b.o.f., w.f.). Slight body turn to R.	
and	Close L.F. to R.F. 5th *pos. front* (b.o.f.). Face diag. centre against L.O.D. (release ball of R.F. from the floor—backward).	
2	Replace R.F. to 5th *pos. rear* (b.o.f., w.f.). Coupé in place	9
3	Release L. hand hold—L.F. diagonally forward against L.O.D. (b.o.f., w.f.). Turning to R. (outwards).	
4	Close R.F. to L.F. 5th *pos. front* (b.o.f.) without weight —take Lady's L. hand in R. hand (Hold No. 2). Face diag. centre down L.O.D.	10
1	R.F. forward down L.O.D. (heel). Turn to R. (inwards).	
and	L.F. to side along L.O.D. (b.o.f.). Face towards wall —Lady's R. hand in L. hand (Double Hold).	
2	Close R.F. to L.F. 5th *pos. front* (b.o.f., w.f.). Almost facing diag. to wall against L.O.D.	11
3	L.F. to side along L.O.D. (b.o.f., w.f.).	
4	Close R.F. to L.F. 3rd *pos. front* (b.o.f., w.f.). Glissade. Partners assume normal Waltz Hold.	12
	Natural Waltzing similar to Bars 13–16 Boston Two Step.	
1 and 2	Natural Rotary Turn, L.F., R.F., L.F. 5th *pos.*	13
3 and 4	Natural Progressive Turn, R.F., L.F., R.F. 5th *pos.*	14
1 and 2	Natural Rotary Turn, L.F., R.F., L.F. 5th *pos.*	15
3 and 4	Pas de Valse forward R.F., L.F., R.F. 3rd *pos. rear.*	16

Lady

Walks and Points—Nat. Waltz Turn (Solo)

1	R.F. forward down L.O.D. (heel).	
2	Point L.F. forward (toe). Slight L. shoulder lead.	1
3	L.F. forward down L.O.D. (heel).	

Count	**Lady**	Bars
4	Point R.F. forward (toe). Slight R. shoulder lead.	2
1	R.F. forward down L.O.D. (heel). Turn to R. (outwards). Hold released.	
and	L.F. to side along L.O.D. (b.o.f.).	
2	Close R.F. to L.F. 5*th pos. front* (b.o.f., w.f.). Face diag. wall against L.O.D.—half turn to R.	3
3	L.F. back down L.O.D. (b.o.f., w.f.) continuing turn to R.	
and	Close R.F. to L.F. 5*th pos. rear* (b.o.f.).	
4	Levé pivot to R. (balls of both feet). Face diag. centre down L.O.D.—L. hand in Man's R. hand—half turn to R.	4

Walk and Zephyr—Rev. Swivel and Zephyr—Walks to Forward Glissade

1	R.F. forward down L.O.D. (heel). R. hand in Man's L. hand (Double Hold No. 5).	
2	Zephyr (swing). L.F. forward down L.O.D. to *low front aerial pos.*	5
3	Swivel to L. (inwards) on ball of R.F. to face diag. centre against L.O.D.—whilst turning close ball of L.F. to R. ankle.	
4	Zephyr (swing). L.F. forward against L.O.D. to *low front aerial pos.* Release hold with L. hand.	6
1, 2	L.F., R.F. forward against L.O.D. (heel).	7
3	L.F. forward against L.O.D. (heel).	
4	Close R.F. to L.F. 3*rd pos. rear* (b.o.f., w.f.).	8

Pas de Basque—Forward Turning Glissé—Rev. Prog. Waltz Turn—Pas Glissade—Natural Waltzing

1	L.F. to side towards wall (b.o.f., w.f.). Slight body turn to L.	
and	Close R.F. to L.F. 5*th pos. front* (b.o.f.), (Release ball L.F. slightly from the floor—backward).	
2	Replace L.F. to 5*th pos. rear* (b.o.f., w.f.). Coupé in place.	9
3	Release R. hand-hold—R.F. diagonally forward against L.O.D. (b.o.f., w.f.). Turning to L. (outwards).	

Count	**Lady**	Bars
4	Close L.F. to R.F. 5*th pos. front* (b.o.f.) without weight L. hand in Man's R. hand. Face diag. wall down L.O.D.	10
1	L.F. forward down L.O.D. (heel). Turn to L. (inwards).	
and	R.F. to side along L.O.D. (b.o.f.), R. hand in Man's L. hand (Double Hold).	
2	Close L.F. to R.F. 5*th pos. front* (b.o.f., w.f.). Almost facing diag. to centre against L.O.D.	11
3	R.F. to side along L.O.D. (b.o.f., w.f.).	
4	Close L.F. to R.F. 3*rd pos. front* (b.o.f., w.f.). At end of step swivel to R. to face centre of room, assuming normal Waltz Hold with partner.	12
	Natural Waltzing similar to bars 13–16 Boston Two Step. Progressive Turn, R.F., L.F., R.F.—Rotary Turn, L.F., R.F., L.F. Progressive Turn, R.F., L.F., R.F.—Rotary Turn, L.F., R.F., L.F. 3*rd pos*.	13–16

WEDGEWOOD BLUE

FRANK NOBLE AND NORA BRAY

TIME 4/4—TEMPO 24

PARTNERS commence—Man facing diag. wall down L.O.D.—Lady facing diag. to centre down L.O.D.—Lady's L. hand in Man's R. hand (Hold No. 2).

Man

Pas de Gavotte—Walks to Check—Walk to Point—Open Rev. Turn

Count		Bars
1	L.F. forward down L.O.D. (b.o.f., w.f.).	
2	Close R.F. to L.F. *3rd pos. rear* (b.o.f., w.f.).	
3	L.F. forward down L.O.D. (b.o.f., w.f.).	
4	R.F. forward to *low front aerial pos.* Headline towards partner	1
1	R.F. forward down L.O.D. (heel). Headline down L.O.D.	
2	L.F. forward down L.O.D. (b.o.f., w.f.).	
3, 4	R.F. forward down L.O.D. (b.o.f., w.f.). Slight R. shoulder lead. Face towards diag. centre down L.O.D. Headline diag. to centre. Check with slight plié. (Quarter turn to L. approx. on last bar.)	2
1	Transfer weight back to L.F. (b.o.f., w.f.).	
2	R.F. forward down L.O.D. (heel)—very short step with body turn to R.	
3, 4	Point L.F. (toe) forward down L.O.D. Headline towards partner. (Quarter turn to R. on last two steps.)	3
1	L.F. forward down L.O.D. (heel). Turn to L. (outwards). R. hand released at end of step.	
2	R.F. to side along L.O.D. (b.o.f., w.f.)—continuing turn to L.	
3	L.F. back down L.O.D. (b.o.f., w.f.). Face against L.O.D.	
4	Close R.F. to L.F. *3rd pos. front*—without weight—Lady's R. hand in L. hand. Face diag. to wall against L.O.D. (three-quarter turn to L. approx.).	4

157

Man

Pas de Gavotte—Open Rev. Turn (Inwards)
Pas de Gavotte—Walks

Count   Bars

1   R.F. forward (b.o.f., w.f.) against L.O.D.—Headline
     against L.O.D.
2   Close L.F. to R.F. *3rd pos. rear* (b.o.f., w.f.).
3   R.F. forward (b.o.f., w.f.) against L.O.D.
4   L.F. forward to *low front aerial pos.* Headline towards
     partner.   5
1   L.F. forward (heel) against L.O.D. Turn to L. (in-
     wards). Release L. hand at end of step.
2   R.F. to side against L.O.D. (b.o.f., w.f.). Face diag.
     wall down L.O.D. ((Lady's L. hand in R. hand—
     L. hand on L. hip.)
3   L.F. back against L.O.D. (b.o.f., w.f.), toe pointing to
     centre of room. Face down L.O.D.
4   Close R.F. to L.F. *3rd pos. front* (b.o.f.) without weight.
     Face diag. to centre down L.O.D. (three-quarter
     turn to L. approx.).   6
1   R.F. forward down L.O.D. (b.o.f., w.f.). Headline
     diag. to centre down L.O.D.
2   Close L.F. to R.F. *3rd pos. rear* (b.o.f., w.f.).
3   R.F. forward down L.O.D. (b.o.f., w.f.).
4   L.F. forward to *low front aerial pos.*   7
1   L.F. forward down L.O.D. (heel). Face down L.O.D.
2   R.F. forward down L.O.D. (b.o.f., w.f.). Turn to R.
     (inwards).
3   L.F. to side along L.O.D. (b.o.f., w.f.). Face wall and
     partner—Lady's R. hand in L. hand (Double
     Hold).
4   Close R.F. to L.F. *3rd pos. front* (b.o.f.) without weight
     (slightly over quarter turn to R. on last 3 steps).   8

Clockwise Circling—Glissade—Gavotte—Waltzing

1   R.F. forward towards wall (b.o.f., w.f.). Slight turn to
     R.
2   L.F. to side (b.o.f., w.f.). Face against L.O.D.
3   R.F. forward against L.O.D. (b.o.f., w.f.) continuing
     curve to R.
4   L.F. to side against L.O.D. (b.o.f., w.f.). Finish facing
     centre of room both hands joined. Face square to
     partner during last 4 steps.   9

WEDGEWOOD BLUE (contd.)

Count	Man	Bars
1	R.F. forward (heel) towards centre of room—slight turn to R. Release L. hand and commence to turn partner to L. under R. hand (Lady's L. hand). Short step.	
2	L.F. forward (b.o.f., w.f.) towards centre of room.	
3	R.F. forward (b.o.f., w.f.) almost down L.O.D.	
4	Close L.F. to R.F. *3rd pos. front* (b.o.f.) without weight. Lady's R. hand in L. hand (Double Hold). Man facing diag. wall down L.O.D. (Lady diag. centre down L.O.D.).	10
1	L.F. forward down L.O.D. (b.o.f., w.f.).	
2	Close R.F. to L.F. *3rd pos. rear* (b.o.f., w.f.). Forward Glissade.	
3	L.F. diag. forward down L.O.D. (b.o.f., w.f.). Turn to R. (inwards).	
4	Close R.F. to L.F. *3rd pos. front* (b.o.f.) without weight. Turning Glissé—quarter turn to R. approx.	11
1	R.F. forward against L.O.D. (b.o.f., w.f.).	
2	Close L.F. to R.F. *3rd pos. rear* (b.o.f., w.f.). Forward Glissade. During next two steps hold is released whilst partner pivots to L.	
3	R.F. diag. forward against L.O.D. (b.o.f., w.f.). Turn to L.	
4	Close L.F. to R.F. *3rd pos. front* (b.o.f.) without weight. Turning Glissé—quarter turn to L. approx.	12
	Finish both partners facing diag. wall down L.O.D. Lady's L. shoulder in front of Man's R. shoulder—L. hand in L. hand—R. hand in R. hand similar to Doris Waltz, Maxina, etc. (Hold No. 3). Headlines down L.O.D.	
	Both partners dance Gavotte Movement commencing L.F.	
1	L.F. forward down L.O.D. (b.o.f., w.f.).	
2	Close R.F. to L.F. *3rd pos. rear* (b.o.f., w.f.).	
3	L.F. forward down L.O.D. (b.o.f., w.f.).	
4	R.F. forward to *low front aerial pos.*	13
	Both partners dance a Natural Progressive Waltz Turn.	
1	R.F. forward down L.O.D. (heel). Turning to R.—L. hands released.	
and	L.F. to side along L.O.D. (b.o.f.). Both hands released.	

Count	**Man**	Bars
2	Close R.F. to L.F. 5*th pos. front* (b.o.f., w.f.).	
	Lady continues with Natural Waltzing whilst Man dances a Glissade.	
3	L.F. to side along L.O.D. (b.o.f., w.f.).	
4	Close R.F. to L.F. 3*rd pos. front* (b.o.f., w.f.). Partners finish assuming normal Waltz Hold.	14
1 and 2	Natural Rotary Waltz Turn, L.F., R.F., L.F. 5*th pos.*	
3 and 4	Natural Progressive Waltz Turn, R.F., L.F., R.F. 5*th pos.*	15
1 and 2	Natural Rotary Waltz Turn, L.F., R.F., L.F. 5*th pos.*	
3 and 4	Pas de Valse, R.F., L.F., R.F.—moving to commencing position.	16
	Last two bars are similar to bars 15–16 La Mascotte.	

Lady

Pas de Gavotte—Walks to Check—Walk to Point—Open Nat. Turn

1	R.F. forward down L.O.D. (b.o.f., w.f.).	
2	Close L.F. to R.F. 3*rd pos. rear* (b.o.f., w.f.).	
3	R.F. forward down L.O.D. (b.o.f., w.f.).	
4	L.F. forward to *low front aerial pos.* Headline towards partner.	1
1	L.F. forward down L.O.D. (heel). Headline down L.O.D.	
2	R.F. forward down L.O.D. (b.o.f., w.f.).	
3, 4	L.F. forward (b.o.f., w.f.). Slight L. shoulder lead. Headline diag. wall down L.O.D. Check with slight plié (quarter turn R. approx.). Face diag. wall down L.O.D.	2
1	Transfer weight back to R.F. (b.o.f., w.f.).	
2	L.F. forward down L.O.D. (heel)—very short step with turn to L.	
3, 4	Point R.F. forward (toe). Headline towards partner (quarter turn L.)	3
1	R.F. forward down L.O.D. (heel). Turn to R. (outwards). Man releases Lady's L. hand.	
2	L.F. to side along L.O.D. continuing turn to R. (b.o.f., w.f.).	
3	R.F. back down L.O.D. (b.o.f., w.f.). Face against L.O.D.	

Count	Lady	Bars
4	Close L.F. to R.F. *3rd pos. front* (b.o.f.) without weight —R. hand in Man's L. hand. Face diag. centre against L.O.D. Three-quarter turn to R. approx. on last 4 steps.	4

Pas de Gavotte—Open Nat. Turn (Inwards)
Pas de Gavotte—Walks

1	L.F. forward (b.o.f., w.f.) against L.O.D.	
2	Close R.F. to L.F. *3rd pos. rear* (b.o.f., w.f.).	
3	L.F. forward (b.o.f., w.f.) against L.O.D.	
4	R.F. forward to *low front aerial pos.* Headline towards partner.	5
1	R.F. forward against L.O.D. (heel). Turn to R. (inwards). Man releases L. hand from Lady's R. hand.	
2	L.F. to side against L.O.D. (b.o.f., w.f.). Face diag. centre down L.O.D.-L. hand in Man's R. hand.	
3	R.F. back against L.O.D. (b.o.f., w.f.). Face down L.O.D.	
4	Close L.F. to R.F. *3rd pos. front* (b.o.f.) without weight —Face diag. wall down L.O.D. three-quarter turn to R. approx. on last 4 steps.	6
1	L.F. forward down L.O.D. (b.o.f., w.f.). Headline diag. wall down L.O.D.	
2	Close R.F. to L.F. *3rd pos. rear* (b.o.f., w.f.).	
3	L.F. forward down L.O.D. (b.o.f., w.f.).	
4	R.F. forward to *low front aerial pos.*	7
1	R.F. forward down L.O.D. (heel).	
2	L.F. forward down L.O.D. (heel), turning to L. (inwards).	
3	R.F. to side along L.O.D. (b.o.f., w.f.). Face centre of room—assume Double Hold—R. hand in Man's L. hand.	
4	Close L.F. to R.F. *3rd pos. rear* (b.o.f., w.f.) with weight. Quarter turn to L. approx. on last 3 steps.	8

Clockwise Circling—Rev. Open Turn (Allemande)— Forward Glissade and Glissé—Forward Glissade— Rev. Pivot

1	R.F. forward towards centre of room (b.o.f., w.f.). Slight turn to R.	

Count	Lady	Bars
2	L.F. to side (b.o.f., w.f.). Face down L.O.D.	
3	R.F. forward almost down L.O.D. (b.o.f., w.f.)—continuing curve to R. to face towards wall.	
4	Close L.F. to R.F. 3rd pos. front. Face square to partner. During next bar turn to L. under Man's R. hand (Lady's L. hand).	9
1	L.F. forward towards wall (b.o.f., w.f.). Turn to L. under hand.	
2	R.F. to side (b.o.f., w.f.). Face down L.O.D.	
3	L.F. back against L.O.D. (b.o.f., w.f.).	
4	Close R.F. to L.F. 3rd pos. front (b.o.f.) without weight. Face diag. centre down L.O.D. both hands joined (Double Hold).	10
1	R.F. forward down L.O.D. (b.o.f., w.f.).	
2	Close L.F. to R.F. 3rd pos. rear (b.o.f., w.f.). Forward Glissade.	
3	R.F. forward down L.O.D. (b.o.f., w.f.). Turn to L. (inwards).	
4	Close L.F. to R.F. 3rd pos. front without weight (b.o.f.).	11
1	L.F. forward against L.O.D. (b.o.f., w.f.). Face against L.O.D.	
2	Close R.F. to L.F. 3rd pos. rear (b.o.f., w.f.).	
3	Release hold—both hands en l'air—L.F. forward against L.O.D. (heel) turning strongly to L. to face diag. wall down L.O.D.	
4	Close R.F. to L.F. 3rd pos. rear (b.o.f., w.f.). Half turn to L. approx. on last two steps. Assume No. 3 Hold, as Doris Waltz.	12

Forward Gavotte—Natural Waltzing

1–4	Both partners dance Gavotte movement—L.F., R.F, L.F., R.F.	13
1	R.F. forward down L.O.D. (heel). Turning to R. (L. hands released).	
and	L.F. to side along L.O.D. (b.o.f.). Both hands en l'air.	
2	Close R.F. to L.F. 5th pos. front (b.o.f., w.f.).	
3 and 4	Natural Rotary Waltz Turn, L.F., R.F., L.F. 5th pos. Partners assume normal Waltz Hold—Natural Waltzing similar to bars 15–16 La Mascotte, etc.	14

162

BAMBI BLUES

DAVID ROLLINSON AND BARBARA HEATHCOTE
TIME 4/4—TEMPO 24/26

PARTNERS commence both facing down L.O.D.—
Lady's L. hip slightly in front of Man's R. hip—L.
hands joined at approx. shoulder height—Man's R.
hand on Lady's R. hip (Lady holds dress in R. hand)
(Hold No. 7). Bars 1/5 are danced on "same leg."

Forward Walks—Rev. Movement—Forward Walks— Nat. Movement

Count	Man and Lady	Bars
SS	L.F., R.F. forward down L.O.D. (heel).	1
Q	L.F. forward down L.O.D. (heel). Turn to L.	
Q	R.F. to side—towards wall. Face diag. centre down L.O.D.	
S	L.F. back diag. wall against L.O.D. Check. One-eighth turn to L.	2
SS	R.F., L.F. forward (heel) diag. to centre down L.O.D.	3
Q	R.F. forward (heel) diag. to centre down L.O.D. Turn to R.	
Q	L.F. to side towards centre of room.	
S	R.F. back diag. to centre against L.O.D.—quarter turn to R.	4

Walks (Lady turns to L.) Backward Open Chassé— Side Chassé

Man

SS	L.F., R.F. forward (heel) diag. to wall down L.O.D.	5
S	L.F. forward diag. wall down L.O.D. (heel). Release L. hand whilst partner turns to L. to back wall.	
S	R.F. forward diag. to wall down L.O.D. (heel). Partners with Double Hold—Lady's hand in R. hand—Lady's R. hand in L. hand. Check.	6

Count	Man	Bars
Q	L.F. back diag. to centre against L.O.D. L. shoulder lead.	
Q	Move R.F. towards L.F. *open parallel pos.*	
S	L.F. back diag. to centre against L.O.D.	7
Q	R.F. to side against L.O.D. Release L. hand hold and commence to turn partner to L. under raised R. hand.	
Q	Close L.F. to R.F. *parallel pos.*	
QQ	Repeat last 2 steps—R.F., L.F. Finish partner's R. hand again in L. hand (Double Hold).	8

Walks and Points—Nat. Rotary Chassé Turn to Side Closes

Q	L.F. diagonally forward down L.O.D. (heel). Face diag. wall down L.O.D. Headline down L.O.D. (*promenade pos.* but with Double Hold).	
Q	Point R.F. forward down L.O.D. (toe). Sway to R.	
Q	R.F. forward down L.O.D. (heel).	
Q	Point L.F. forward (toe). Sway to L.	9
QQQQ	Repeat last four steps—L.F., R.F., R.F., L.F.	10
Q	With body turn to R. L.F. to side towards wall assuming normal Ballroom Hold with partner.	
Q	Close R.F. to L.F. *parallel pos.* Back down L.O.D., partners square.	
S	L.F. back down L.O.D. continuing turn to R. to face centre of room.	11
Q	R.F. to side along L.O.D. (Man on outside—Lady on inside of room.)	
Q	Close L.F. to R.F. *parallel pos.*	
QQ	Repeat last two steps—R.F., L.F. Finish preparing to adopt Double Hold again.	12

Walks and Points—Nat. Chassé Turn— Forward Closes

Q	R.F. diagonally forward down L.O.D. (heel). Headline down L.O.D. (continuing *promenade pos.* but with Double Hold).	
Q	Point L.F. forward down L.O.D. (toe). Sway to L.	
Q	L.F. forward down L.O.D. (heel).	
Q	Point R.F. forward (toe). Sway to R.	13

BAMBI BLUES (*contd.*)

Count	**Man**	Bars
QQQQ	Repeat last four steps—R.F., L.F., L.F., R.F.	14
Q	R.F. to side towards wall. Slight turn to R.—assume normal Ballroom Hold with partner.	
Q	Close L.F. to R.F. *parallel pos.* Face down L.O.D. Partners square.	
S	R.F. forward down L.O.D. (heel) between partner's feet—preparing to release hold.	15
Q	L.F. forward—slightly diag. to centre down L.O.D.	
Q	Close R.F. to L.F. *parallel pos.*	
Q	L.F. forward down L.O.D.	
Q	Close R.F. to L.F. *parallel pos.* with weight—assume hold as at commencement of Dance.	16

Walks—Rev. Twinkle—Forward Open Chassé— Rev. Telemark (Allemande)

Lady

SS	L.F., R.F. forward (heel) diag. to wall down L.O.D.	5
Q	L.F. forward (heel) diag. wall down L.O.D. Turn strongly to L. to back diag. wall down L.O.D. Hold released.	
Q	Close R.F. to L.F. *parallel pos.* (half turn to L.).	
S	L.F. back diag. to wall down L.O.D. Headline to L. L. hand in Man's R. hand—R. hand in Man's L. hand (Double Hold).	6
Q	R.F. forward diag. to centre against L.O.D.	
Q	Move L.F. towards R.F. *open parallel pos.*	
S	R.F. forward diag. centre against L.O.D.—Finish brushing L.F. towards R.F. preparing to turn to L.	7
Q	L.F. forward (heel) against L.O.D. Turning to L. under Man's R. hand (Lady's L. hand). Face wall.	
Q	R.F. to side against L.O.D.	
Q	Continue turn to L. (ball of R.F.) to face centre of room. L.F. to side against L.O.D.	
Q	Close R.F. to L.F. *parallel pos.* without weight. Resume Double Hold (R. hand in Man's L. hand).	8

Walks and Points—Nat. Chassé Turn—Side Closes

Q	R.F. diagonally forward down L.O.D. (heel). Face diag. centre down L.O.D. Headline down L.O.D. (*promenade pos.* but with Double Hold).	

BAMBI BLUES (contd.)

Count	Lady	Bars
Q	Point L.F. forward down L.O.D. (toe). Sway to L.	
Q	L.F. forward down L.O.D. (heel).	
Q	Point R.F. forward (toe). Sway to R.	9
QQQQ	Repeat last four steps—R.F., L.F., L.F., R.F.	10
Q	R.F. to side towards wall. Turn slightly to R. Assume normal Ballroom Hold.	
Q	Close L.F. to R.F. *parallel pos.* Face down L.O.D. square to partner.	
S	R.F. forward down L.O.D. (heel) between partner's feet—continuing turn to R. to face towards wall.	11
Q	L.F. to side along L.O.D. (Lady on inside of room.)	
Q	Close R.F. to L.F. *parallel pos.*	
QQ	Repeat last two steps—L.F., R.F.—preparing to adopt Double Hold again.	12

Walks and Points—Nat. Rotary Chassé—Closed Finish

Count	Lady	Bars
Q	L.F. diagonally forward down L.O.D. (heel).	
Q	Point R.F. forward (toe). Sway to R.	
Q	R.F. forward down L.O.D. (heel).	
Q	Point L.F. forward (toe). Sway to L.	13
QQQQ	Repeat last four steps—L.F., R.F., R.F., L.F.	14
Q	L.F. to side towards wall with body turn to R. Assuming normal Ballroom Hold with partner.	
Q	Close R.F. to L.F. *parallel pos.* Back down L.O.D.	
S	L.F. back down L.O.D. Continuing turn to R. to face diag. centre down L.O.D.	15
Q	R.F. to side along L.O.D. (toe pointing down L.O.D.). Hold released.	
Q	Close L.F. to R.F. *parallel pos.* Face down L.O.D.	
Q	R.F. forward down L.O.D.	
Q	Close L.F. to R.F. *parallel pos.* without weight. Resume commencing hold and position.	16

TANGO EL CID

KEN PARK
TIME 2/4—TEMPO 32

Partners dance throughout with modern Tango Hold.
Commence Man facing, Lady backing L.O.D.

Forward Walks—Basic Rev. Turn—Four Step—
Nat. Twist Turn—Promenade Walks—Double Close

Count	Man	Bars
S	L.F. forward down L.O.D. (heel).	
S	R.F. forward down L.O.D. R. shoulder lead (slight turn to L.).	1
Q	L.F. forward (heel) diag. centre down L.O.D. Turning to L.	
Q	R.F. to side along L.O.D. (b.o.f., w.f.). Back down L.O.D. at end of step.	
S	Lock (cross) L.F. over front of R.F. (b.o.f., w.f.).	2
Q	R.F. back down L.O.D. (b.o.f., w.f.). Turning to L.	
Q	L.F. to side along L.O.D. (w.f.).	
S	Close R.F. to L.F (w.f.). Close with ball of R.F. by instep of L.F., feet parallel. Face diag. to wall down L.O.D.	3
Q	L.F. forward (heel) diag. to wall down L.O.D.	
Q	R.F. to side against L.O.D. (b.o.f., w.f.)—short step.	
Q	L.F. back (b.o.f., w.f.). Partner towards R. side (R. hip to R. hip). Turn partner to R. at end of step.	
Q	Close R.F. to L.F. *parallel pos.* (b.o.f., w.f.). *Promenade pos.* (ball of R.F. by instep on L.F.).	4
S	L.F. to side along L.O.D. in *promenade pos.* (heel).	
Q	R.F. forward down L.O.D. in *promenade pos.* (heel). Turn to R.	
Q	L.F. to side towards diag. wall down L.O.D. (Lady R.F. forward between Man's feet.) Back down L.O.D. at end of step.	5
S	Loosely cross R.F. in behind L.F. (b.o.f., w.f.)	
QQ	With feet in place, turn to R. to face diag. wall down L.O.D. (turn with floor pressure on L. heel and ball of R.F.). Lady moves forward round Man. Finish in *promenade pos.*	6

167

Count	**Man**	Bars
S	L.F. to side along L.O.D. in *promenade pos.* (heel).	
S	R.F. forward (heel) down L.O.D. in *promenade pos.*—slight turn to L.	7
Q	L.F. to side (w.f.) towards centre of room—*promenade pos.*—headline to L.	
Q	Close R.F. to L.F. (ball of R.F. by instep of L.F.).	
Q	L.F. to side (w.f.) almost facing diag. centre down L.O.D. Turn partner square.	
Q	Close R.F. to L.F. (ball of R.F. by instep of L.F.). Face diag. centre down L.O.D.	8

Rev. Turn to Oversway and Promenade Position—Open Promenade to Outside Swivel—Promenade Tap—Nat. Promenade Turn—Nat. Rock Turn—Back Rev. Turn

Q	L.F. forward (heel) diag. to centre down L.O.D.—Turn to L.	
Q	R.F. to side (b.o.f., w.f.) towards centre of room (Lady heel turn). Back down L.O.D. at end of step.	
S	L.F. back down L.O.D. (b.o.f., w.f.). Strong L. shoulder lead.	9
S	Hold footline and slightly flex L. knee with oversway of bodyline leftwards—bodyline towards wall—headline over Lady's L. shoulder.	
S	Transfer weight to R.F. against L.O.D. (heel). Turn to L. to face diag. wall down L.O.D.—partners in *promenade pos.*	10
S	L.F. to side along L.O.D. in *promenade pos.* (heel).	
Q	R.F. forward in *promenade pos.* (heel). Turn partner square at end of step.	
Q	L.F. to side along L.O.D. (w.f.).	11
S	R.F. forward (heel) towards wall. Check on R. side of partner.	
S	Transfer weight back to L.F. (b.o.f., w.f.) diag. centre against L.O.D. Turn partner to *promenade pos.* At end of step loosely cross R.F. over front of L.F. without weight.	12
Q	R.F. forward down L.O.D. in *promenade pos.* (heel).	
Q	Tap L.F. to R.F. (without weight) feet parallel and a few inches apart.	

168

Count	**Man**	Bars
S	L.F. to side along L.O.D. in *promenade pos.* (heel).	13
Q	R.F. forward (heel) down L.O.D. in *promenade pos.* Turn to R.	
Q	L.F. to side towards diag. wall down L.O.D. (Lady R.F. forward between Man's feet.) At end of step turn strongly to R. to face almost down L.O.D. Pivot action of almost a half turn.	
S	R.F. forward down L.O.D. (heel)—partners square— continue turn slightly to R.	14
Q	L.F. to side along L.O.D. (b.o.f., w.f.) (slightly back in relation to the body). Face diag. wall down L.O.D.	
Q	Rock forward to R.F. (heel). R. shoulder lead. Face towards wall.	
S	L.F. back (b.o.f., w.f.). L. shoulder lead—towards centre of room.	15
Q	R.F. back (b.o.f., w.f.)—turning to L.	
Q	L.F. to side and slightly forward (w.f.) toe pointing down L.O.D.	
S	Close R.F. to L.F. (w.f.). Face down L.O.D. (ball of R.F. by instep of L.F.).	16

Backward Walks—Basic Rev. Turn—Four Step— Nat. Twist Turn—Promenade Walks—Double Close

Lady

S	R.F. back down L.O.D. (b.o.f., w.f.).	
S	L.F. back down L.O.D. L. shoulder lead (b.o.f., w.f.).	1
Q	R.F. back diag. to centre down L.O.D. (b.o.f., w.f.)— turning to L.	
Q	L.F. diagonally forward down L.O.D. (b.o.f., w.f.).	
S	Close R.F. to L.F. (w.f.) feet parallel (ball of R.F. by instep of L.F.). Face down L.O.D.	2
Q	L.F. forward (heel) down L.O.D. continuing turn to L.	
Q	R.F. to side along L.O.D. (b.o.f., w.f.).	
S	Close L.F. to R.F. (w.f.). Back diag. wall down L.O.D. (Instep of L.F. by ball of R.F.)	3
Q	R.F. back diag. to wall down L.O.D. (b.o.f., w.f.).	
Q	L.F. to side against L.O.D. (w.f.). Slightly wider step than Man.	
Q	R.F. forward (heel) on R. side of partner (R. hip to R. hip) diag. to centre against L.O.D. At end of step turn to R. to face diag. centre down L.O.D.	

169

Count	**Lady**	Bars
Q	Close L.F. to R.F. *parallel pos.* (w.f.), *promenade pos.*	4
S	R.F. to side along L.O.D. in *promenade pos.* (heel).	
Q	L.F. forward down L.O.D. (heel) face down L.O.D. at end of step.	
Q	R.F. forward (heel) down L.O.D. between partner's feet.	5
S	L.F. forward down L.O.D. (heel). L. shoulder lead. Face diag. wall down L.O.D.—preparing to step outside partner.	
Q	R.F. forward (heel)towards wall on R. side of partner (R. hip to R. hip).	
Q	Turn strongly to R. on ball of R.F. to face diag. centre down L.O.D.—Close L.F. to R.F. *parallel pos.* (b.o.f., w.f.), partners in *promenade pos.* Seven-eighths turn to R. on last 3 steps.	6
S	R.F. to side along L.O.D. in *promenade pos.* (heel).	
S	L.F. forward down L.O.D. in *promenade pos.* (heel). Slight turn to L.	7
Q	R.F. to side towards centre of room (w.f.). Headline to R.	
Q	Close L.F. to R.F. *parallel pos.* (w.f.), *promenade pos.*	
Q	R.F. to side towards centre (w.f.). Turn to L. now square to partner.	
Q	Close L.F. to R.F. *parallel pos.* (w.f.). Backing diag. to centre down L.O.D.	8

Rev. Turn—Oversway to Promenade Position— Open Promenade to Outside Swivel— Promenade Tap—Promenade Turn—Nat. Rock Turn— Forward Rev. Turn

Q	R.F. back diag. to centre down L.O.D. Turning to L.	
Q	Close L.F. to R.F. *parallel pos.* (heel turn). Face down L.O.D.	
S	R.F. forward down L.O.D. (heel). R. shoulder lead.	9
S	With feet in place overswing bodyline to L. Headline to L.	
S	Replace weight to L.F. against L.O.D. (heel)—turning to R. to face diag. centre down L.O.D.— partners in *promenade pos.*	10
S	R.F. to side along L.O.D. in *promenade pos.* (heel).	

TANGO EL CID (*contd.*)

Count	Lady	Bars
Q	L.F. forward down L.O.D. (heel). Turn to L. to back towards wall.	
Q	R.F. to side along L.O.D. (b.o.f., w.f.). Back diag. wall down L.O.D.	11
S	L.F. back diag. wall down L.O.D. (b.o.f., w.f.). Check with partner towards R. side.	
S	R.F forward (heel) diag. to centre against L.O.D.—turning to R. to face diag. centre down L.O.D. At end of step close L.F. to R.F. without weight—partners in *promenade pos.*	12
Q	L.F. forward down L.O.D. in *promenade pos.* (heel).	
Q	Tap R.F. to L.F. (without weight), feet parallel and a few inches apart.	
S	R.F. to side along L.O.D. in *promenade pos.*	13
Q	L.F. forward down L.O.D. (heel) *promenade pos.*	
Q	R.F. forward (heel) down L.O.D. between partner's feet. Pivot strongly to R. almost a half turn to back down L.O.D.	
S	L.F back down L.O.D. (b.o.f., w.f.), continuing turn to R.	14
Q	Rock forward to R.F. (heel), moving foot towards centre of room between partner's feet—R. shoulder lead.	
Q	Rock back to L.F. (b.o.f., w.f.)—L. shoulder lead.	
S	R.F. forward (heel) slightly diag. to centre down L.O.D.	15
⎱	L.F. forward (heel)—turning to L.	
⎰	R.F. to side towards centre of room (b.o.f., w.f.).	
	Close L.F. to R.F. *parallel pos.* (b.o.f., w.f.). Back down L.O.D.	16

TANGO SERIDA

RITA POVER

TIME 2/4—TEMPO 32

PARTNERS commence both facing down L.O.D. L. hands joined—Man's R. hand on Lady's R. hip— Lady holds dress in R. hand. (Hold No. 7). Bars 1–4 are danced on "same leg."

Forward and Backward Walks—Forward Chassé— Backward Chassé

Count	Man and Lady	Bars
SS	L.F., R.F. forward down L.O.D. (heel). Slight plié on R.F.	1
S	L.F. back against L.O.D.	
S	R.F. back against L.O.D. Slight R. shoulder lead.	2
Q	L.F. forward down L.O.D. (heel). L. shoulder lead.	
Q	Close R.F. to L.F. *parallel pos.*	
S	L.F. forward down L.O.D. (heel). Check with slight plié action.	3

Man

Q	R.F. diagonally back against L.O.D. Release hold whilst partner turns to R.	
Q	Close L.F. to R.F. *parallel pos.* Face diag. wall down L.O.D.	
S	R.F. to side against L.O.D. Adopt normal Tango Hold in *promenade pos.*	4

Lady (4th bar)

Q	With body turn to R.—R.F. to side against L.O.D. Face wall.	
Q	Close L.F. to R.F. *parallel pos.* Face diag. wall against L.O.D.	
Q	R.F. forward against L.O.D. (heel). Turn strongly to	

Count	Lady	Bars
	R. to face diag. centre down L.O.D.	
Q	Close L.F. to R.F. *parallel pos.*	4

Promenade Link—Lunge—Backward Chassé— Side Chassé to Promenade Position

Man

S	L.F. to side along L.O.D. in *promenade pos.* (heel).	
Q	R.F. forward down L.O.D. (heel). Turn partner sharply to L.	
Q	Tap L.F. parallel to R.F. feet a few inches apart. Partner square. `	5
S	L.F. forward (heel) diag. to wall down L.O.D.	
S	R.F. forward (heel). R. shoulder lead. Slight plié. Headline towards partner's L, shoulder.	6
Q	L.F. back diag. to centre against L.O.D.	
Q	Close R.F. towards L.F.	
S	L.F. back. L. shoulder lead.	7
Q	R.F. to side against L.O.D.—slight turn to R.	
Q	Close L.F. to R.F. *parallel pos.* Face diag. wall down L.O.D. partners in *promenade pos.*	
S	R.F. to side against L.O.D. (L.F. extended sideways along L.O.D.)	8

Promenade Walks—Telemark Turn (Solo)— Promenade Link—Contra Check

S	L.F. to side along L.O.D. (heel). Very open *promenade pos.*	
S	R.F. forward down L.O.D. Release hold and lower arms to sides of body.	9
Q	L.F. forward down L.O.D. (heel)—turning to L.	
Q	R.F. to side along L.O.D. Face diag. centre against L.O.D.	
Q	Continue turn to L. on ball of R.F. to face wall—L.F. to side along L.O.D.	
Q	Close R.F. to L.F. *parallel pos.* Face diag. wall down L.O.D. Normal Tango Hold in *promenade pos.*	10
SQQ	Repeat 5th bar—Promenade Link—L.F., R.F., L.F.	11
S	L.F. forward (heel), diag. wall down L.O.D.—Contra check.	
S	R.F. back diag. centre against L.O.D.	12

173

Backward and Forward Chassés—Hesitation—
Double Side Close

Count	Man	Bars

QQS Repeat 7th bar—Back Chassé—L.F., R.F., L.F. 13

Q R.F. forward (heel) diag. wall down L.O.D., short step.

Q Close L.F. to R.F. *parallel pos.*

Q R.F. forward (heel), short step.

Q Close L.F. to R.F. *parallel pos.*

During above bar Lady turns gradually to R. to face down L.O.D. 14

QQ Hesitate with feet in place (weight on L.F.) whilst partner dances Solo turn to R. (L. hand on L. hip).

S R.F. forward (heel) towards diag. wall down L.O.D. Lady's L. hand in R. hand—both partners facing towards L.O.D. Headlines to R. 15

Q Replace weight to L.F. towards centre of room.

Q Close R.F. to L.F. *parallel pos.*, transferring Lady's L. hand to L. hand.

Q L.F. to side—short step.

Q Close R.F. to L.F., *parallel pos.*—R. hand on Lady's R. hip resuming commencing hold. 16

Promenade Link—Lunge—Forward Chassé—
Side Chassé to Promenade Position

Lady

S R.F. to side along L.O.D. in *promenade pos.* (heel).

Q L.F. forward down L.O.D. (heel)—turning to L. Back diag. wall down L.O.D.

Q Tap R.F. parallel to L.F., feet a few inches apart—partners square. 5

S R.F. back—diag. to wall down L.O.D.

S L.F. back—L. shoulder lead—headline to L. (lunge). 6

Q R.F. forward (heel) diag. centre against L.O.D.

Q Close L.F. to R.F.

S R.F. forward diag. centre against L.O.D. (heel). 7

Q With body turn to R.—L.F. to side against L.O.D.

Q Close R.F. to L.F. *parallel pos.* Face diag. centre down L.O.D.—partners in *promenade pos.*

S L.F. to side against L.O.D. (R.F. extended sideways). 8

174

TANGO SERIDA (*contd.*)

Promenade Walks—Telemark Turn (Solo)
Promenade Link—Contra Check

Count	Lady	Bars
S	R.F. to side along L.O.D. (heel)—very open *promenade pos.*	
S	L.F. forward down L.O.D. (heel). Release hold and lower arms to sides of body.	9
Q	R.F. forward down L.O.D. (heel)—turning to R.	
Q	L.F. to side along L.O.D.—Face diag. wall against L.O.D.	
Q	Continue turn to R. on ball of L.F. to face centre of room—R.F. to side along L.O.D.	
Q	Close L.F. to R.F. *parallel pos.* Face diag. centre down L.O.D. Normal Tango Hold in *promenade pos.*	10
SQQ	Repeat 5th bar—Promenade Link, R.F., L.F., R.F.	11
S	R.F. back—diag. wall down L.O.D. Headline to L.—Check.	
S	L.F. forward (heel)—diag. to centre against L.O.D.	12

Forward Chassé—Curving Chassé to Natural Solo Turn

QQS	Repeat 7th bar—R.F., L.F., R.F.	13
	Next bar moves backward—curving to R.	
Q	L.F. back diag. to wall down L.O.D.	
Q	Close R.F. to L.F. *parallel pos.* Face diag. centre down L.O.D.	
Q	L.F. back. Face down L.O.D.	
Q	Brush (close) R.F. to L.F. *parallel pos.*—without weight. Face diag. wall down L.O.D.—release R. hand.	14
Q	R.F. forward (heel)—diag. wall down L.O.D. (Release Hold)—turning strongly to R.—face against L.O.D.	
Q	L.F. to side towards wall.	
S	Continue turn to R. on ball of L.F. to face down L.O.D. R.F. sideways towards diag. wall down L.O.D. Lunge line—R. arm extended to R., hand lowered, Headline to R., L. hand in Man's R. hand.	15
Q	L.F. to side towards centre of room.	

175

Count	**Lady**	Bars
Q	Close R.F to L.F. *parallel pos*. L. hand in Man's L. hand.	
Q	L.F. to side—L. hip in front of Man's R. hip.	
Q	Close R.F. to L.F *parallel pos*. Commencing hold and position.	16

TRELAWNEY TANGO

STAN ROSS
TIME 2/4—TEMPO 32

PARTNERS commence with normal Tango Hold—Man facing—Lady backing L.O.D.

Walks—Rev. Movement—Double Close—Walks
Nat. Movement—Double Close to Promenade Position

Count	Man	Bars
SS	L.F., R.F. forward down L.O.D. (heel).	1
Q	L.F. forward (heel) turning to L.	
Q	R.F. to side towards wall. Face diag. centre down L.O.D.	
S	L.F. back diag. to wall against L.O.D. (one-eighth turn L.). Check with partner towards R. side (R. hip to R. hip).	2
SS	R.F., L.F. diag. centre down L.O.D. (heel).	3
Q	R.F. forward (heel) on R. side of partner—turning to R.	
Q	Close L.F. to R.F. *parallel pos.* Face down L.O.D., partners square.	
Q	R.F. to side towards wall.	
Q	Close L.F. to R.F. *parallel pos.* (one-eighth turn R.).	4
SS	R.F., L.F. forward down L.O.D. (heel).	5
Q	R.F. forward down L.O.D. (heel)—turning to R.	
Q	L.F. to side towards centre of room. Face diag. wall down L.O.D.	
S	R.F. back diag. to centre against L.O.D. (one-eighth turn R.). Check with partner towards L. side (L. hip to L. hip).	6
SS	L.F., R.F. forward (heel) diag. to wall down L.O.D.	7
Q	L.F. forward (heel) on L. side of partner—turning to L.	
Q	Close R.F. to L.F. *parallel pos.* (quarter turn to L.). Lady does not turn.	
Q	L.F. to side towards centre of room (heel) in *promenade pos.*	
Q	Close R.F. to L.F. *parallel pos.*	8

TRELAWNEY TANGO (*contd.*)

Promenade Twist to Left (Outwards) Point—
Reverse Oversway

Count	Man	Bars
S	L.F. to side in *promenade pos.* (heel)—partners moving square to centre of room.	
S	Cross R.F. forward (heel) well across front of L.F. (Release Hold).	9
S	With feet in place twist (swivel) to L.—feet flat to face towards wall—five-eighths turn to L. approx. Headline towards wall.	
S	*Point* L.F. forward (toe). Lady's R. hand in L. hand.	10
Q	L.F forward towards wall (heel). Turn to L. (inwards).	
Q	Close R.F. to L.F. *parallel pos.* Lady's L. hand in R. hand (Double Hold)—quarter turn to L. approx. Partners square.	
Q	L.F. to side towards centre of room.	
Q	Close R.F. to L.F. *parallel pos.* Release R. hand and assume normal Tango Hold.	11
S	L.F. back against L.O.D. L. shoulder lead.	
S	Hesitate with feet in place with slight overswing of bodyline to L. Headline over Lady's L. shoulder.	12

Promenade Movement to Side Step—Closed Finish

Q	Turning partner square—R.F. forward down L.O.D. (heel) with slight turn to R.	
Q	L.F. to side along L.O.D. (heel) in *promenade pos.*	
S	Close R.F. to L.F. *parallel pos.* Face diag. wall down L.O.D.	13
Q	L.F. forward down L.O.D. (heel). Face down L.O.D. releasing hold at end of step.	
Q	R.F. forward down L.O.D. (heel). Slightly shorter step than partner.	
S	Close L.F. to R.F. *parallel pos.* Without weight. R. hand on Lady's R. hip—Partners L. hand in L. hand (Hold No. 7). Partners dance on "same leg" during next bar.	14
Q	L.F. forward down L.O.D. (heel) across front of R.F., moving slightly diag. to wall down L.O.D. (C.B.M.P.).	
Q	R.F. to side towards wall.	

Count	**Man**	Bars
S	L.F. back against L.O.D.—Check (C.B.M.P.)—Headlines to R.	15
Q	R.F. forward (heel) and slightly leftwards—Release Hold whilst partner turns to R.	
Q	L.F. forward down L.O.D. (heel).	
S	Close R.F. to L.F. *parallel pos.*—assuming normal Tango hold.	16

Walks—Rev. Movement—Double Close—Walks—Nat. Movement—Double Close to Promenade Position

Lady

SS	R.F., L.F. back down L.O.D.	1
Q	R.F. back down L.O.D. turning to L.	
Q	L.F. to side towards wall. Back diag. centre down L.O.D.	
S	R.F. forward (heel) diag. to wall against L.O.D. Check on R. side of partner—one-eighth turn L.	2
SS	L.F., R.F. back diag. centre down L.O.D.	3
Q	L.F. back partner on R. side—turning to R.	
Q	Close R.F. to L.F. *parallel pos.* Back L.O.D. square to partner.	
Q	L.F. to side towards wall.	
Q	Close R.F. to L.F. *parallel pos.*—one-eighth turn R.	4
SS	L.F., R.F. back down L.O.D.	5
Q	L.F. back down L.O.D.—turning to R.	
Q	R.F. to side towards centre of room—Back diag. wall down L.O.D.	
S	L.F. forward (heel) diag. centre against L.O.D. Check on L. side of partner.	6
SS	R.F., L.F. back diag. to wall down L.O.D.	7
Q	R.F. back diag. wall down L.O.D. (no turn).	
Q	Close L.F. to R.F. *parallel pos.*	
Q	R.F. to side in *promenade pos.* (heel), moving square to centre of room.	
Q	Close L.F. to R.F. *parallel pos.*	8

Promenade Twist to Right (Outwards) Point—Rev. Oversway

S	R.F. to side in *promenade pos.* (heel).	
S	Cross L.F. forward (heel) well across front of R.F. Partners release hold.	9

Count	**Lady**	Bars
S	With feet in place twist (swivel) to R. to face towards wall—five-eighths turn approx. Headline towards wall.	
S	*Point* R.F. forward (toe), R. hand in Man's L. hand.	10
Q	R.F. forward towards wall (heel)—turning to R. (inwards).	
Q	Close L.F. to R.F. *parallel pos.* Lady's L. hand in Man's R. hand (Double Hold).	
Q	R.F. to side towards centre of room—Backing L.O.D.	
Q	Close L.F. to R.F. *parallel pos.*—normal Tango hold.	11
S	R.F. forward against L.O.D. (heel). R. shoulder lead.	
S	Oversway bodyline to L. with feet in place—Headline to L.	12

Promenade Movement to Side Step—Solo Turn to Right

Q	L.F. back down L.O.D. turning strongly to R. to face towards diag. centre down L.O.D.—partners in *promenade pos.*	
Q	R.F. to side along L.O.D. in *promenade pos.*	
S	Close L.F. to R.F. *parallel pos.*	13
Q	R.F. forward down L.O.D. (heel)—hold released.	
Q	L.F. forward down L.O.D. (heel), slightly longer step than partner.	
S	Close R.F. to L.F. *parallel pos.* with weight. Partners L. hands joined—R. hand holds dress (Hold No.7).	14
Q	L.F. forward down L.O.D. (heel).	
Q	R.F. to side towards wall.	
S	L.F. back against L.O.D. Check. Headline to R.	15
Q	R.F. forward down L.O.D. (heel), turning to R. Hold released.	
Q	L.F. to side along L.O.D. Face diag. wall against L.O.D. at end of step.	
Q	R.F. to side towards centre of room—Back down L.O.D. now facing partner.	
Q	Close L.F. to R.F. *parallel pos.*	16

DREAM WALTZ

ROBERT STEWART
TIME 3/4—TEMPO 32

NORMAL Ballroom Hold throughout. Commence Man facing—Lady backing diag. to centre down L.O.D.

Reverse Turn—Checked Open Finish—Left Side Check —Rev. Chassé—Natural Turn—Checked Open Finish—Right Side Check—Nat. Chassé

Count	Man	Bars
1	L.F. forward (heel) diag. centre down L.O.D. Turn to L.	
2	R.F. to side towards centre of room.	
3	Close L.F. to R.F. *parallel pos*. Back down L.O.D. Three-eighths turn L.	1
1	R.F. back down L.O.D. continuing turn to L.	
2	L.F. to side along L.O.D. Face diag. wall down L.O.D.	
3	R.F. forward—diag. wall down L.O.D. Check on R. side of partner (R. hip to R. hip). Three-eighths turn L. Headline to R.	2
1	L.F. back diag. centre against L.O.D. Turn to R.	
2	R.F. to side against L.O.D. Face diag. wall against L.O.D.	
3	L.F. forward—diag. wall against L.O.D. Check on L. side of partner (L. hip to L. hip). Quarter turn R. Headline to R.	3
1	R.F. back diag. centre down L.O.D. Turn to L.	
2	L.F. to side along L.O.D. Partners square.	
and	Close R.F. to L.F. *parallel pos*. Face diag. wall down L.O.D.	
3	L.F. to side along L.O.D. Preparing to step outside partner—quarter turn L.	4
1	R.F. forward (heel) diag. wall down L.O.D. on R. side of partner. Turn to R.	
2	L.F. to side towards wall—partners square.	

181

DREAM WALTZ (*contd.*)

Count	Man	Bars
3	Close R.F. to L.F. *parallel pos.* Back down L.O.D. Three-eighths turn.	5
1	L.F. back down L.O.D. continuing turn to R.	
2	R.F. to side along L.O.D. Face diag. centre down L.O.D.	
3	L.F. forward diag. centre down L.O.D. Check on L. side of partner. Headline to L. Three-eighths turn to R.	6
1	R.F. back diag. wall against L.O.D. Turn to L.	
2	L.F. to side against L.O.D. Face diag. centre against L.O.D.	
3	R.F. forward diag. centre against L.O.D. Check on R. side of partner. Quarter turn to L.	7
1	L.F. back diag. wall down L.O.D. Turn to R.	
2	R.F. to side (toe pointing down L.O.D.).	
and	Close L.F. to R.F. *parallel pos.*—partners square.	
3	R.F. diagonally forward—short step—three-eighths turn to R.	8

Link Change to Promenade Position—Weave to Promenade Position—Chassé

Count	Man	Bars
1	L.F. forward down L.O.D. Square to partner (heel).	
2	Close R.F. to L.F. *parallel pos.* Turn partner to *promenade pos.*	
3	L.F. diagonally forward (*promenade pos.*)—moving diag. centre down L.O.D. Headline to L.	9
1	R.F. forward (heel)—commencing to turn partner square.	
2	L.F. forward—diag. centre down L.O.D. between partner's feet—turning to L.	
3	R.F. to side along L.O.D.—Back down L.O.D. at end of step.	10
1	L.F. back down L.O.D. Partner on R. side.	
2	R.F. back down L.O.D. Partners square—turn to L.	
3	L.F. to side along L.O.D. Face diag. wall down L.O.D. at end of step. Partners in *promenade pos.* Seven-eighths turn to L. approx. on last two bars.	11
1	R.F. forward down L.O.D. in *promenade pos.* Turn partner square.	
2	L.F. to side along L.O.D. Partners square.	
and	Close R.F. to L.F. *parallel pos.*	

Count	**Man**	Bars
3	L.F. to side along L.O.D. (Lady backing diag. wall down L.O.D.)	12

Forward Natural Turn—Backward Open Change— Back Reverse Turn—Rev. Chassé

1	R.F. forward (heel) diag. wall down L.O.D. on R. side of partner—turning to R.	
2	L.F. to side along L.O.D. Partners square.	
3	Close R.F. to L.F. *parallel pos.* Back diag. centre down L.O.D. Quarter turn to R.	13
1	L.F. back diag. centre down L.O.D. Curve to R.	
2	R.F. back—preparing to lead partner to R. side.	
3	L.F. back down L.O.D. Partner on R. side. One-eighth turn to R.	14
1	R.F. back down L.O.D. Partner square. Turn to L.	
2	L.F. to side along L.O.D.	
3	Close R.F. to L.F. *parallel pos.* Face diag. wall down L.O.D. Three-eighths turn to L.	15
1	L.F. forward (heel) diag. wall down L.O.D. Turn to L.	
2	R.F. to side along L.O.D. Almost facing diag. centre down L.O.D.	
and	Close L.F. to R.F. *parallel pos.*	
3	R.F. to side along L.O.D., short step—Face diag. centre down L.O.D. At end of step brush L.F. towards R.F. *parallel pos.* Quarter turn L.	16

Reverse Turn—Checked Open Finish—Left Side Check —Rev. Chassé—Nat. Turn—Checked Open Finish—Right Side Check—Nat. Chassé

Lady

1	R.F. back diag. centre down L.O.D. Turn to L.	
2	L.F. to side towards centre of room.	
3	Close R.F. to L.F. *parallel pos.* Face down L.O.D. Three-eighths turn L.	1
1	L.F. forward (heel) down L.O.D. continuing turn to L.	
2	R.F. to side along L.O.D.—Back diag. wall down L.O.D.	

DREAM WALTZ (*contd.*)

Count	Lady	Bars
3	L.F. back—diag. wall down L.O.D. Check with partner on R. side. Headline to L.	2
1	R.F. forward (heel) diag. centre against L.O.D. Turn to R.	
2	L.F. to side against L.O.D. Back diag. wall against L.O.D.	
3	R.F. back diag. wall against L.O.D. Check with partner on L. side. Headline to R. Quarter turn to R.	3
1	L.F. forward (heel) diag. centre down L.O.D. Turn to L.	
2	R.F. to side along L.O.D.—partners square.	
and	Close L.F. to R.F. *parallel pos.* Back diag. wall down L.O.D.	
3	R.F. to side along L.O.D. Quarter turn to L.	4
1	L.F. back diag. wall down L.O.D. Turn to R.—partner on R. side.	
2	R.F. to side towards wall—partners square.	
3	Close L.F. to R.F. *parallel pos.* Face down L.O.D. Three-eighths turn to R.	5
1	R.F. forward down L.O.D. (heel) continuing turn to R.	
2	L.F. to side along L.O.D. Back diag. centre down L.O.D.	
3	R.F. back. Check with partner on L. side. Headline to R. Three-eighths turn to R.	6
1	L.F. forward (heel) diag. wall against L.O.D. Turn to L.	
2	R.F. to side against L.O.D. Back diag. centre against L.O.D.	
3	L.F. back diag. centre against L.O.D. Check with partner on R. side. Headline to L. Quarter turn to L.	7
1	R.F. forward (heel) diag. wall down L.O.D. Turn to R.	
2	L.F. to side towards wall—partners square.	
and	Close R.F. to L.F. *parallel pos.* Almost backing L.O.D.	
3	L.F. back down L.O.D.—short step.	8

Link Change to Promenade Position—Weave to Promenade Position—Chassé

1	R.F. back down L.O.D.	
2	Close L.F. to R.F. *parallel pos.* Turn to R.—*promenade pos.*	

DREAM WALTZ (*contd.*)

Count	Lady	Bars
3	R.F. to side in *promenade pos*. Moving diag. to centre down L.O.D. Headline to R.	9
1	L.F. forward (heel) *promenade pos*. Turn to L. to back diag. centre down L.O.D.	
2	R.F. back—continue turn to L. to face down L.O.D.	
3	L.F. forward down L.O.D.	10
1	R.F. forward down L.O.D. on R. side of partner.	
2	L.F. forward down L.O.D.—square to partner (no turn).	
3	R.F. to side along L.O.D. in *promenade pos*.	11
1	L.F. forward (heel) *promenade pos*.—turning to L.	
2	R.F. to side along L.O.D.—partners square—back diag. wall down L.O.D.	
and	Close L.F. to R.F. *parallel pos*.	
3	R.F. to side along L.O.D.	12

Backward Nat. Turn—Open Change— Forward Rev. Turn—Rev. Chassé

Count	Lady	Bars
1	L.F. back diag. wall down L.O.D.—partner on R. side. Turn to R.	
2	R.F. to side along L.O.D.—partners square.	
3	Close L.F. to R.F. *parallel pos*. Face diag. centre down L.O.D. Quarter turn to R.	13
1	R.F. forward (heel) diag. centre down L.O.D. Curve to R.	
2	L.F. forward. L. shoulder lead.	
3	R.F. forward down L.O.D. on R. side of partner. One-eighth turn R.	14
1	L.F. forward down L.O.D.—square to partner— turning to L.	
2	R.F. to side along L.O.D.	
3	Close L.F. to R.F. *parallel pos*. Back diag. wall down L.O.D.	15
1	R.F. back diag. wall down L.O.D.—turning to L.	
2	L.F. to side along L.O.D. Back diag. centre down L.O.D. at end of step.	
and	Close R.F. to L.F. *parallel pos*.	
3	L.F. to side along L.O.D. At end of step brush R.F. towards L.F. without weight—commencing position.	16

WOODSIDE WALTZ

J. FANNING

TIME 3/4—TEMPO 30

PARTNERS dance with normal Ballroom Hold throughout. Commence Man facing—Lady backing diag. to wall down L.O.D.

Forward Change—Nat. Spin Turn—
Turning Lock Step—Nat. Hesitation Change—
Reverse Turn

Count	Man	Bars
1	L.F. forward (heel) diag. wall down L.O.D.	
2	R.F. to side towards wall.	
3	Close L.F. to R.F. *parallel pos*.	1
1	R.F. forward (heel) diag. wall down L.O.D.—turning to R.	
2	L.F. to side towards wall.	
3	Close R.F. to L.F. *parallel pos*. Back down L.O.D.	2
1	L.F. back down L.O.D.—turning strongly to R. (pivot action).	
2	R.F. forward down L.O.D. (heel)—continuing turn to R.	
3	L.F. to side along L.O.D.—backing diag. to centre down L.O.D. Seven-eighths turn to R. on last 3 steps.	3
1	R.F. back diag. centre down L.O.D. R. shoulder lead.	
and	Lock (cross) L.F. in front of R.F.	
2	R.F. back turning to L.—partner square.	
3	L.F. to side along L.O.D. Face diag. wall down L.O.D.	4
1	R.F. forward (heel) diag. wall down L.O.D. on R. side of partner (R. hip to R. hip). Turn to R.	
2	L.F. to side towards wall—partners square.	
3	Close R.F. to L.F. *parallel pos*. Back down L.O.D. Three-eighths turn to R.	5
1	L.F. back down L.O.D.—turning to R.	

Count	**Man**	Bars
2	R.F. to side along L.O.D.—feet a few inches apart (pull step).	
3	Brush (close) L.F. to R.F. without weight. Face diag. centre down L.O.D. Three-eighths turn to R.	6
1	L.F. forward (heel)—turning to L.	
2	R.F. to side towards centre of room.	
3	Close L.F. to R.F. *parallel pos*. Back down L.O.D. Three-eighths turn to L.	7
1	R.F back down L.O.D. continuing turn to L.	
2	L.F. to side along L.O.D.	
3	Close R.F. to L.F. *parallel pos*. Face diag. wall down L.O.D. Three-eighths turn to L.	8

Whisk—Wing—Open Telemark—Hover—Contra Check —Nat. Turn to Back Whisk—Closed Finish

1	L.F. forward (heel) diag. to wall down L.O.D.	
2	R.F. to side towards wall. Face down L.O.D. Turn partner to promenade position.	
3	Whisk (cross) L.F. in behind R.F. (Lady facing centre of room).	9
1	R.F. forward (heel) towards diag. centre—leading partner forward towards L. side.	
2, 3	Close L.F. to R.F. *parallel pos*. without weight. Finish facing diag. to centre down L.O.D. Partner on L. side (L. hip to L. hip).	10
1	L.F. forward (heel) diag. centre on L. side of Lady— turning to L.	
2	R.F. to side towards centre of room (Lady heel turn).	
3	Continue turn to L. on ball of R.F. to face diag. wall down L.O.D. L.F. to side along L.O.D.—partners in *promenade pos*. (partner does not turn on last step).	11
1	R.F. forward (heel) down L.O.D. in *promenade pos*. Turn to R.	
2	L.F. to side along L.O.D. Partners square.	
3	Transfer weight to R.F.—rising to toes of both feet. Quarter turn to R. approx. Face diag. wall against L.O.D.	12
1	L.F. forward (heel) diag. wall against L.O.D. Knee line slightly flexed—headline to R. over Lady's L. shoulder. Check.	
2	Transfer weight back to R.F. with body turn to L.	

Count	**Man**	Bars
3	L.F. to side along L.O.D. Face diag. wall down L.O.D.	13
1	R.F. forward (heel) on R. side of partner—Turn to R.	
2	L.F. to side towards wall—partners square.	
3	Close R.F. to L.F. *parallel pos*. Back diag. wall down L.O.D. Half turn to R. on last three steps.	14
1	L.F. back diag. wall down L.O.D. Turn to R. (turn partner strongly to R.).	
2	R.F. to side. Face diag. centre down L.O.D. (short step).	
3	Whisk (cross) L.F. in behind R.F.—partners in *promenade pos*.	15
1	R.F. forward (heel) *promenade pos*. Turn to R. to get square to partner.	
2	L.F. to side along L.O.D. Face diag. wall down L.O.D.	
3	Close R.F. to L.F. *parallel pos*.	16

Change Step—Nat. Spin Turn—Turning Lock Step—Nat. Hesitation Change—Reverse Turn

Lady

1	R.F. back diag. wall down L.O.D.	
2	L.F. to side towards wall.	
3	Close R.F. to L.F. *parallel pos*.	1
1	L.F. back—diag. wall down L.O.D. Turn to R.	
2	R.F. to side towards wall.	
3	Close L.F. to R.F *parallel pos*. Face down L.O.D. Three-eighths turn to R.	2
1	R.F. forward down L.O.D. (heel)—turning strongly to R.	
2	L.F. sideways along L.O.D. continuing turn to R. to face centre of room.	
and	Brush (close) R.F. towards L.F.	
3	R.F. forward, diag. to centre down L.O.D. Seven-eighths turn to R. on last 4 steps.	3
1	L.F. forward—L. shoulder lead.	
and	Lock (cross) R.F. in behind L.F.	
2	L.F. forward—diag. centre down L.O.D.—turning to L.	
3	R.F. to side along L.O.D. Backing diag. wall down L.O.D.	4

Count	**Lady**	Bars
1	L.F. back—partner towards R. side. Turn to R.	
2	R.F. to side towards wall.	
3	Close L.F. to R.F. *parallel pos.* Face down L.O.D. square to partner. Three-eighths turn to R.	5
1	R.F. forward down L.O.D. Turning to R.	
2	L.F. to side along L.O.D. back diag. centre down L.O.D.	
3	Brush (close) R.F. to L.F. without weight.	6
1	R.F. back diag. centre down L.O.D. Turn to L.	
2	L.F. to side towards centre of room.	
3	Close R.F. to L.F. *parallel pos.* Face down L.O.D.	7
1	L.F. forward (heel) down L.O.D. continuing turn to L.	
2	R.F. to side along L.O.D.	
3	Close L.F. to R.F. *parallel pos.* Back diag. wall down L.O.D.	8

Whisk—Wing—Open Telemark—Hover—Contra Check —Nat. Turn to Turning Whisk—Closed Finish

1	R.F. back. Slight turn to R. to face towards centre of room.	
2	L.F. to side towards wall.	
3	Whisk (cross) R.F. in behind L.F. (*promenade pos.*). On next three steps move forward curving to L. (anticlockwise) to back diag. centre down L.O.D.	9
1	L.F. forward. Face centre of room (heel).	
2	R.F. forward. Face diag. centre against L.O.D.	
3	L.F. forward. Face diag. wall against L.O.D. Check on L. side of partner (L. hip to L. hip).	10
1	R.F. back diag. centre down L.O.D. Turn to L.	
2	Close L.F. to R.F. (heel turn). Face down L.O.D.	
3	R.F. diagonally forward down L.O.D. Face diag. centre down L.O.D. in promenade pos. Half turn to L. approx. on last 3 steps.	11
1	L.F. forward (heel) down L.O.D.	
2	R.F. forward—short step (Man turns square to Lady).	
3	Transfer weight back to L.F. rising to toes of both feet. Hover action. Finish with weight on L.F.	12
1	R.F. back diag. to wall against L.O.D.—partner square. Headline to L. Knee-line slightly flexed (C.B.M.P.).	
2	Transfer weight forward to L.F. (heel). Turn to L.	

WOODSIDE WALTZ (*contd.*)

Count	**Lady**	Bars
3	R.F. to side along L.O.D. Back diag. wall down L.O.D. Quarter turn L.	13
1	L.F. back diag. wall down L.O.D. partner on R. side —turning to R.	
2	R.F. to side towards wall.	
3	Close L.F. to R.F. *parallel pos*. Face diag. wall down L.O.D. Half turn to R. on last 3 steps.	14
1	R.F. forward (heel) diag. wall down L.O.D. Turn strongly to R.	
2	L.F. to side towards wall. Continue turn to R. to face centre of room.	
3	Whisk (cross) R.F. in behind L.F. Face towards diag. centre down L.O.D. Three-quarter turn to R. approx. on last 3 steps.	15
1	L.F. forward (heel) *promenade pos*. Slight turn to L.	
2	R.F. to side along L.O.D. backing diag. wall down L.O.D.	
3	Close L.F. to R.F. *parallel pos*. Partners square.	16

HELENA QUICKSTEP

TIME 4/4—TEMPO 46

PARTNERS commence with normal Ballroom Hold in promenade position.   Man facing diag. wall down L.O.D.—Lady diag. centre down L.O.D.

Promenade Chassé—Points—Forward Lock Step— Points—Rev. and Nat. Telemarks (Solo)

Count	Man	Bars
Q	L.F. to side along L.O.D. in *promenade pos.*	
Q	Close R.F. to L.F. *parallel pos.*	
S	L.F. to side along L.O.D.—a forward action.	1
S	Point R.F. forward down L.O.D. Sway to R.	
S	Point R.F. back against L.O.D. Sway to L.	2
Q	R.F. forward down L.O.D. Very open *promenade pos.*	
Q	Lock (cross) L.F. in behind R.F.	
S	R.F. forward down L.O.D.	3
S	Point L.F. forward. Sway to R.	
S	Point L.F. back against L.O.D. Correct body sway.	4
S	L.F. forward down L.O.D. (heel). Release Hold. Turn to L. (outwards).	
S	R.F. to side along L.O.D. Face towards centre of room.	5
S	Continue turn to L. on ball of R.F. to face wall L.F. to side along L.O.D.	
S	Close R.F. to L.F. *parallel pos.* without weight—both hands joined (Hold No. 5). Hesitation action.	6
S	R.F. forward against L.O.D. Turn to R. Hold released.	
S	L.F. to side against L.O.D. Face towards centre of room.	7
S	Continue turn to R. on ball of L.F. to face wall—R.F. to side against L.O.D.	
S	Close L.F. to R.F. *parallel pos.* without weight. Adopt normal Ballroom Hold—continuing turn to R.	8

Natural Rotary Chassé Turn—Reverse Swivel and Point—Natural Swivel and Point Left Side Rock and Reverse Swivel—Forward Lock Step—Closed Finish

Count	Man	Bars
Q	L.F. to side towards wall—partner square. Turn to R.	
Q	Close R.F. to L.F. *parallel pos.* Back L.O.D.	
S	L.F. back down L.O.D. Turn strongly to R. to face almost down L.O.D.	9
Q	R.F. to side towards wall—short step.	
Q	Close L.F. to R.F. *parallel pos.*	
S	R.F. forward—moving towards diag. wall down L.O.D. Finish facing diag. wall down L.O.D.	10
S	L.F. forward (heel) diag. wall on L. side of partner (L. hip to L. hip).	
S	R.F. to side without weight—Swivel to L. on L.F. to face diag. centre down L.O.D. (quarter turn approx.).	11
S	R.F. forward diag. centre down L.O.D. (heel) on R. side of partner (R. hip to R. hip).	
S	L.F. to side without weight. Swivel to R. to face diag. wall down L.O.D. (quarter turn).	12
S	L.F. forward (heel) on L. side of partner—headline to L. over Lady's R. shoulder—slight sway to R.	
S	Transfer weight back to R.F. Check—Rock action.	13
S	L.F. forward (heel) diag. wall down L.O.D. on L. side of partner—turning to L.	
S	Close R.F. to L.F. *parallel pos.*—without weight—Face diag. centre down L.O.D. (quarter turn to L.).	14
Q	R.F. forward diag. centre down L.O.D. on R. side of partner. Slight turn to R.	
Q	Lock (cross) L.F. in behind R.F. Face down L.O.D.	
S	R.F. forward down L.O.D. on R. side of partner. Turn partner to R. at end of step.	15
S	L.F. to side along L.O.D.—partners in *promenade pos.*	
S	Close R.F. to L.F. *parallel pos.*—commencing position.	16

Promenade Chassé—Points—Forward Lock Step— Points—Nat. and Rev. Telemarks (Solo)

Lady

Q	R.F. to side along L.O.D. in *promenade pos.*	
Q	Close L.F. to R.F. *parallel pos.*	
S	R.F. to side along L.O.D. A forward action.	1

Count	**Lady**	Bars
S	*Point* L.F. forward down L.O.D. Sway to L.	
S	*Point* L.F. back against L.O.D. Sway to R.	2
Q	L.F. forward down L.O.D.—very open *promenade pos.*	
Q	Lock (cross) R.F. in behind L.F.	
S	L.F. forward down L.O.D.	3
S	*Point* R.F. forward. Sway to L.	
S	*Point* R.F. back against L.O.D., correcting sway.	4
S	R.F. forward down L.O.D. (heel). Turn to R. (outwards). Hold released.	
S	L.F. to side along L.O.D. Face wall.	5
S	Continue turn to R. on ball of L.F. to face centre of room—R.F. to side along L.O.D.	
S	Close L.F. to R.F. *parallel pos.* without weight—Both hands joined—three-quarter turn to R.	6
S	L.F. forward against L.O.D. Turn to L. Hold released.	
S	R.F. to side against L.O.D. Face towards wall.	7
S	Continue turn to L. on ball of R.F. to face diag. centre down L.O.D. L.F. to side against L.O.D.	
S	Close R.F. to L.F. *parallel pos.* without weight. Partners assume normal Ballroom Hold.	8

Nat. Rotary Chassé Turn—Rev. Swivel and Point—Nat. Swivel and Point—Left Side Rock and Rev. Swivel—Back Lock Step—Promenade Finish

Q	R.F. sideways towards wall.	
Q	Close L.F. to R.F. *parallel pos.* Face down L.O.D.	
S	R.F. forward down L.O.D. (heel)—turning to R. to back diag. centre down L.O.D.	9
Q	L.F. to side towards wall.	
Q	Close R.F. to L.F. *parallel pos.* Back down L.O.D.	
S	L.F. back down L.O.D. Almost backing diag. wall down L.O.D.	10
S	R.F. back towards diag. wall down L.O.D. Partner towards L. side.	
S	L.F. to side—without weight. Swivel on R.F. to back diag. centre down L.O.D.—quarter turn to L. approx.	11
S	L.F. back diag. centre down L.O.D. Partner towards R. side.	

Count	**Lady**	Bars
S	R.F. to side without weight. Swivel to R. on ball of L.F. to back diag. wall down L.O.D.—quarter turn to R.	12
S	R.F. back diag. wall down L.O.D.—partner towards L. side—headline to R.	
S	Transfer weight forward to L.F. (heel). Rock action.	13
S	R.F. back—diag. wall down L.O.D.—turning to L. to back diag. centre down·L.O.D.	
S	Close L.F. to R.F. *parallel pos.* without weight—quarter turn L.	14
Q	L.F. back diag. centre down L.O.D.—partner towards R. side.	
Q	Lock (cross) R.F. in front of L.F. Slight turn to R. to back down L.O.D.	
S	L.F. back down L.O.D. Turn to R. to face diag. centre down L.O.D.	15
S	R.F. to side along L.O.D. *promenade pos.*	
S	Close L.F. to R.F. *parallel pos.*	16

OLYMPIC QUICKSTEP

LEWIS WILSON
TIME 4/4—TEMPO 46

PARTNERS dance with normal Ballroom Hold throughout. Commence Man facing—Lady backing diag. to wall down L.O.D.

Walk—Nat. Open Impetus Turn—Wing—
Rev. Chassé—Back Fishtail

Count	**Man**	Bars
S	L.F. forward diag. wall down L.O.D. (heel).	
S	R.F. forward (heel)—turning to R.	1
Q	L.F. to side towards wall—Face diag. wall against L.O.D.	
Q	Close R.F. to L.F. *parallel pos.*—Face against L.O.D.	
S	L.F. back down L.O.D.—turning to R.	2
S	Close R.F. to L.F. (heel turn)—continuing turn to R. to face diag. centre down L.O.D.	
S	L.F. to side in *promenade pos.* moving diag. to centre down L.O.D.	3
S	R.F. forward in *promenade pos.*—leading partner forward towards L. side.	
QQ	Close L.F. to R.F. *parallel pos.* without weight. Finish with partner on L. side (L. hip to L. hip).	4
S	L.F. forward (heel) on L. side of partner. Turn to L.	
Q	R.F. to side along L.O.D. Face centre of room—partners square.	
Q	Close L.F. to R.F. *parallel pos.*—backing diag. wall down L.O.D.	5
S	R.F. to side—a short step.	
S	L.F. back diag. wall down L.O.D. Partner on R. side (R. hip to R. hip).	6
Q	Lock (cross) R.F. in front of L.F.	
Q	L.F. back—very slightly leftwards.	
Q	R.F. back—diag. wall down L.O.D.	
Q	Lock (cross) L.F. in front of R.F.	7

Count	Man	Bars
S	R.F. back diag. wall down L.O.D.	
S	L.F. back—partner on R. side.	8

Rev. Movement—Forward Fishtail—Chassé Left and Right—Side Close

Count	Man	Bars
Q	R.F. back diag. wall down L.O.D. Turn to L.—partner square.	
Q	L.F. to side towards wall. Face against L.O.D.	
S	R.F. forward diag. to wall against L.O.D. on R. side of partner.	9
Q	L.F. forward—turn to L.—square to partner.	
Q	R.F. to side against L.O.D.—short step.	
S	L.F. back towards centre of room—partner on R. side.	10
Q	R.F. back towards centre of room—partner square. Turn to L.	
Q	L.F. to side along L.O.D.	
S	R.F. forward (heel) diag. to wall down L.O.D. on R. side of partner.	11
Q	Lock (cross) L.F. behind R.F.	
Q	R.F. forward—very slightly rightwards.	
Q	L.F. forward—diag. to wall down L.O.D.	
Q	Lock (cross) R.F. in behind L.F.	12
S	L.F. forward—diag. to wall down L.O.D.	
S	R.F. forward (heel) on R. side of partner.	13
Q	L.F. to side towards diag. centre down L.O.D. Still facing diag. to wall down L.O.D.	
Q	Close R.F. to L.F. *parallel pos.*	
S	L.F. to side—a short step. Sway to L. Check.	14
Q	R.F. to side towards diag. wall against L.O.D.—still facing diag. to wall down L.O.D.	
Q	Close L.F. to R.F. *parallel pos.*	
S	R.F. to side—a short step. Sway to R. Check.	15
S	L.F. to side towards diag. centre down L.O.D.	
S	Close R.F. to L.F. *parallel pos.*	16

Walk—Open Impetus Turn—Rev. Chassé—Forward Fishtail

Lady

Count	Lady	Bars
S	R.F. back diag. to wall down L.O.D.	
S	L.F. back—turning to R.	1

Count	Lady	Bars
Q	R.F. to side towards diag. wall down L.O.D.	
Q	Close L.F. to R.F. *parallel pos.* Face down L.O.D.	
S	R.F. forward down L.O.D.—turning to R. (heel).	2
S	L.F. to side across L.O.D.—still turning to R. (At end of step brush R.F. towards L.F. without weight.)	
S	R.F. to side in *promenade pos.* towards diag. centre down L.O.D. Three-quarter turn to R. approx. on last 3 steps.	3
S	L.F. forward (heel) *promenade pos.*—curving to L.	
Q	R.F. forward—diag. to centre against L.O.D.	
Q	L.F. forward—diag. to wall against L.O.D. Check on L. side of partner (L. hip to L. hip). Three-eighths turn to L. approx. on Wing.	4
S	R.F. back diag. to centre down L.O.D. Turn to L.	
Q	L.F. to side along L.O.D. Face towards wall.	
Q	Close R.F. to L.F. *parallel pos.* Face diag. wall down L.O.D.	5
S	L.F. to side along L.O.D.	
S	R.F. forward (heel) diag. to wall down L.O.D. on R. side of partner (R. hip to R. hip).	6
Q	Lock (cross) L.F. in behind R.F.	
Q	R.F. forward diag. wall down L.O.D. (very slightly rightwards).	
Q	L.F. forward—diag. wall down L.O.D.	
Q	Lock (cross) R.F. in behind L.F.	7
S	L.F. forward—diag. to wall down L.O.D.	
S	R.F. forward (heel) on R. side of partner.	8

Reverse Movement—Back Fishtail—Chassé to Right and Left—Side Close

Count	Lady	Bars
Q	L.F. forward diag. wall down L.O.D.—square to partner. Turn to L.	
Q	R.F. to side towards wall. Back against L.O.D.	
S	L.F. back—diag. to wall against L.O.D.—partner on R. side.	9
Q	R.F. back—diag. wall against L.O.D.—partner square. Turn to L.	
Q	L.F. to side—towards centre of room.	
S	R.F. forward—towards centre on R. side of partner.	10
Q	L.F. forward—square to partner continuing turn to L.	

Count	Lady	Bars
Q	R.F. to side along L.O.D.	
S	L.F. back—diag. to wall down L.O.D. partner on R. side.	11
Q	Lock (cross) R.F. in front of L.F.	
QQ	L.F.—R.F. back—diag. to wall down L.O.D.	
Q	Lock (cross) L.F. in front of R.F.	12
S	R.F. back diag. to wall down L.O.D.	
S	L.F. back—partner towards R. side.	13
Q	R.F. to side towards diag. centre down L.O.D. (partners square).	
Q	Close L.F. to R.F. *parallel pos.*	
S	R.F. to side—short step. Sway to R. Check.	14
Q	L.F. to side—diag. to wall against L.O.D.	
Q	Close R.F. to L.F. *parallel pos.*	
S	L.F. to side—short step. Sway to L. Check.	15
S	R.F. to side towards diag. centre down L.O.D.	
S	Close L.F. to R.F. *parallel pos.*	16

AZALEA FOXTROT

JACQUELINE JAY
TIME 4/4—TEMPO 32

Feather Step—Check—Back Feather—Left Sidecheck—Feather to Centre—Rev. Turn

Count	Man	Bars
S	R.F. forward (heel) diag. centre down L.O.D.	
Q	L.F. forward—slight L. shoulder lead.	
Q	R.F. forward. Check on R. side of partner (R. hip to R. hip).	1
S	L.F. back diag. to wall against L.O.D. Turn to R.	
Q	R.F. to side towards wall.	
Q	L.F. forward diag. to wall down L.O.D. Check on L. side of partner (L. hip to L. hip).	2
S	R.F. back diag. to centre against L.O.D. Turn to L.	
Q	L.F. to side towards centre of room.	
Q	R.F. forward diag. centre down L.O.D. on R. side of partner.	3
S	L.F. forward (heel) diag. to centre. Square to partner. Turn to L.	
Q	R.F. to side across L.O.D. Almost backing L.O.D.	
Q	L.F. back down L.O.D. Three-eighths turn to L.	4

Back Feather—Right Side Check—Back Feather—Left Side Check—Back Rev. Turn to Whisk

Count	Man	Bars
S	R.F. back down L.O.D. Slight turn to L.	
Q	L.F. to side towards wall.	
Q	R.F. forward diag. wall against L.O.D. Check on R. side of partner.	5
S	L.F. back diag. centre down L.O.D. Slight turn to R.	
Q	R.F. to side towards centre of room.	
Q	L.F. forward diag. to centre against L.O.D. Check on L. side of partner.	6
S	R.F. back—almost down L.O.D.—turning to L.	
Q	L.F. to side along L.O.D. Face towards wall.	
Q	R.F. forward diag. wall down L.O.D. on R. side of partner.	7

AZALEA FOXTROT *(contd.)*

Count	**Man**	Bars
S	L.F. forward (heel)—square to partner. Turn to L.	
Q	R.F. to side towards wall. Face down L.O.D.	
Q	Whisk (cross) L.F. in behind R.F. Face towards diag. centre down L.O.D.—partners in *promenade pos.*	8

Feather Step—Open Telemark—Passing Right Turn—Outside Swivel

S	R.F. forward (heel) diag. to centre down L.O.D. Turn partner square.	
Q	L.F. forward. Slight L. shoulder lead.	
Q	R.F. forward diag. centre down L.O.D. on R. side of partner.	9
S	L.F. forward (heel)—square to partner. Turn to L.	
Q	R.F. to side, slightly across L.O.D.	
Q	Continue turn to L. on ball of R.F. to face wall—L.F. to side along L.O.D. Face towards diag. wall down L.O.D. Partners in *promenade pos.* Half turn to L. approx.	10
S	R.F. forward (heel) towards diag. wall down L.O.D. Turning to R.	
Q	L.F. to side towards wall. Back down L.O.D. (Lady R.F. forward between Man's feet.)	
Q	R.F. back diag. to wall down L.O.D. Three-eighths turn to R. approx.	11
S	L.F. back diag. to wall down L.O.D. Partner towards R. side. Turn Lady strongly to R. Finish Crossing R.F. over front of L.F. without weight—*promenade pos.*	
S	R.F. forward (heel) diag. centre against L.O.D. Turn partner to L.	12

Reverse Weave to Contra Check—Natural Pivots—Oversway

Q	L.F. forward diag. centre against L.O.D. (between partner's feet). Turn to L.	
Q	R.F. to side towards centre of room.	
Q	L.F. back almost diag. to centre down L.O.D.—partner towards R. side.	
Q	R.F. back diag. centre—partner square—continue turn to L.	13
Q	L.F. to side along L.O.D. Face towards wall.	

Count	Man	Bars
Q	R.F. forward diag. to wall down L.O.D. on R. side of partner. Half turn to L. on last 6 steps.	
S	L.F. forward (heel) diag. to wall down L.O.D.—partners square—kneeline relaxed slightly—headline over Lady's L. shoulder, Slight R. shoulder lead (L. shoulder tends to move backward).	14
Q	Transfer weight back to R.F.—correct oversway of shoulderline.	
Q	L.F. back—short step commencing to turn to R. Face diag. to wall against L.O.D. at end of step.	
Q	R.F. forward (heel)—very short step between partner's feet—continuing to turn to R. Face diag. centre against L.O.D.	
Q	L.F. to side towards diag. wall against L.O.D.—continuing turn to R. to face diag. centre down L.O.D. Three-quarter turn to R. on last three steps.	15
S	R.F. back diag. wall against L.O.D.	
S	L.F. back. Check with L. shoulder lead and oversway of bodyline to L. Headline over partner's L. shoulder.	16

Back Feather—Check—Forward Feather— Left Side Check—Feather to Rev. Turn

Lady

S	L.F. back diag. to centre down L.O.D.	
Q	R.F. back—Slight R. shoulder lead.	
Q	L.F. back—Check with partner towards R. side (R. hip to R. hip).	1
S	R.F. forward (heel) diag. wall against L.O.D. Turn to R.	
Q	L.F. to side towards wall.	
Q	R.F. back—check backing diag. wall down L.O.D.—partner towards L. side—quarter turn to R. approx.	2
S	L.F. forward (heel) diag. centre against L.O.D. Turn to L.	
Q	R.F. to side towards centre of room.	
Q	L.F. back diag. centre down L.O.D.—partner on R. side—quarter turn to L.	3
S	R.F. back diag. centre down L.O.D.—turning to L.—partners square.	

AZALEA FOXTROT (*contd.*)

Count	Lady	Bars
Q	Close L.F. to R.F. *parallel pos.* (heel turn).	
Q	R.F. forward down L.O.D. Face down L.O.D.—three-eighths turn to L.	4

Feather—Check—Forward Feather—Left Side Check—Forward Reverse Turn to Whisk

S	L.F. forward down L.O.D. Slight turn to L.	
Q	R.F. to side towards wall.	
Q	L.F. back diag. to wall against L.O.D. Check with partner towards R. side.	5
S	R.F. forward (heel) diag. centre down L.O.D. Turn to R.	
Q	L.F. to side towards centre.	
Q	R.F. back diag. to centre against L.O.D. Check with partner towards L. side.	6
S	L.F. forward (heel)—turning to L.	
Q	R.F. to side along L.O.D.—backing towards wall.	
Q	L.F. back—diag. to wall down L.O.D.—partner on R. side.	7
S	R.F. back diag. wall down L.O.D.—partner square.	
Q	L.F. to side—slight turn to R.	
Q	Whisk (cross) R.F. in behind L.F. Face towards centre of room.	8

Reverse Feather Step—Open Telemark—Three Step—Outside Swivel—Reverse Weave to Contra Check—Natural Pivots to Oversway

S	L.F. forward (heel)—turning to L. face partner.	
Q	R.F. to side—moving towards diag. centre down L.O.D.	
Q	L.F. back diag. centre down L.O.D.—partner towards R. side—three-eighths turn to L.	9
S	R.F. back diag. centre down L.O.D. Turn to L.	
Q	Close L.F to R.F. (heel turn). Face diag. wall down L.O.D.	
Q	R.F. diagonally forward down L.O.D. in *promenade pos.*—quarter turn to L. approx.	10
S	L.F. forward (heel) in *promenade pos.*	
Q	R.F. forward between partner's feet.	

Count	**Lady**	Bars
Q	L.F. forward diag. to wall down L.O.D. preparing to step forward outside partner.	11
S	R.F. forward (heel) on R. side of partner (R. hip to R. hip). Turn strongly to R. to face against L.O.D. at end of step. Close L.F. to R.F. without weight (*promenade pos.*).	
S	L.F. forward (heel)—commencing to turn to L.	12
Q	R.F. diagonally back—towards diag. centre against L.O.D. Turn to L. to face almost down L.O.D. (Man steps L.F. forward between Lady's feet.)	
Q	L.F. to side and slightly forward down L.O.D.	
Q	R.F. forward diag. to centre down L.O.D. on R. side of partner.	
Q	L.F. forward—square to partner—continuing turn to L.	13
Q	R.F. to side along L.O.D. Back towards diag. wall down L.O.D.	
Q	L.F. back—diag. wall down L.O.D.—partner towards R. side.	
S	R.F. back—headline to L.—kneeline slightly relaxed. Check—partners square.	14
Q	Transfer weight forward to L.F. Correct Overswing of bodyline.	
Q	R.F. forward (heel) between Man's feet—turning to R.	
Q	L.F. to side along L.O.D. short step—Face diag. wall down L.O.D.	
Q	Move R.F. forward (heel) towards diag. wall against L.O.D. (footline between partner's feet).	15
S	L.F. forward (heel) diag. to wall against L.O.D.	
S	R.F. forward (heel). R. shoulder lead. Overswing bodyline to L. —headline to L.	16

TANGO SOLAIR

ROBERT STEWART
TIME 2/4—TEMPO 32—16 BAR SEQUENCE

Commence with normal Tango Hold. Man facing—
Lady backing L.O.D.

Walks—Link—Outside Swivel—Reverse Turn

Count	Man	Bars
SS	L.F., R.F., forward down L.O.D. (heel).	1
Q	L.F. forward down L.O.D. (heel) commencing to turn partner to prom. pos.	
Q	Close R.F. to L.F. parallel pos. (b.o.f., w.f.) prom. pos. (Lady facing centre of room).	
S	L.F. to side towards diag. centre down L.O.D. (heel) prom. pos.	2
S	R.F. forward diag. to centre down L.O.D. (heel) prom. pos. turning partner to L. and square—check. $\frac{1}{8}$th turn to L.	
S	L.F. back diag. to wall against L.O.D. (b.o.f., w.f.). Lady on R. side (R. hip to R. hip).	3
Q	R.F. back to wall turning L. Partner square. $\frac{1}{8}$th turn.	
Q	L.F. to side and slightly forward (b.o.f., w.f.) facing against L.O.D. $\frac{1}{4}$ turn to L.	
S	Close R.F. to L.F. parallel pos. (b.o.f., w.f.).	4
SS	L.F., R.F., forward against L.O.D. (heel).	5
Q	L.F. forward against L.O.D. (heel) commencing to turn partner to prom. pos.	
Q	Close R.F. to L.F. parallel pos. (b.o.f., w.f.) prom. pos. (Lady faces wall).	
S	L.F. to side diag. to wall against L.O.D. (heel) prom. pos.	6
S	R.F. forward diag. to wall against L.O.D. (heel) prom. pos. turning partner to L. and square—check. $\frac{1}{8}$th turn to L.	
S	L.F. back diag. to centre down L.O.D. (b.o.f., w.f.). Lady on R. side (R. hip to R. hip).	7

Q   R.F. back diag. to centre down L.O.D. (b.o.f., w.f.). Slight turn to L. to prom. pos. Partner square.

Q   L.F. to side along L.O.D. in prom. pos. (b.o.f., w.f.).

S   Close R.F. to L.F. parallel pos. (b.o.f., w.f.) facing diag. to wall down L.O.D. in prom. pos. (Lady facing diag. to centre down L.O.D.)—release hold.   8

Solo Rev. and Nat. Turn—Zig Zag—Contra Check—Prom. Walks—Same Foot Lunge—Prom. Chassé—Closed Finish

S   L.F. forward down L.O.D. (heel) turning to L. (Lady to R.). Arms lowered to side. ⅛th turn.

Q   R.F. to side along L.O.D. (b.o.f., w.f.) facing diag. to centre down L.O.D. ⅛th turn to L.

Q   Close L.F. to R.F. parallel pos. (b.o.f., w.f.).   9

S   R.F. forward down L.O.D. (heel) turning R. (Lady to L.)—inwards. ⅛th turn.

Q   L.F. to side along L.O.D. (b.o.f., w.f.) facing wall. ¼ turn to R.

Q   Close R.F. to L.F. parallel pos. (b.o.f., w.f.). Assume normal Tango Hold.   10

Q   L.F. forward to wall (heel) commencing to turn to L.

Q   R.F. to side and slightly back (b.o.f., w.f.) facing diag. to wall down L.O.D.

Q   L.F. back diag. to centre against L.O.D. (b.o.f., w.f.) commencing to turn to R. (Lady on R. side.) (R. hip to R. hip).

Q   R.F. to side against L.O.D. (b.o.f., w.f.) facing wall—partner square.   11

S   L.F. forward to wall (heel) R. shoulder lead. Flex knees slightly—Contra Check action.

Q   Transfer weight back to R.F. to centre of room (b.o.f., w.f.) commencing to turn partner to prom. pos.

Q   Close L.F. to R.F. parallel pos. without weight (b.o.f.) facing diag. to wall in prom. pos. ⅛th turn to L. on last 2 steps.   12

S   L.F. to side along L.O.D. in prom. pos. (heel).

S   R.F. forward down L.O.D. in prom pos. (heel) commencing to turn to R. Release Hold.   13

Q   L.F. to side along L.O.D. (b.o.f., w.f.) facing wall. (Lady R.F. forward down L.O.D. turning to R).

Q   Close R.F. to L.F. parallel pos. (b.o.f.) without weight. Join L. hands. Both now facing wall—Man behind Lady.

S	R.F. to side against L.O.D. (b.o.f., w.f.). Flex R. knee—Same foot Lunge. R. hands extended to side and downwards—Check.	14
Q	Place R. hand on Lady's R. hip. L.F. to side along L.O.D. (heel) facing diag. to wall down L.O.D.	
Q	Close R.F. to L.F. parallel pos. (b.o.f., w.f.).	
S	L.F. to side along L.O.D. (heel). Hold released at end of step.	15
Q	R.F. forward diag. to wall down L.O.D. (heel). (Lady R.F. forward turning strongly to R.).	
Q	Close L.F. to R.F. parallel pos. without weight. (b.o.f.). Partner square.	
Q	L.F. to side towards centre of room (b.o.f., w.f.) turning to L. ⅛th turn, facing down L.O.D. Assume normal Tango Hold.	
Q	Close R.F. to L.F. parallel pos. (b.o.f., w.f.) facing L.O.D. Commencing position.	16

Walks—Link—Outside Swivel—Reverse Turn
Lady

SS	R.F., L.F. back down L.O.D. (b.o.f., w.f.).	1
Q	R.F. back down L.O.D. (b.o.f., w.f.) turning to R. to prom. pos.	
Q	Close L.F. to R.F. parallel pos. (b.o.f., w.f.) facing centre of room. ¼ turn to R.	
S	R.F. to side diag. to centre down L.O.D. in prom. pos. (heel).	2
S	L.F. forward diag. to centre down L.O.D. in prom. pos. (heel) turning strongly to L. on ball of L.F. to face diag. wall against L.O.D. R.F. ends diag. back without weight. This is a sharp action with slight flexing of L. knee. Headline to R.	
S	R.F. forward diag. to wall against L.O.D. (heel) on R. side of partner (R. hip to R. hip).	3
Q	L.F. forward to wall (heel) turning to L.—square to partner.	
Q	R.F. to side and slightly back (b.o.f., w.f.) backing against L.O.D. ¼ turn to L.	
S	Close L.F. to R.F. parallel pos. (b.o.f., w.f.).	4
SS	R.F., L.F. back against L.O.D. (b.o.f., w.f.).	5
Q	R.F. back against L.O.D. (b.o.f., w.f.) turning to prom. pos.	

Q   Close L.F. to R.F. parallel pos. (b.o.f., w.f.) facing wall in prom. pos. $\frac{1}{4}$ turn to R.

S   R.F. to side diag. to wall against L.O.D. in prom. pos. (heel).   6

S   L.F. forward diag. to wall against L.O.D. in prom. pos. (heel) turning strongly to L. on ball of L.F. to face diag. to centre down L.O.D. ($\frac{1}{2}$ turn) R.F. ends diag. back without weight. This is a sharp action with slight flexing of L. knee. Headline to R.

S   R.F. forward diag. to centre down L.O.D. (heel) on R. side of partner (R. hip to R. hip).   7

Q   L.F. forward diag. to centre down L.O.D. (heel) partner turning to prom. pos.

Q   R.F. to side along L.O.D. in prom. pos. (b.o.f., w.f.).

S   Close L.F. to R.F. parallel pos. (b.o.f., w.f.) in prom. pos. facing diag. to centre down L.O.D. Release hold.   8

Solo Nat. and Rev. Turns—Zig Zag—Contra Check—Prom. Walks—Same Foot Lunge—Prom. Chassé—Nat. Turn to Closed Finish

S   R.F. forward down L.O.D. (heel) turning to R. (Man turns to L.). Arms lowered to side. $\frac{1}{8}$th turn.

Q   L.F. to side along L.O.D. (b.o.f., w.f.) facing diag. to wall down L.O.D. $\frac{1}{8}$th turn.

Q   Close R.F. to L.F. parallel pos. (b.o.f., w.f.).   9

S   L.F. forward down L.O.D. (heel) turning to L. (Man turns to R.). Inwards— $\frac{1}{8}$th turn.

Q   R.F. to side along L.O.D. (b.o.f., w.f.) facing centre of room. $\frac{1}{4}$ turn to L.

Q   Close L.F. to R.F. parallel pos. (b.o.f., w.f.). Assume normal Tango Hold.   10

Q   R.F. back to wall (b.o.f., w.f.) commencing to turn to L.

Q   L.F. to side and slightly forward (b.o.f., w.f.) facing diag. to centre against L.O.D.

Q   R.F. forward diag. to centre against L.O.D. (heel) commencing to turn to R. on R. side of partner (R. hip to R. hip).

Q   L.F. to side against L.O.D. (b.o.f.) square to partner, facing centre.   11

S   R.F. back to wall (b.o.f., w.f.) L. shoulder lead—knees slightly flexed (Contra Check)—Check.

Q   Transfer weight forward to L.F. to centre of room (heel) turning to R. to prom. pos. facing diag. to centre down L.O.D.

Q   Close R.F. to L.F. parallel pos. without weight (b.o.f., w.f.) facing diag. to centre in prom. pos. $\frac{1}{8}$th turn on last 2 steps.   12

S   R.F. to side along L.O.D. in prom pos. (heel).

S   L.F. forward down L.O.D. in prom. pos. commencing to turn to R. Release Hold.   13

Q   R.F. forward down L.O.D. turning to R. (heel).

Q   Close L.F. to R.F. parellel pos. (b.o.f., w.f.). Join L. hands. Both facing wall. $\frac{1}{4}$ turn on last 2 steps.

S   R.F. to side against L.O.D. (b.o.f., w.f.) slightly flex R. knee—same foot Lunge—R. hands extended to side and downwards.   14

Q   L.F. to side along L.O.D. (heel) facing diag. to wall down L.O.D.

Q   Close R.F. to L.F. parallel pos. (b.o.f.).

S   L.F. to side along L.O.D. (heel). Hold released at end of step.   15

Q   R.F. forward diag. to wall down L.O.D. (heel) turning strongly to R. to back diag. wall down L.O.D. $\frac{1}{2}$ turn.

Q   Close L.F. to R.F. parallel pos. (b.o.f., w.f.). Partner square.

Q   R.F. to side towards centre of room (b.o.f., w.f.) $\frac{1}{8}$th turn to L. Assume normal Tango Hold.

Q   Close L.F. to R.F. parallel pos. (b.o.f., w.f.) backing L.O.D. Commencing position.   16

Description is printed by Courtesy of the Official Board of Ballroom Dancing.

SAUNTER REVÉ

RITA POVER
TIME 4/4—TEMPO 28—16 BAR SEQUENCE

Commence with normal ballroom Hold—Man facing—
Lady backing L.O.D. Bars 5/8 are dances on 'same
foot'.

Forward Waltz—Half Square—Promenade Chassé to No. 7 Hold.

Count	Man	Bars
SS	L.F., R.F. forward down L.O.D. (heel).	1
Q	L.F. to side towards centre of room (b.o.f., w.f.).	
Q	Close R.F. to L.F. parallel pos. (b.o.f., w.f.).	
S	L.F. back against L.O.D. (b.o.f., w.f.) L. shoulder lead—body rise. Headline to R. over lady's L. shoulder. (Slight upward Lilt).	2
Q	R.F. forward down L.O.D. (heel) turn partner strongly to R.	
Q	Close L.F. to R.F. (b.o.f.) without weight—brushing action. prom. pos.—face diag. to wall down L.O.D.—Lady diag. to centre down L.O.D.	
Q	L.F. to side along L.O.D. (b.o.f., w.f.) prom. pos.	
Q	Close R.F. to L.F. Parallel pos. (w.f.).	3
S	L.F. to side along L.O.D. (heel) face diag. to wall—release hold.	
Q	R.F. forward down L.O.D. (heel) short step—Lady's L. hand in Man's L. hand. (Lady turns slightly to R. to face down L.O.D.).	
Q	Close (Brush) L.F. to R.F. parallel pos. (b.o.f.) without weight. Finish with R. hand on Lady's R. hip—Hold No. 7 similar to Gainsborough Glide.	4

Forward Walks—Backward Lock Steps
Man and Lady

S	L.F. forward (heel) diag. to wall down L.O.D.	
S	R.F. forward (heel) slight plié action (relax).	5
Q	L.F. back diag. to centre against L.O.D. (b.o.f., w.f.).	

Q	Cross (Lock) R.F. in front of L.F. (b.o.f., w.f.).
Q	L.F. back diag. to centre against L.O.D. (b.o.f.).
Q	Close R.F. to L.F. parallel pos. (b.o.f., w.f.). Swivel to L. to face diag. centre down L.O.D.— ¼ turn. 6

Most dancers of Modern will turn with an action similar to a Rev. Slip Pivot.

SS	L.F., R.F. forward (heel) diag. to centre down L.O.D. 7
Q	L.F. back diag. to wall against L.O.D. (b.o.f., w.f.).
Q	Cross (Lock) R.F. in front of L.F. (b.o.f., w.f.).
Q	L.F. back (b.o.f.) swivel to R. to face down L.O.D.— ⅛ turn.
Q	Close R.F. to L.F. parallel pos. (w.f.).

Most dancers of Modern will dance last 2 steps similar to a Pull Step. 8

Forward Walk (Lady Solo Turn to R.)
Sways and Chassés

Man

S	L.F. forward down L.O.D. (heel) release hold.
Q	R.F. forward (heel) turn to R. to face wall.
Q	Close (Brush) L.F. to R.F. parallel pos. without weight. Assume Double Hold—Lady's R. hand in Man's L. hand—Lady's L. hand in Man's R. hand (Hold No. 5). 9
S	L.F. to side along L.O.D. (b.o.f., w.f.). Sway to L.
S	Transfer weight back to R.F. (b.o.f., w.f.). 10
Q	L.F. to side along L.O.D. (b.o.f., w.f.).
Q	Close R.F. to L.F. (w.f.) parallel pos.
S	L.F. to side along L.O.D. (b.o.f., w.f.). 11
Q	R.F. to side against L.O.D. (b.o.f., w.f.).
Q	Close L.F. to R.F. parallel pos. (w.f.).
S	R.F. to side against L.O.D. (b.o.f., w.f.) slight turn to L. to face diag. wall down L.O.D. (L.F. in place—prom. pos.) 12

Nat. Promenade Turn—Side Chassés

S	L.F. to side along L.O.D. (heel) prom. pos.
S	R.F. forward down L.O.D. (heel) turning to R. 13
S	L.F. to side across L.O.D. (b.o.f., w.f.) towards wall. Back L.O.D. at end of step (Lady's R.F. forward between Man's feet.) Take normal Ballroom Hold.
S	Continue turn to R. (ball of L.F.) to face diag. centre down L.O.D.—R.F. forward diag. to centre down L.O.D. (heel). ¾ turn to R. approx. on last 3 steps. 14

Q	L.F. to side towards centre of room (b.o.f., w.f.).	
Q	Close R.F. to L.F. parallel pos. (b.o.f., w.f.) face down L.O.D.	
S	L.F. to side (b.o.f., w.f.) R.F. veers towards L.F.	15
Q	R.F. to side towards wall (b.o.f., w.f.).	
Q	Close L.F. to R.F. parallel pos. (b.o.f., w.f.).	
Q	R.F. to side (b.o.f., w.f.) towards wall.	
Q	Close L.F. to R.F. (b.o.f.) parallel pos. without weight.	16

Backward Walks—Half Square—Promenade Chassé to No. 7 Hold

Lady

SS	R.F., L.F. back down L.O.D. (b.o.f., w.f.).	1
Q	R.F. to side towards centre of room (b.o.f., w.f.).	
Q	Close L.F. to R.F. parallel pos. (b.o.f., w.f.).	
S	R.F. forward against L.O.D. (heel) R. shoulder lead—body rise. Headline to L. (Slight upward Lilt).	2
Q	L.F. back down L.O.D. turning strongly to R. to prom. pos.	
Q	Close R.F. to L.F. without weight (brushing action)—prom. pos. face diag. to centre down L.O.D.	
Q	R.F. to side along L.O.D. (b.o.f., w.f.) prom. pos.	
Q	Close L.F. to R.F. parallel pos. (w.f.).	3
S	R.F. to side along L.O.D. (heel) face diag. to centre down L.O.D.—prom. pos.—release hold.	
Q	L.F. forward down L.O.D. (heel) turning to R. to face down L.O.D. Man takes Lady's L. hand in his L. hand.	
Q	Close R.F. to L.F. parallel pos. Finish with Man's R. hand on Lady's R. hip. Man and Lady now side by side—Lady slightly in front of Man. Hold No. 7 similar to Gainsborough Glide.	4

Walk—Solo Turn to R. Sways and Chassés to Promenade Turn

S	L.F. forward down L.O.D. (heel) release hold.	
Q	R.F. forward down L.O.D. (heel) turning very strongly to R.	
Q	Close L.F. to R.F. parallel pos. (b.o.f., w.f.) face centre of room. Assume Double Hold—L. hand in Man's R. hand—R. hand in Man's L. hand. $\frac{3}{4}$ turn to R. on last 2 steps.	9

S	R.F. to side along L.O.D. (b.o.f., w.f.). Sway to R.	
S	Transfer weight back to L.F. (b.o.f., w.f.).	10
Q	R.F. to side along L.O.D. (b.o.f., w.f.).	
Q	Close L.F. to R.F. parallel pos. (b.o.f., w.f.).	
S	R.F. to side along L.O.D. (b.o.f., w.f.).	11
Q	L.F. to side against L.O.D. (b.o.f., w.f.).	
Q	Close R.F. to L.F. parallel pos. (b.o.f., w.f.).	
S	L.F. to side against L.O.D. (b.o.f., w.f.) slight turn to R. to face diag. centre down L.O.D. (R.F. in place—prom. pos.).	12

Nat. Promenade Turn—Side Chassés

S	R.F. to side along L.O.D. (heel) prom. pos.	
S	L.F. forward down L.O.D. (heel) commence to turn to R.	13
S	R.F. forward down L.O.D. (heel) turning strongly to R. (footline between partner's feet). Take normal Ballroom Hold.	
S	L.F. back diag. to centre down L.O.D. (b.o.f., w.f.) C.B.M.P. $\frac{1}{2}$ turn to R. on last 3 steps.	14
Q	R.F. to side towards centre of room (b.o.f., w.f.).	
Q	Close L.F. to R.F. parallel pos. (b.o.f., w.f.) backing L.O.D.	
S	R.F. to side (b.o.f., w.f.) L.F. veers towards R.F.	15
Q	L.F. to side towards wall (b.o.f., w.f.).	
Q	Close R.F. to L.F. parallel pos. (b.o.f., w.f.).	
Q	L.F. to side towards wall (b.o.f., w.f.).	
Q	Close R.F. to L.F. parallel pos. without weight (b.o.f.)	16

Description is printed by courtesy of the Official Board of Ballroom Dancing.

REGIS WALTZ

RITA POVER

TIME 3/4—TEMPO 42—16 BAR SEQUENCE

Commencing position similar to Veleta (No. 2 Hold).
Lady's L. hand in Man's R. hand. Man facing diag. to
wall down L.O.D.—Lady facing diag. to centre down
L.O.D.

Walk and Point—Nat. Open Turn (Inwards)—Back Lock Step—Rev. Rotary Waltz Turn

Count	Man	Bars
1/2	L.F. forward down L.O.D. (heel).	
3	Point R.F. forward down L.O.D. (toe). Headline to R. towards partner.	1
1/2	R.F. forward down L.O.D. (heel) turn to R. (Inwards).	
3	L.F. to side along L.O.D. (b.o.f., w.f.) continuing turn to R. to back down L.O.D.—Hold released— ½ turn to R. approx.	2
1/2	R.F. back down L.O.D. (b.o.f.) Lady's R. hand in Man's L. hand. Headline to L. towards partner.	
3	Cross (Lock) L.F. in front of R.F. (b.o.f., w.f.).	3
1	R.F. back down L.O.D. (b.o.f., w.f.) turning to L.	
2	Close L.F. to R.F. 5th pos. rear (b.o.f.) release hold at end of step.	
3	Pivot to L. on balls of both feet to face diag. wall down L.O.D.—Lady's L. hand in Man's R. hand. Slightly under ½ turn to L.	4

Rev. Open Turn (Outwards)—Rear Glissé—Glissade—Glisse

Count	Man	Bars
1/2	L.F. forward down L.O.D. (heel) turn to L. (Outwards)—hold released.	
3	R.F. to side along L.O.D. (b.o.f., w.f.) diag. back in relation to the body—face diag. centre against L.O.D.— ½ turn to L.	5

213

1	L.F. Back down L.O.D. (b.o.f., w.f.) toe pointing towards wall—face diag. to wall against L.O.D. preparing to take Double Hold (No. 5).	
2/3	Close R.F. to L.F. 3rd pos. front (b.o.f.) without weight (Glissé). Take Double Hold—Lady's L. hand in Man's R. hand—Lady's R. hand in Man's L. hand.	6
1	R.F. to side against L.O.D. (b.o.f., w.f.) toe pointing towards wall (body turn to L.).	
2/3	Close L.F. to R.F. 3rd pos. front (b.o.f., w.f.) (Glissade)	7
1	R.F. to side against L.O.D. (b.o.f., w.f.).	
2/3	Close L.F. to R.F. 3rd pos. rear (b.o.f.) without weight.	8

Backward Pas de Valse and Balancé—Forward Pas de Valse and Balancé—Nat. Waltz Turns

	Next 2 bars move on a line diag. to centre down L.O.D.	
1	With slight body turn to R.—L.F. back diag. to centre down L.O.D. (b.o.f., w.f.).	
2	R.F. back diag. to centre down L.O.D. (b.o.f.) R. shoulder lead.	
3	Close L.F. to R.F. 3rd pos. front (b.o.f., w.f.).	9
1	R.F. back diag. to centre down L.O.D. (b.o.f., w.f.).	
2/3	Close L.F. to R.F. 3rd pos. front (b.o.f.) without weight. Rise to ball of R.F. (Balancé) slight sway to R.	10
1	L.F. forward (heel) diag. to wall against L.O.D. slight turn to L.	
2	R.F. forward (b.o.f.) R. shoulder lead.	
3	Close L.F. to R.F. 3rd pos. rear (b.o.f., w.f.).	11
1	R.F. forward (heel) diag. to wall against L.O.D.	
2/3	Close L.F. to R.F. 3rd pos. rear (b.o.f.) without weight. Rise to ball of R.F. (Balancé) slight sway to L. Finish assuming normal Waltz Hold.	12
	Nat. Waltzing similar to bars 13/16 Veleta etc.	
123	Nat. Rotary Waltz Turn—L.F., R.F., L.F., 5th pos.	
123	Nat. Prog. Waltz Turn—R.F., L.F., R.F., 5th pos.	
123	Nat. Rotary Waltz Turn—L.F., R.F., L.F., 5th pos.	
1	R.F. forward down L.O.D. (heel) release hold.	
2	L.F. forward (b.o.f.) towards diag. centre down L.O.D.	

3   Close R.F. to L.F. 3rd pos. rear (b.o.f., w.f.) face diag. to wall down L.O.D. opening out to commencing position and hold.   13/16

Walk and Point—Rev. Open Turn (Inwards)—Back Lock Step—Nat. Rotary Waltz Turn

Lady

1/2   R.F. forward down L.O.D. (heel).

3   Point L.F. forward (toe). Headline to L. towards partner.   1

1/2   L.F. forward down L.O.D. (heel) turn to L. (Inwards).

3   R.F. to side along L.O.D. (b.o.f., w.f.) continuing turn to L. to back down L.O.D.—Hold released—$\frac{1}{2}$ turn to L. approx.   2

1/2   L.F. back down L.O.D. (b.o.f.) R. hand in Man's L. hand. Headline to R. towards partner.

3   Cross (Lock) R.F. in front of L.F. (b.o.f., w.f.).   3

1   L.F. back down L.O.D. (b.o.f., w.f.) turning to R.

2   Close R.F. to L.F. 5th pos. rear (b.o.f.) release hold.

3   Pivot to R. on balls of both feet to face diag. centre down L.O.D.—L. hand in Man's R. hand.   4

Nat. Open Turn (Outwards)—Rear Glissé—Glissade—Glissé

1/2   R.F. forward down L.O.D. (heel) turn to R. (Outwards)—hold released.

3   L.F. to side along L.O.D. (b.o.f., w.f.) diag. back in relation to the body—face diag. wall against L.O.D.   5

1   R.F. back down L.O.D. (b.o.f.) toe pointing to centre of room—face diag. centre against L.O.D. preparing to take Double Hold.

2/3   Close L.F. to R.F. 3rd pos. front (b.o.f.) without weight (Glissé) L. hand in Man's R. hand—R. hand in Man's L. hand. (Double Hold—No. 5).   6

1   L.F. to side against L.O.D. (b.o.f., w.f.) toe pointing towards centre of room (body turn to R.).

2/3   Close R.F. to L.F. 3rd pos. front (b.o.f., w.f.) (Glissade)   7

1   L.F. to side against L.O.D. (b.o.f., w.f.).

2/   Close R.F. to L.F. 3rd pos. front (b.o.f.) without weight (Glissé).   8

REGIS WALTZ (*contd.*)

Forward Pas de Valse and Balancé—Backward Pas de Valse and Balancé—Nat. Waltz Turns

1	With slight body turn to R.—R.F. forward diag. to centre down L.O.D. (heel).	
2	L.F. forward (b.o.f.) diag. to centre down L.O.D. L. shoulder lead.	
3	Close R.F. to L.F. 3rd pos. rear (b.o.f., w.f.) (Pas de Valse).	9
1	L.F. forward (heel) diag. to centre down L.O.D.	
2/3	Close R.F. to L.F. 3rd pos. rear (b.o.f.) without weight. Rise to ball of L.F. (Balancé).	10
1	R.F. back diag. to wall against L.O.D. (b.o.f., w.f.).	
2	L.F. back diag. to wall against L.O.D. (b.o.f.) L. shoulder lead.	
3	Close R.F. to L.F. 3rd pos. front (b.o.f., w.f.) (Pas de Valse)	11
1	L.F. back diag. to wall against L.O.D. (b.o.f., w.f.).	
2/3	Close R.F. to L.F. 3rd pos. front (b.o.f.) without weight. Rise to ball of L.F. (Balancé).	
	Finish assuming normal Waltz Hold.	12
	Nat. Waltzing similar to 13/16 bars Veleta etc.	
123	Nat. Prog. Waltz Turn—R.F., L.F., R.F., 5th pos.	
123	Nat. Rotary Waltz Turn—L.F., R.F., L.F., 5th pos.	
123	Nat. Prog. Waltz Turn—R.F., L.F., R.F., 5th pos.	
123	Nat. Rotary Waltz Turn—L.F., R.F., L.F., 3rd pos.	
	Opening out to commencing position (Hold No. 2). 13/16	

Description is printed by courtesy of the Official Board of Ballroom Dancing.

WALTZ CAMAY

PATRICIA JOSS

TIME 3/4—TEMPO 42—16 BAR SEQUENCE

Partners commence with Double Hold—Man facing
diag. to wall down L.O.D.—Lady backing diag. to wall
down L.O.D.—Lady's R. hand in Man's L. hand—L.
hand in Man's R. hand.

Forward and Backward Balancés—Rev. (Solo) Waltz Turn

Count	Man	Bars
1	L.F. forward diag. to wall down L.O.D. (heel).	
2/3	Close R.F. to L.F. 3rd pos. rear (b.o.f.) without weight. Rise to ball of L.F.	1
1	R.F. back (b.o.f., w.f.) diag. to centre against L.O.D.	
2/3	Close L.F. to R.F. 3rd pos. front (b.o.f.) without weight. Rise to ball of R.F. Release lady's R. hand from L. hand turning to promenade position.	2
1 2 3	Release Hold. Rev. Prog. Waltz Turn (Outwards) L.F., R.F., L.F.	3
1 2 3	Rotary Waltz Turn R.F., L.F., R.F. Partners finish with Double Hold—Man facing diag. wall down L.O.D.—Lady facing diag. to centre down L.O.D.	4

Zephyr Turns—Point—Pas de Valse—Lock Step Movement

1	L.F. forward down L.O.D. (heel).	
2/3	Swing (Zephyr) R.F. forward to low aerial pos.	5
1	Turn inwards to R. on ball of L.F.	
2/3	Swing (Zephyr) R.F. against L.O.D. to low aerial pos. backing L.O.D. ½ turn.	6
1	R.F. back down L.O.D. (b.o.f., w.f.) turning to L. (inwards).	
2/3	L.F. forward down L.O.D. (b.o.f., w.f.) ½ turn.	7
1	R.F. forward down L.O.D. (heel).	
2/3	Point L.F. forward (toe) 4th pos. front.	8

123	Pas de Valse down L.O.D. (release lady's R. hand from L. hand) L.F., R.F., L.F., (similar to 1st bar of Veleta).	9
1	R.F. forward down L.O.D. (heel).	
2/3	Cross (Lock) L.F. over front of R.F. (b.o.f., w.f.)—outside edges of feet almost in contact.	10
1	R.F. back against L.O.D. (b.o.f., w.f.).	
2/3	Cross (Lock) L.F. in behind R.F. (b.o.f., w.f.). (Similar action to a Whisk position).	11
1	R.F. forward down L.O.D. (heel).	
2/3	Point L.F. forward down L.O.D. (toe)	12

Rev. (Solo) Waltz Turn—Nat. Rotary Waltz Turn—Pas de Valse

1/6	Repeat bars 3 and 4. L.F., R.F., L.F.—R.F., L.F., R.F. 3rd pos. Finish assuming normal Waltz Hold.	13/14
123	Nat. Rotary Waltz Turn L.F., R.F., L.F.	15
123	Pas de Valse forward—R.F., L.F., R.F.— ¼ turn to R. to face diag. wall down L.O.D.	16
	During last bar Man releases R. hand and re-assumes Double Hold as at the commencement of the dance.	

Backward and Forward Balancés—Nat. (Solo) Waltz Turn

Count	**Lady**	Bars
1	R.F. back diag. to wall down L.O.D. (b.o.f., w.f.).	
2/3	Close L.F. to R.F. 3rd pos. front (b.o.f.) without weight. Rise to ball of R.F.	1
1	L.F. forward (heel) diag. to centre against L.O.D.— body turn to R. to face diag. centre down L.O.D.	
2/3	Close R.F. to L.F. 3rd pos. front (b.o.f.) without weight. Rise to ball of L.F. Release R. hand from partner's L. hand.	2
123	Nat. Prog. Waltz Turn (Solo) outwards—R.F., L.F., R.F. Hold released.	3
123	Nat. Rotary Waltz Turn—L.F., R.F., L.F. Resume Double Hold with partner. Finish facing towards diag. centre down L.O.D.	4

Zephyr Turns—Point—Pas de Valse—Lock Step Movement

| 1 | R.F. forward down L.O.D. (heel). | |
| 2/3 | Zephyr (Swing) L.F. forward to low aerial pos. | 5 |

WALTZ CAMAY (*contd.*)

1	Turn inwards to L. on ball of R.F.	
2/3	Zephyr (Swing) L.F. forward against L.O.D. to low aerial pos. backing L.O.D. ½ turn.	6
1	L.F. back down L.O.D. (b.o.f., w.f.) turning R. (Inwards).	
2/3	R.F. forward down L.O.D. (b.o.f., w.f.) ½ turn.	7
1	L.F. forward down L.O.D. (heel).	
2/3	Point R.F. forward (toe) 4th pos. front.	8
123	Pas de Valse down L.O.D. (R. hand released from Man's L. hand) R.F., L.F., R.F. (similar to 1st bar Veleta).	9
1	L.F. forward down L.O.D. (heel).	
2/3	Cross (Lock) R.F. over front of L.F. (b.o.f., w.f.)—outside edges of feet almost in contact.	10
1	L.F. back against L.O.D. (b.o.f., w.f.).	
2/3	Cross (Lock) R.F. in behind L.F. (b.o.f., w.f.). (Similar action to a Whisk position).	11
1	L.F. forward down L.O.D. (heel).	
2/3	Point R.F. forward down L.O.D. (toe).	12

Nat. (Solo) Waltz Turn—Prog. Waltz Turn—Pas de Valse

1/6	Repeat bars 3 and 4. R.F., L.F., R.F.,—L.F., R.F., L.F. Assuming normal Waltz Hold at end.	13/14
1/3	Nat. Prog. Waltz Turn—R.F., L.F., R.F.	15
123	Backward Pas de Valse turning to R. to back diag. to wall down L.O.D.— ¼ turn approx.	16
	During last bar re-assume Double Hold as at commencement of the dance.	

NORTHERN STAR WALTZ

GILBERT DANIELS

TIME 3/4—TEMPO 40/42—16 BAR SEQUENCE

Commence with normal Ballroom Hold. Man facing—
Lady backing diag. to wall down L.O.D.

Rev. Prog. Waltz Turn—Backward Pas de Valse—Balancés
Nat. Rotary Waltz Turn—Forward Pas de Valse—Balancé

Count	Man	Bars
1	L.F. forward diag. to wall down L.O.D. (heel) turn to L.	
2	R.F. to side along L.O.D. (b.o.f.).	
3	Close L.F. to R.F. 5th pos. front (b.o.f., w.f.) backing diag. to wall down L.O.D. ½ turn to L.	1
1	R.F. back (b.o.f., w.f.) curving to L.	
2	L.F. back L. shoulder lead.	
3	Close R.F. to L.F. 3rd pos. front (b.o.f., w.f.) backing diag. to centre down L.O.D. ¼ turn to L.	2
1	L.F. back diag. to centre down L.O.D. (b.o.f., w.f.).	
2/3	Close R.F. to L.F. 3rd pos. front (b.o.f.) without weight. Rise to ball of L.F. (Balancé).	3
1	R.F. forward diag. to wall against L.O.D. (heel).	
2/3	Close L.F. to R.F. 3rd pos. rear (b.o.f.) without weight. Rise to ball of R.F. (Balancé).	4
1	L.F. back diag. to centre down L.O.D. (b.o.f., w.f.) turning to R.	
2	Close R.F. to L.F. 5th pos. rear (b.o.f.).	
3	Pivot to R. on balls of both feet to face diag. centre down L.O.D. ½ turn to R.	5
1	R.F. forward diag. to centre (heel) curving to R.	
2	L.F. forward down L.O.D. (b.o.f.) L. shoulder lead.	
3	Close R.F. to L.F. 3rd pos. rear (b.o.f., w.f.) face diag. wall down L.O.D. ¼ turn to R.	6
1	L.F. forward diag. to wall down L.O.D. (heel).	
2/3	Close R.F. to L.F. 3rd pos. rear (b.o.f.) without weight (Balancé). Release Hold.	7

| 1 | R.F. back diag. to centre against L.O.D. (b.o.f., w.f.) (Lady turns to R). | |
| 2/3 | Close L.F. to R.F. 3rd pos. front (b.o.f.) without weight. Finish facing diag. to wall down L.O.D.—Lady's L. hand in Man's R. hand—No. 2 Hold, similar to Veleta commencing position. (Lady faces diag. to centre down L.O.D.). | 8 |

Rev. Open Turn—Nat. Rotary Waltz Turn—Walk and Point—Forward Pas de Valse—Nat. Waltz Turn—Walk and Point

1	L.F. forward down L.O.D. (heel) turning to L. Release Hold.	
2/3	R.F. diag. back down L.O.D. (b.o.f., w.f.) facing diag. to centre against L.O.D.	9
1	L.F. back down L.O.D. (b.o.f., w.f.) L. shoulder lead—Lady's R. hand in Man's L. hand.	
2/3	Close R.F. to L.F. 3rd pos. front (b.o.f., w.f.) face diag. to wall against L.O.D. $\frac{3}{4}$ turn to L. on last 2 bars.	10
1	L.F. back down L.O.D. (b.o.f., w.f.) turning to R.	
2	Close R.F. to L.F. 5th pos. rear (b.o.f.). Release Hold.	
3	Pivot to R. on balls of both feet to face diag. centre down L.O.D. $\frac{1}{2}$ turn to R.	11
1	R.F. forward down L.O.D. (heel). Lady's L. hand in Man's R. hand—Turn to R.	
2/3	Point L.F. forward down L.O.D. (toe) facing diag. to wall down L.O.D. $\frac{1}{4}$ turn to R.—Headline towards partner.	12
1	L.F. forward down L.O.D. (heel)—body turn to L.	
2	R.F. forward down L.O.D. (b.o.f.) R. shoulder lead.	
3	Close L.F. to R.F. 3rd pos. rear (b.o.f., w.f.) face diag. to centre down L.O.D. $\frac{1}{4}$ turn to L.	13
1	R.F. forward down L.O.D. (heel) turning to R.	
2	L.F. to side along L.O.D. (b.o.f.).	
3	Close R.F. to L.F. 5th pos. front (b.o.f., w.f.) face diag. to wall against L.O.D. $\frac{1}{2}$ turn to R.—Adopt normal Waltz Hold.	14
1	L.F. diag. back down L.O.D. (b.o.f., w.f.) turning to R.	
2	Close R.F. to L.F. 5th pos. rear (b.o.f.).	
3	Pivot to R. on balls of both feet to face diag. centre down L.O.D. $\frac{1}{2}$ turn to R.	15
1	R.F. forward down L.O.D. (heel) slight turn to R.	
2/3	Point L.F. forward down L.O.D. (toe) facing diag. to wall down L.O.D. $\frac{1}{4}$ turn to R.	16

Rev. Rotary Waltz Turn—Forward Pas de Valse—Balancés
Nat. Prog. Waltz Turn—Backward Pas de Valse—Balancé
Lady

1	R.F. diag. back down L.O.D. (b.o.f., w.f.) turning to L.	
2	Close L.F. to R.F. 5th pos. rear (b.o.f.).	
3	Pivot to L. on balls of both feet to face diag. wall down L.O.D. ½ turn to L.	1
1	L.F. forward (heel) curving to L.	
2	R.F. forward (b.o.f.) R. shoulder lead.	
3	Close L.F. to R.F. 3rd pos. rear (b.o.f., w.f.) face diag. to centre down L.O.D. ¼ turn to L.	2
1	R.F. forward (heel) diag. to centre down L.O.D.	
2/3	Close L.F. to R.F. 3rd pos. rear (b.o.f.) without weight. Rise to ball of R.F. (Balancé).	3
1	L.F. back diag. to wall against L.O.D. (b.o.f., w.f.).	
2/3	Close R.F. to L.F. 3rd pos. front (b.o.f.) without weight. Rise to ball of L.F. (Balancé).	4
1	R.F. forward (heel) diag. to centre down L.O.D.—turn to R.	
2	L.F. to side along L.O.D. (b.o.f.) face wall approximately.	
3	Close R.F. to L.F. 5th pos. front (b.o.f., w.f.) facing diag. to wall against L.O.D. ½ turn to R.	5
1	L.F. back down L.O.D. (b.o.f., w.f.) curving to R.	
2	R.F. back down L.O.D. (b.o.f.) R. shoulder L.	
3	Close L.F. to R.F. 3rd pos. front (b.o.f., w.f.) backing diag. wall down L.O.D. ¼ turn to R.	6
1	R.F. back diag. to wall down L.O.D. (b.o.f., w.f.).	
2/3	Close L.F. to R.F. 3rd pos. front (b.o.f.) without weight. Rise to ball of R.F.—Release Hold.	7
1	With body turn to R.—L.F. diag. forward (b.o.f., w.f.) towards diag. wall against L.O.D.—Sideways action.	
2/3	Close R.F. to L.F. 3rd pos. front (b.o.f.) without weight. Finish facing diag. to centre down L.O.D.—L. hand in Man's R. hand—Hold No. 2.	8

Nat. Open Turn—Rev. Rotary Waltz Turn—Walk and Point—Forward Pas de Valse—Prog. Nat. Waltz Turn—Walk and Point

1	R.F. forward down L.O.D. (heel) turning to R. Release Hold.

2/3	L.F. diag. back down L.O.D. (b.o.f., w.f.) face diag. wall against L.O.D.	9
1	R.F. back down L.O.D. (b.o.f., w.f.) R. shoulder lead. R. hand in Man's L. hand.	
2/3	Close L.F. to R.F. 3rd pos. front (b.o.f., w.f.) face diag. centre against L.O.D. ¾ turn to R. on last 2 bars.	10
1	R.F. back down L.O.D. (b.o.f., w.f.) turning to L.	
2	Close L.F. to R.F. 5th pos. rear (b.o.f.). Release Hold.	
3	Pivot to L. on balls of both feet to face diag. to wall down L.O.D. ½ turn to L.	11
1	L.F. forward down L.O.D. (heel) L. hand in Man's R. hand—body turn to L.	
2/3	Point R.F. forward down L.O.D. (toe) face diag. centre down L.O.D. ¼ turn to L.—Headline towards partner.	12
1	R.F. forward down L.O.D. (heel) body turn to R.	
2	L.F. forward down L.O.D. (b.o.f.) L. shoulder lead.	
3	Close R.F. to L.F. 3rd pos. rear (b.o.f., w.f.) face diag. wall down L.O.D. ¼ turn to R.	13
1	L.F. forward down L.O.D. (heel) body turn to L.	
2	R.F. forward down L.O.D. (b.o.f.) R. shoulder lead.	
3	Close L.F. to R.F. 3rd pos. rear (b.o.f., w.f.) face diag. centre down L.O.D. ¼ turn to L. Adopt normal Waltz Hold with partner.	14
1	R.F. forward down L.O.D. (heel) turning to R.	
2	L.F. to side along L.O.D. (b.o.f.).	
3	Close R.F. to L.F. 5th pos. front (b.o.f., w.f.) backing diag. to centre down L.O.D. ½ turn to R.	15
1	L.F. back down L.O.D. (b.o.f., w.f.) body turn to R.	
2/3	Point R.F. back (toe) backing diag. to wall down L.O.D.— ¼ turn to R.	16

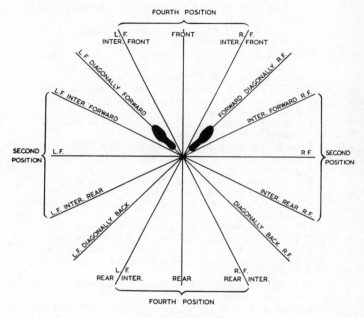

INTERMEDIATE OPEN POSITIONS

NOTES ON THE FOOT POSITIONS

THERE are no closed *intermediate positions*. An *intermediate position* is a position formed between *2nd* and *4th position*. Note that in the accompanying chart the *intermediate position* is shown as diagonal, this term is more descriptive of the step in relation to the body.

Classes of Position—

    (*a*) Toe (point).
    (*b*) Ball of foot.
    (*c*) Flat (whole foot).
    (*d*) Aerial. Any position in which the foot is off the ground—

        (1) Low aerial—ankle height.
        (2) Medium—calf height.
        (3) High—knee height.

Professional candidates should note that the Official Board of Ballroom Dancing clarified the foot positions as follows (the angle at which the feet are placed in the *1st pos.* must be maintained throughout)—

1st pos. Heels together, toes turned out at an angle of 45 degrees from the Line of Direction, that is 90 degrees in relation of one foot to the other.

2nd pos. Either foot placed to the side neither in advance nor rearward of the standing foot.

3rd pos. Place the heel of one foot to the instep of the other.

4th pos. Extend the foot forward directly opposite *1st pos.*

5th pos. The heel of one foot placed at the side of the big toe of the opposite foot.

Rear pos. Any position taken behind the standing foot.

GLOSSARY

À Coin (ah-kwahn). To the corner.

À Côté (ah-ko-tay). To the side.

À Droite (ah-droo-aht). To the right.

Advance and Retire. Three steps forward and close to *3rd position rear* without weight. Three steps backwards and close *3rd position front* or *1st position*.

Aerial. A position where the foot is in the air.

À Gauche (ah-gohsh). To the left.

Allé (ah-lay). A step taken with the heel meeting the floor first.

Allemande (ahlmahnd). Either partner turning under the raised arms; it is more usual for the lady to turn underneath.

Arrière (ah-ree-air). Rear or backward.

Assemblé (ah-sahm-blay). To bring together, i.e. bring the foot from an open to a closed position, or from one closed position to another closed position.

Avant (ah-vahn). To the front—forward.

À vos Places (ah-vo-plahs). Regain your places.

Balance. The correct distribution of the weight of the body.

Balancé (bah-lahn-say). A rising and falling movement on the ball of one foot whilst the other foot is brought to a closed position without weight.

Ballonné (bah-lonnay). Taken from an aerial position. Bend the knee of the moving leg, bringing the foot towards the supporting leg with a temps levé, re-extend the foot again. (Can be taken in–out–in or out–in–out.) A step in which the moving foot appears as if it were passing over a ball.

Battements (baht-mahn). Beatings.

Bow. Acknowledgment for the man. Form of salutation by the man equivalent to the lady's curtsy.

Chaîne des Dames (-day-dahm). Ladies' Chain.

Chassé (shahs-say). A chasing movement consisting of three steps—step, close, step.

Chassé Battu (bahttu). A beaten chassé.

Chassé Croisé. Chassé crossing. Partners chassé across, man behind lady. Closing in *3rd position front*.

Coin (kwahn). Corner.

Counter or Contra Promenade. Promenade position but man's left hip in contact with lady's right hip.

226

COUPÉ (koo-pay). Cutting movement in which the weight of the body is cut from one foot to the other.

CROISÉ. Traversé (*q.v.*).

CURTSY. Acknowledgment for the lady. Form of salutation by the lady usually to her partner.

DEDANS (de-dahn). Inwardly, inward.

DÉGAGÉ (day-gah-jhay). A disengagement of the foot from a closed position to an open position with or without weight.

DEHORS (de-or). Outwardly, outward.

DEMI (deh-me). Half.

DERRIÈRE. Behind.

DESSOUS (des-soo). Under or to the rear.

DESSUS (dessu). Over or to the front.

DEVANT. In front.

DOS À DOS (doh-za-doh). Back to back.

DROIT (droo-ah). Right.

ELEVATIONS. Raisings, movements in which the foot and leg are raised from the floor.

EN ARRIÈRE (ahn ah-ree-air). To the rear or to retire.

EN AVANT. To the front or advance.

EN DEDANS. Inward.

EN DEHORS. Outward.

EN L'AIR (ahn-lair). A movement off the ground—in the air.

EN PASSANT (ahn-pahssan). In passing.

EN TERRE (ahn-tahr). The foot on the floor.

ENTRÉE (ahn-tray). The opening of a dance—entry.

ÉPAULEMENT (ay-pole-mahn). The shoulder.

FLEXION. Bending of the joints.

FONDU. A bending of the supporting leg.

FOUETTÉ (foo-ett-ay). A whipping movement of the raised foot as it passes rapidly before or behind the supporting leg.

GAUCHE (gohsh). Left.

GLISSÉ. A gliding movement in any direction.

JETÉ (jhettay). A thrown step in which a springing off is made from one foot alighting on to the other foot.

L'ENVERS. Reverse, sometimes called *à rebours*.

LEVÉ (lev-ay). A levering movement, rising on to the ball of one foot or the balls of both feet.

LEVÉ, SAUTÉ. A jump, falling on one foot while the other remains raised.

LEVÉ, TEMPS. A rising time. Raising one leg with some movement of the other leg—a low hop.

LINE OF DANCE. The normal forward progression round the ballroom, anticlockwise—the line that is parallel to the four walls.

MARCHÉ (marshay). A forward step—toe or ball of foot touching the floor first.

OUVERT (oo-vair). Legs open sideways to left or right.

PAS (pah). A step.

PAS ALLÉ. A normal walking step, heel touching the floor first.

PAS DE BASQUE (pah-der-bahsk). Jeté with demi-rondé to *2nd position*. Assemblé to *5th front* (ball of foot). Slight plié and coupé in place, finishing *5th en l'air* with toe pointing to the floor.

PAS DE GAVOTTE (gah-vot). Glide either foot forward, close the other foot to *3rd position rear*, glide first foot forward, pass the second foot through *1st* to *4th aerial position* in front. (A *4th point position* is frequently substituted for the *aerial position*.)

PAS GLISSADE. Step in any direction—glide other foot to *3rd position*, lowering heel and transferring weight. Is generally understood as a step to the side, closing other foot to a *3rd front position* with weight, then moving the first foot again.

PAS GLISSÉ. Step in any direction, glide opposite foot to *3rd position* without weight. Is generally understood as a step to the side, closing other foot to *3rd front position* without transference of weight, then moving the closing foot into another position or movement.

PAS MARCHÉ. A marching step—toe or ball of foot touching the floor first.

PAS DE MAZURKA. Step forward, close foot to *3rd rear position*, temps levé and fouetté with front foot to *3rd rear aerial position*.

PAS DE VALSE. A movement of three steps taken forward or backward, commencing with either foot: forward to *4th position*, forward to *4th position*, and close to *3rd position rear*. Backward to *4th position*, backward to *4th position*, close to *3rd position front*.

PAS DE ZÉPHYR. A stretched or sweeping movement from *4th position rear* to *4th position forward*, or vice versa.

PETITE (pet-eet). Small.

PIQUÉ (pee-kay). Describes movements in the steps of which only the heel meets the floor.

PIROUETTE (pee-roo-et). A turn. One or more complete turns on the toe or ball of one foot.

PIVOT. To turn on one or both feet.

PLIÉ (plee-ay). Flexion or bending of one or both knees.

POINT. Toe pointed to the floor, the foot fully stretched, with the weight of the body sustained on the other foot.

POINTÉ DE TALON. Movements made with the point of the heel.

POISE. Carriage of the body.

PROMENADE POSITION. Relative positions of the man's and the lady's bodies. Man's right hip in contact with partner's left hip, the other sides of the bodies opened out forming a V shape.

REBOURS (re-boor). Reverse.

REBROUSSALE (re-broo-sal). The heel position of the foot.

RELEVÉ (rel-avay). Relifting or straightening of the knee.

RETRAVERSÉ (re-trah-vair-say). To go over the same place—recross.

RHYTHM. The regular accentuation of a certain beat or beats in the bars of the music.

ROND. Any movement in a circle.

ROND DE JAMBE(rawn-der-jhahmb). Rounding the leg in a circle either inwards or outwards, on the floor or raised.

RUEMENT (ru-mahn). To kick—forcibly throwing the leg into an open position.

SAUTÉ (sotay). A springing movement with progression. In practice a hop during which the body travels, the body rising more than in a temps levé.

SLIP PIVOT. Used by lady to turn from a fall away position to get body square to man. She turns on the ball of foot, brushing the other foot towards the "turning" foot as the turn is made, then moves the foot forward between her partner's feet.

SOUTENU (soo-ter-noo). Sustained or supported.

SUR PLACE. In place—on the spot.

TACET. Musical direction indicating silence.

TEMPO. The speed at which the music is played—the number of bars of music per minute.

TEMPS (tahm). Part of a step.

TEMPS LEVÉ. A hop without progression—a low hop on the spot.

TENDRE (tahndr). To stretch. The opposite of plié.

TENDU, PAS (tahndu). A stretched step.

TERRE À TERRE(tehr-ah-tehr). A movement on the ground—a gliding style of dancing, small steps connected with each other lightly gliding over the floor. Nearly all ballroom steps are so danced in contradistinction to steps taken *en l'air*.

TIME. The division of a piece of music into bars or measures, i.e. number of beats in a bar of music.

TOUR (toor). A round movement whether executed in place or moving away.

TOUR DE CORPS. Turn of the body.

TOUR EN L'AIR. Turn in the air.

TOUR DES MAIN (toor day ma(n)). Turn of the hands. A couple with hands joined make a circle round the joined hands.

TOURNÉ (toor-nay). A movement by which the whole leg is turned inward or outward.

TOURNURE. When presenting a hand to partner turn the body to "look" at partner or other person.

TRAVERSÉ (trah-ver-say). To cross—similar to retraversé (*per se*).

TWINKLE. A movement of three steps, can be commenced with either foot—forward, close back or back close, forward.

TWO STEP. Chassé backward, forward, or turning. Rotary chassé is generally understood to be a Two Step.

VIS À VIS. Facing or opposite.

ZEPHYR. A light step in which the toe lightly touches the floor in passing from one raised extended position to another extended position.

GRAMOPHONE RECORDS

There are some excellent records available by prominent bands who specialize in recording for the sequence dancer.

Phil Tate
Ted Taylor
Victor Sylvester
Bryan Smith
Ken Turner
Tony Evans

A list can be obtained from
IDTA Sales Ltd., 76 Bennett Road, Brighton BN25 JL

NOTE ON THE OFFICIAL BOARD
OF BALLROOM DANCING

THE Board is composed primarily of prominent teachers of dancing selected by members of the profession.

The following organizations are the principal dancing societies—

Allied Association of Teachers of Dancing
British Association of Teachers of Dancing
Imperial Society of Teachers of Dancing
International Dance Teachers Association
National Association of Teachers of Dancing
Northern Counties Dance Teachers Association
Scottish Dance Teachers Alliance
United Kingdom Dance Teachers Alliance

The above Societies are represented on The Sequence Dance Committee of the Official Board of Ballroom Dancing.

The Official Board recommends Dances for the purposes of Championship Competitions, and the Societies have individual Examinations for professional purposes, as well as Amateur Medal Tests—Bronze—Silver and Gold awards.

As the dances selected by the various Societies are liable to alteration from time to time, it is recommended that direct application should be made to the Society of selection for information on the current syllabus.

ALPHABETICAL INDEX OF DANCES